W9-BHU-840

BRIDE'S BOOK
OF ETIQUETTE

1) Bride
2) Groom
3) Best Dude
4) maid honor

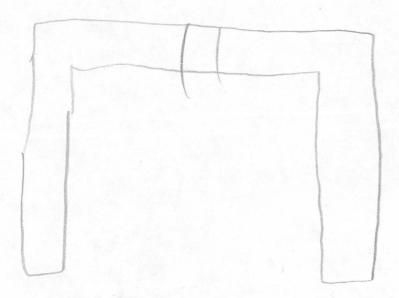

BRIDE'S BOOK OF ETIQUETTE

GOLDEN ANNIVERSARY EDITION

THE EDITORS OF *BRIDE'S MAGAZINE*
with
KATHY C. MULLINS

A PERIGEE BOOK

Perigee Books
are published by
The Putnam Publishing Group
200 Madison Avenue
New York, New York 10016

Copyright © 1984, 1981, 1973, 1967, 1948 by The Condé Nast Publications Inc.
All rights reserved. This book, or parts thereof,
may not be reproduced in any form without permission.
Published simultaneously in Canada by
General Publishing Co. Limited, Toronto.

Library of Congress Cataloging in Publication Data

Main entry under title:

Bride's book of etiquette.

Rev. ed. of: The New bride's book of etiquette.
4th ed., rev. and updated. c1981.
Includes index.
1. Wedding etiquette.   I. Bride's magazine.
II. New bride's book of etiquette.
BJ2051.B7   1984   395'.22   84-7058
ISBN 0-399-51096-6
ISBN 0-399-51084-2 (pbk.)

Sketches by Susan Gray
Back cover photograph by Barbara Bersell
Front cover photograph by Andrea Alberts reprinted from BRIDE'S.
Copyright © 1982 by The Condé Nast Publications Inc.

Four previous editions by Grosset & Dunlap
Printed in the United States of America
7   8   9   10

ACKNOWLEDGMENTS

BRIDE'S acknowledges contributions on this *BRIDE'S Book of Etiquette* from staff members Elizabeth Thayer Verney, Yvonne Vera, Heidi Benson, Maribeth Maher, Andrea Furey, and Susan Kuziak, with special thanks to Andrea Feld, Copy and Features Editor, whose heartfelt dedication to BRIDE'S and brides is evident in every word of this book, and Sharon Bonanni, whose daily correspondence with our readers gives us a window on the world that is unparalleled.

Contents

Foreword

I n this, the fiftieth year of BRIDE'S magazine, the Editors felt that a major revision of this classic book of etiquette was both timely and necessary. At no time in our long and historic publishing career have there been such variations in manners and mores of marrying. And yet, both the dream and the reality of each wedding is a personal statement for the couple who make it come true. This Golden Anniversary Edition of *BRIDE'S Book of Etiquette* respects not only tradition but also the individual. It is designed to help you plan a wedding celebration that is both joyous and solemn . . . and filled with a lifetime of memories.

As a woman and man who have agreed to marry, you are about to embark upon one of life's richest and most rewarding adventures. No one, of course, thinks marriage is easy anymore. We have scores of bleak statistics to prove that failure is possible, and problems certainly probable. And yet we persist. Why?

Because marriage—reexamined, restructured, modernized and custom-made—is the best (though admittedly imperfect) institution of total personal commitment. And without commitment, without the daily interaction of two dedicated personalities, most of us feel vaguely empty and unfulfilled, without distinct roots or purpose. Private agreements between loving couples are frequent and temporarily effective. Yet no tacit understanding can substitute for the joyous pride a couple can feel in pledging their love and devotion before the immediate world, and then in recognizing the responsibility to make their marriage work.

Our society, buffeted as it is by revolution and change, yearns for the security that comes from trusting in our own humanity. What better promise for the future than to "love, honor, and cherish"? What more nourishing platform for growth and development than the strength that two human beings can give each other—through tenderness, discipline, and will.

Of course there is a lighter tone to this book. The *BRIDE'S Book of Etiquette* is about invitations and receiving lines, about photographs and receptions, about showers and gifts and going-away clothes. But it is also about feelings—those subtle courtesies and kindnesses that smooth relationships between families and friends . . . and between two very special friends—you and your fiancé.

Read between the lines as you look up information about announcing your engagement, personalizing your ceremony, choosing your attendants as well as the guest list. Notice how this, the Fifth Edition of the *BRIDE'S Book of Etiquette*, with its newly revised and updated text, avoids clichés and rigid rules, depending instead upon good taste and common sense for its authority. There is a chapter specifically for those who are starting married life again, as well as for those who wish to reaffirm their vows after many years together. Within these pages is a wealth of information for those who have never planned a party, much less a formal wedding for two hundred guests.

This book is designed to answer your every question and anticipate your needs. Whether you're in doubt about inviting your four-year-old niece to be a flower girl, or wondering where your divorced father-in-law (to-be) should sit at the reception, depend upon us to come up with an understanding—and sensible—solution.

All of us who have been connected with this book (including other brides and grooms whose ideas have appeared in BRIDE'S magazine over the years and are incorporated in this volume) wish you and your future husband a very special toast:

Health, happiness, and prosperity . . . and plenty of time to enjoy them!

BARBARA TOBER
Editor-in-Chief
BRIDE'S magazine

BRIDE'S BOOK
OF ETIQUETTE

1
Your Engagement

Getting engaged! It happens suddenly when he "pops the question"; slowly, as you grow more confident of each other's love; or, it happens with flair, when you look up to see a skywriter spelling out "Sue, will you marry me?" No matter how it happens, getting engaged sets in motion a whirlwind of emotion that heightens your daydreams and catapults you into the future.

Parties and plans and the delightful feeling of being the bride—these are some of the things you can look forward to once the news that you're going to be married is out. But first, of course, you'll want to share your excitement with your family and friends. Imagine now the cry of joy from your roommate or the quiet smile that will tug at the corners of your father's mouth. Telling everyone is just the beginning of all the fun of a wedding.

YOUR FAMILIES FIRST

Your families should be the first to hear the good news. How you go about letting them in on your decision is up to you.

If your parents know your fiancé extremely well, and he's visited their home often, you might choose a time when you're all together, saying perhaps, "Dad, Mom . . . Bill and I have something we'd like to share with you. . . ." Chances are, you won't even get to finish your sentence—you'll be buried in good wishes! Living far away from your parents means you may not be able to wait and see them in person. In this case, do put in a joint telephone call. At the same time, make arrangements to visit your parents as soon as possible.

If your parents aren't acquainted with your fiancé yet, a letter or note asking them to please "invite someone very special" for a weekend or holiday works nicely. You needn't say anything until your fiancé feels comfortable and at

13

home—rest assured, your parents will have a hint of your plans. (Incidentally, even if you are already sharing an apartment or house, you shouldn't expect to share a room in your parents' home if this makes them uneasy.) If your fiancé's schedule doesn't permit a visit or you're not sure how they'll react to your decision, then you might tell them of your upcoming marriage yourself, before you bring him into the picture.

No matter what your situation, speaking with your family alone gives them—and you—the opportunity to express yourselves freely, crying a bit and laughing, and may seem the best way to inform them of your plans.

Your fiancé may still want to speak privately with your father. Not so much to ask for your hand—although some fathers appreciate this old-fashioned courtesy—as to receive congratulations, some loving thoughts about you, and a warm welcome to the family.

But your fiancé might do well to anticipate any worries or questions your father may have, just in case there is a serious discussion. Some parental anxiety can be expected, so don't mistake this for lack of trust in your judgment. Your parents will want to know about your fiancé's career plans, where you two will live, and how you are dealing with major differences, such as religion, education, nationality. Probably both sets of parents are eager to be just as excited as the two of you are, and your straightforward information will help them be at ease concerning these issues.

If your father is no longer alive, your mother, stepfather, guardian, or whoever raised you may talk with your fiancé. If your parents are divorced, he can see one parent, then the other.

He'll want, of course, to tell his parents right away, too. Again, how he lets them know is up to him.

His family, too, may have reservations. They will want to feel they know you and that you've both thought through potential problems in advance. For instance, if you are divorced with custody of two children, his parents may have trouble visualizing their son as an "instant dad." Once they get to know you, pay a few visits with the children so they can see how well their son gets along with them.

If one of you is divorced, the other's parents may be uneasy about what went wrong with the first marriage. It's possible to offer a simple, reassuring statement about your first marriage ("It wasn't until after we were married that he admitted he never wanted children") without feeling that your privacy has been invaded.

Once your fiancé tells his parents, they traditionally "call on" your parents, so everyone can get acquainted. His mother might drop your mother a note, or phone to invite your parents for drinks, brunch, or dinner. Any way his parents usually entertain their friends is a good way for them to get to know your parents. If your parents are divorced, your fiancé's family might first extend their invitation to the person who raised you. If your families live in different towns, a note from your fiancé's mother to your mother saying how pleased she is that you'll be a member of the family is a thoughtful gesture. In this case, your fiancé's parents may also ask you to spend a few days with them. Accept right away. Not only will you meet your fiancé's family, but if you haven't already, you will have a chance to see where he grew up, getting to know and appreciate the man you're marrying much better.

Even if your parents and his are old friends, this is the perfect excuse for them to have dinner together and toast the occasion. You two—and your brothers and sisters—may or may not be included. Now is the time for a small gathering. The bigger party can come when your engagement is officially announced.

Your fiancé's parents haven't contacted your parents? Then your mother might make the first move, perhaps calling to invite them over for a drink.

Perhaps you and your fiancé are in a better position than either set of parents to entertain, so just go ahead and get everyone together. There's no need to stand on ceremony—as long as the families are getting off to a good start.

When one of you has children, you should make telling them a top priority. You want your child to hear the news from you. Then, too, if your news will take a little getting used to, you'll be able to talk things over before someone's "Isn't little Susie thrilled?" gets a blunt "No!" from little Susie. Probably if you've been spending a great deal of time with your fiancé, and including the child in your outings, he or she will not really be surprised. Yet each child will react in his or her own way, partly according to age—one will be worried, another happy, yet another angry.

You can anticipate some of your child's worries: Will you still have time for him? Will she still see her own father? Does he have to change his name? Will the stepfather make curfew rules? Will her father still pay for college? Does this mean you will move? Make the announcement time as comfortable as possible, allowing lots of time for discussion and airing of all those troubled feelings. And try not to be hurt if your child is less than overjoyed. Time and love will work it out.

In addition to children and parents, there may be other special people to tell personally. Your boss and co-workers will be excited to hear your news, but the office is a functional place. A bride- and groom-to-be may be shocked by the assumption that they'll be less efficient on the job just because they're getting married. You can deflect this kind of thinking when you make your announcement: "Well, I'm finally settling down to the comfortable supportive home life you've raved about all these years—Gary and I are getting married June fifteenth. And, I'm requesting five vacation days next month to tackle most of the wedding arrangements." Do reassure everyone that you'll use lunch hours for other wedding chores, that your fiancé is supportive of your career, that a move or children are not in the immediate future.

Depending on your present relationship, you might drop your ex-spouse a note or telephone the news that you are remarrying. It is best if the news comes directly from you. If there are children involved, it is even more important to speak together so you can answer any questions your ex-spouse has. Otherwise children become the conveyors of news and may have to answer too many awkward questions.

LENGTH OF ENGAGEMENT

You can consider yourselves engaged as soon as you decide to marry and to inform your parents. But you might wait to announce your engagement to everyone else until you begin making plans for your wedding (usually six to ten months before the ceremony; in some areas, up to a year). This may be a good idea if your fiancé has to complete his military service, or if you both look forward to graduating from college. Questions from well-meaning friends—"When are you going to have your first baby?" "How will you support yourselves?"—start the moment the word of your upcoming marriage gets around. You may prefer some time to yourselves to settle issues like these between you, and to get to know one another as fully as you should in a relaxed way.

PUBLISHING THE NEWS

Once you've decided to make your plans known to everyone, your engagement may be announced in both your hometown newspapers and in other pertinent papers, such as those of the city where you both work.

You and your parents may tell your closest friends and relatives somewhat before the announcement appears (rather than send printed cards, you should phone, speak, or write to them personally). Or you may time an engagement party for this purpose to coincide with the announcement release date.

Since policies vary from paper to paper, it's best to check with the society editor in advance about the proper form, deadlines, photograph requirements, and such. Some newspapers, for example, accept information over the phone, while others require that you submit a special printed form at least ten days prior to publication. Some papers publish wedding pictures only, while others publish either wedding or engagement pictures, but not both. If your newspaper does not supply forms, send the necessary information to the societyeditor. Type it, double-spaced, on one side of an 8½ × 11-inch sheet of paper. In the upper right-hand corner be sure to include the name, address, and phone number of your parents or someone in the community who can be contacted to verify the information. Include the date on which you would like the announcement to appear. Instead of indicating a Sunday—a very popular day—you might put under the phone number: "For release Wednesday, May 26, 1985."

The simplest and customary form:

Mr. and Mrs. Dennis Brown of Dayton Avenue announce the engagement of their daughter, Ann Marie, to Mr. John Smith, the son of Mr. and Mrs. Thomas Smith of St. Louis. No date has been set for the wedding. [Or, The wedding will take place in December.]

Note that the city is mentioned only when it is not the same as where the paper is published.

If your parents are divorced, the announcement is made by the parent with whom you've lived, but both parents are mentioned. (A divorced mother's name is traditionally a combination of her maiden and married surnames: "Mrs. Hoyt Brown." But she might prefer the more contemporary pairing of her given name and married surname: "Mrs. Jean Brown.")

Mrs. Hoyt Brown announces the engagement of her daughter, Ann Marie, to Mr. John Smith, the son of Mr. and Mrs. Thomas Smith of St. Louis. Miss Brown is also the daughter of Mr. Dennis Brown of Tulsa.

If your parents are divorced but friendly, they might wish to announce the news together:

Mr. Dennis Brown of Tulsa and Mrs. Hoyt Brown of Dayton Avenue, Chicago, announce the engagement of their daughter, Ann Marie, to Mr. John Smith, the son of Mr. and Mrs. Thomas Smith of St. Louis.

If your mother has remarried, she uses her current married name: "Mrs. Raymond Jones."

Mr. and Mrs. Raymond Jones announce the engagement of Mrs. Jones's daughter, Ann Marie Brown, to Mr. John Smith, the son of Mr. and Mrs. Thomas Smith of St. Louis. Miss Brown is also the daughter of Mr. Dennis Brown of Tulsa.

If one of your parents has died, your announcement might read:

The engagement of Miss Ann Marie Brown, daughter of Mrs. Dennis Brown and the late Mr. Brown, to Mr. John Smith, the son of Mr. and Mrs. Thomas Smith of St. Louis, is announced by the bride's mother.

If both of your parents are dead, the announcement is usually made by an older brother or sister or any close relative—even a close friend:

Mr. Jason Hoyt of Pittsburgh announces the engagement of his niece, Miss Ann Marie Brown, to Mr. John Smith, the son of Mr. and Mrs. Thomas Smith of St. Louis. Miss Brown is the daughter of the late Mr. and Mrs. Dennis Brown.

If you are sponsoring the wedding yourselves, you might still have your parents announce the engagement, or announce it yourselves as follows:

Susan Elizabeth Scott, newscaster for WBIX-TV, is to be married in June to James J. Sampson, vice-president, trust accounts, for First National Bank of Denver. Miss Scott is the daughter of John Z. Scott of Atlanta, Georgia, and Sarah Newberry Scott of New York City. Mr. Sampson is the son of Mr. and Mrs. Dudley P. Sampson of Cleveland, Ohio.

Your fiancé's parents do not announce the engagement, even when the news appears in their hometown paper.

Should your fiancé be the one whose parents are dead or divorced, you can adapt the appropriate wording to suit his situation.

Nowadays, it is quite common for remarriage engagements to be announced in the same public way the first engagements are publicized. Once, second marriages were quiet events, but now every aspect of remarriage is a celebration. Word it in the usual way, using the bride-to-be's legal name:

Mr. and Mrs. Alvin G. Dunlap announce the engagement of their daughter, Anne Dunlap Crosby, to Joseph G. Riggs, son of Mr. and Mrs. G. Denton Riggs.

There is no need to mention a previous marriage, although your newspaper may want to include this information. If, however, you've only been divorced a short while or your first spouse has died quite recently, wait and announce your wedding only.

Death in either family, or someone critically ill, means you will probably want to put off announcing your engagement until the worry has passed, unless the sick person is anxious to share in your happiness now.

Each newspaper has its own style for announcements, which you can determine by reading a few issues. The newspaper will usually supply a standard form indicating whether they want to know about military service, club memberships, or college associations. You may expect some changing trends will affect your newspaper. Some papers are running pictures of the engaged couple, not just the bride-to-be. The article will probably devote more attention to your careers and professional associations than to social background. Some newspapers are using first names for all persons mentioned; for example, "the daughter of Sarah G. Hopkins" rather than "the daughter of Mrs. James G. Hopkins."

Listing the family's specific street address and the date of your wedding may invite theft. If you send a photograph with your announcement, it should be an 8 × 10-inch glossy portrait (5 × 7 inches is also acceptable). Be sure to attach a line of identification and to protect your photo with a piece of stiff cardboard.

Newspapers usually charge a fee for printing announcements; before you send anything in, check with the society editor on this.

AN ENGAGEMENT PARTY

Anyone may give a party in your honor, but your parents are the ones most likely to be looking forward to this pleasure. If they do have a party, it should be the first one celebrating your engagement. It may be held shortly before, after, or perhaps on the very day your engagement announcement appears in the newspapers.

Any sort of party gathering is appropriate: a buffet, a cocktail party, even a backyard picnic. "In honor of Howard and Carol" might be written on the invitations, and you two might greet guests in an informal receiving line with your parents and your fiancé's.

What about gifts? If your engagement announcement is a surprise, guests would not bring gifts; after all, how would they know why you've gathered them together? But if you've already spread the good news around, or if it's called an "engagement party," some will no doubt mark the occasion with a gift. But, traditionally, gifts should not be expected. (It is wise, once you know you're getting married, to list your choices at your favorite department store's Wedding Gift Registry. For more information, see Chapter 17.) Whether it's a surprise announcement or not, your father might choose a natural break in the festivities to propose a toast to you and your fiancé. As whenever a toast is proposed to you, you refrain from raising your glass or taking even a sip. But after that, it's the custom for your fiancé to respond by drinking to you and your parents. Another toast from you might be a loving gesture.

Your fiancé's parents may want to give a party to introduce you to their family and friends, too. This might be a luncheon, a cocktail party, or a dinner, but it should not be a shower, since the hosts this time are members of your groom's immediate family, who should not appear to be asking for gifts for you.

Be sure to thank in writing anyone who entertains for you, even if it has been as simple as a picnic outing with brothers, sisters, and cousins your own age. A sincere note, perhaps with a gift of flowers as well, will show everyone your thoughtfulness and consideration.

By the way, somewhere among the partying, your mother-in-law-to-be will probably suggest, "Oh, call me Marjorie!" (or "Mom" or "Mother B"). Or she may ask you what you would like to call her. You might suggest her first name or whatever your fiancé calls her, unless that is what you call your own mother. She hasn't brought it up? If you're still feeling a bit unsure in your relationship with her, have your fiancé drop a gentle suggestion. But chances are, you'll be comfortable enough to say, "We're getting to know one another really well, and you've already made me feel like a part of your family. Jack calls you Mom—may I call you Mom, too?"

An engagement may also raise the question of what stepparents/stepchildren will call each other. Take it slow and let children lead. One child may want to call his or her stepfather "Dad" and his or her parent "Father." It's best to talk about what feels comfortable and leave options open for growing more affectionate as time goes on: "You can call me Sam now, but I'll answer to 'Dad' if you ever feel like calling me that."

ENGAGEMENT PRESENTS

Your first engagement gift will probably be your ring, though a ring is not necessary to being engaged. A single diamond symbolizing love and fidelity is the classic choice, but other precious and semiprecious stones—from opals to emeralds—are also beautifully appropriate. When your budget is very limited, you may prefer to do without the engagement ring in favor of a really handsome wedding ring; some couples (men and women alike) choose engagement rings they will wear as wedding rings, too. Your engagement ring needn't be new. Your fiancé may wish to honor you with an heirloom ring from his family, or to have family stones reset in a style you select.

You do not have to give your fiancé an engagement gift, but many brides choose to do so. It is usually something personal and lasting, perhaps a wristwatch or leather-bound edition of his favorite book, or even a man's engagement ring. Your jeweler will show you some of the popular current styles men are wearing to display their happy about-to-be married status.

In addition to your ring—or in place of it—your fiancé may give you another gift. Such a gift may be anything you like, though choices tend to be sentimental (pearls, jewelry box) rather than practical (money, cars, clothing).

As far as family and friends are concerned, an engagement need not be a gift-giving occasion. But those particularly close to you may surprise you with household or trousseau items. Whatever you receive, respond promptly with a written note of thanks, even if you expressed your appreciation in person when you opened the gift.

ENGAGEMENT CUSTOMS

For centuries engaged couples just like you have had similar needs—to get to know each other's families, to decide where to live, and to begin assembling furnishings. Customs all over the world help couples accomplish these things. Here are some traditions you may have wondered about.

Why an engagement ring? The betrothal ring dates back to the days of marriage by purchase, when it served as both partial payment for the bride and as a symbol of the groom's honorable intentions. The gimmal ring was of three parts, and at betrothal the woman, the man, and their witness each donned a portion to wear until wedding day, when the pieces were reunited as a single ring for the bride. A "regard" ring spelled out a message of love (DEAR) with precious stones such as diamonds, emeralds, amethysts, and rubies. The diamond, first incorporated into engagement rings in medieval Italy, was, because of its hardness, chosen to stand for enduring love. Now that men and women are enjoying equal roles in their relationships, a bride may be as likely to give an engagement ring to her groom as vice versa.

Why the bridal shower? Tradition has it that the first bridal shower took place in Holland when a maiden fell in love with a poor miller. Her father forbade the marriage, denying her the customary bridal dowry. So the miller's friends "showered" the bride with gifts (just as your friends will do before your wedding) to help the young couple set up housekeeping.

What is a matchmaker? In countries where marriages are arranged, "go-betweens" play a prescribed and respected role. In China, a matchmaker must determine if astrological signs are compatible. In Uganda, the bride's elder brother and paternal uncle speak to prospective grooms and barter for the family. Do find a way to honor someone who introduced you to your fiancé, or an especially supportive friend, with a special seat at the wedding, with a corsage, small gift, or thank-you toast.

What are love tokens? Welsh and Pennsylvania Dutch couples once gave each other handcrafted gifts, useful for their future home. Such things as cake molds, butter prints, and carved spoons were covered with symbols and announcements of love. Why not give yourselves a romantic gift? Borrow an English custom: Hang a painted porcelain rolling pin over the kitchen door to use only for baking on "special days."

What was a flouncing? In Guernsey, England, a betrothal party, called a "flouncing," was held for the engaged couple to meet friends of both families. The "flouncing" established a formal contract and marked an abrupt change of status. Afterward, the couple could not be seen with or talk to other suitors. Following this formal declaration, if either changed his or her mind about the marriage, the other could lay claim to half his or her property.

Formal engagement ceremonies or parties, common in many cultures, bestowed responsibilities (a concept which grew into "breach of promise" lawsuits). For instance, in China, betrothal was a family obligation. If an engaged man died before the wedding, his intended bride was treated like a widow.

Today, your parents will want to schedule their own contemporary version of "flouncing," a chance to get together to meet each other.

Why did brides go collecting? A Finnish bride-to-be was considered snobbish if she did not go door-to-door to receive her gifts in a pillowcase. An old married man (symbolizing long-lasting marriage), in a top hat and carrying an umbrella (representing shelter), came along and was given a drink at each door! Today's bride would travel right to her department store's Wedding Gift Registry to list preferences and make shopping easier for her friends. She receives gifts at a bridal shower, where an umbrella is often a decoration, symbolizing "protection."

What is a hope chest? The bride's family once began preparing for her marriage when she was born. They collected, embroidered, and crafted items to store in a striking piece of furniture, a marriage chest. Today the groom's or bride's family might purchase the similar hope chest, which is a serviceable place to store gifts and purchases and can be a beautiful addition to your new home.

BROKEN ENGAGEMENTS

If you decide to call off your engagement, send a release to every newspaper that published your announcement, stating quite simply:

> *The engagement of Miss Ann Marie Brown and Mr. John Smith
> has been terminated by mutual consent.*

Return any gifts that were given to you for your engagement, including your ring. Your former fiancé's family will especially appreciate getting back any heirlooms that may have been given to you, but you may keep any other birthday or holiday presents you have received.

If it's a last-minute decision, wedding invitations will have to be recalled by notes, telephone calls, or telegrams (see Chapter 5), and all wedding gifts returned. A brief personal note from you to close family friends and relatives is thoughtful, but there is no need to go into details.

In the unfortunate case of a fiancé's death before the wedding, the gifts must also be returned. Someone in the bride's family may assume this task, in consideration of the bride's feelings and those of the fiancé's parents and other relatives.

WEDDINGS AND PARENTS

A wedding is a tradition as much for parents, in a sense, as it is for the couple. Not only will a man and woman look at themselves and one another in a different way once they are husband and wife, but their parents will as well. Marriage means two people are taking new roles in society. Marking this occasion with a special celebration makes it easier for everyone to adjust. Couples who choose not to involve parents, and parents who wish, for whatever reason, not to involve themselves, fail to help the adjustment process along. Even if there are misgivings, they should be put aside after they have been voiced, and everyone should try to take part in the plans.

Most situations can be helped by talking with a third party, perhaps a trusted member of the clergy or a family friend. This may be especially desirable when conflict develops over the choice of a partner of another nationality, race, or religion (see Chapter 9 for information about interfaith services). If you know that your parents will object, smooth the way ahead of time. Don't just spring an announcement on them; instead, give them a chance to get to know this special man in relaxed situations. Line up an ally—a family friend, a sister, a grand-mother who will speak on your behalf.

Practical matters such as where you'll live, how you'll support yourselves, are really your concerns. But parents do have an emotional interest in your plans. Try to be understanding. Your ability to discuss things as an adult will help your parents perceive you as a married woman.

Wedding planning can become a tug-of-war between your parents and yourself if each of you has strong feelings about what kind of wedding it will be. You and your fiancé should decide first what things are important, then talk to your mothers and fathers about their ideas. It is your day, but it's theirs also, and you'll want to be sure that everyone's happy with the plans, no matter who pays the bills. If you want extras, and they are not in the budget, do consider paying for them yourselves. As brides are rediscovering, societal and family traditions play a meaningful role in weddings and family cooperation is to be valued.

No matter how small and intimate the ceremony, a wedding is a time of transition, a time for building toward happy relationships in the future.

2
Wedding Customs

W edding customs evolve from a wish to symbolize all the good things marriage means to the couple and to their community: happiness, commitment, sharing. Every culture has its own wedding customs. The old ones are updated to accommodate changing values and ideals; new ones are created to enrich everyone's experience of the marriage celebration.

CONTEMPORARY CUSTOMS

Your wedding dress, your veil, your flowers—all have traditional significance and, in a way, mean as much to others as they mean to you. Here are the whys and wherefores of many of our modern American marriage traditions.

Why a wedding ring? The circular shape of the wedding ring has suggested unending love since the days of the early Egyptians. Primitive brides wore rings of rushes or hemp which had to be replaced every year. Early Romans chose more durable iron to symbolize the permanence of marriage. The current favorite is, of course, gold, with its lasting beauty and purity. And, again, husbands as well as wives now wear wedding bands proudly—and forever.

Why the third finger, left hand? Ancient peoples believed that the vein in the third finger of the left hand ran directly to the heart. Medieval bridegrooms placed the ring on three of the bride's fingers in turn to symbolize the Trinity: "the Father, the Son, and the Holy Spirit." The ring remained on the third finger, and that has since become the customary ring finger for all English-speaking cultures. However, in many European countries, the wedding ring is worn on the right hand. A Greek woman wears her ring on her left hand while she is engaged, moving it to her right hand after she is married.

Why does the bride wear a veil? Originally, the bride's veil symbolized her youth and virginity. Even today, in Arab countries, for instance, a young man conducts his entire courtship with his bride-to-be while she is veiled, and never is permitted to see her face until after the wedding. Early Greek and Roman brides wore flame-red veils. The red (probably representing fire) was thought to ward off demons. Early Christian brides wore white (indicating purity, celebration) or blue (symbol of the Virgin Mary's purity). It is said that Nellie Custis (Martha Washington's granddaughter, whom she later adopted as her own "daughter") began the fashion for the lacy white veil of today when she chose to wear a long scarf to her wedding to President Washington's aide, Major Lawrence Lewis. Her decision stemmed from the flattering comments her fiancé made after glimpsing her through a lace curtain at an open window. Fresh (or silk) flowers caught with a wisp of veil or a hat tied with veiling are modern interpretations of this wedding classic.

Why does the bride wear white? White has been a symbol of celebration since Roman times. In Victorian times, it was a sign of affluence. But at the turn of the century, the idea of white for purity took precedence. Happily, the white wedding gown holds its original meaning of joy today and women marrying again may choose among many shades of white, such as ecru, eggshell, or cameo.

Why does the bride carry flowers? Flowers have long stood for a variety of emotions and values—lilies for virtue, roses for love, and so on. Early Roman brides carried bunches of herbs under their veils to symbolize fidelity. The Greeks used ivy as a sign of indissoluble love. Our modern orange blossoms were originally chosen by the ancient Saracens to represent fulfillment and happiness, as the orange tree blooms and bears fruit at the same time.

Why do the bridesmaids and the groom have flowers too? Early bridesmaids' bouquets were made of pungent herbs such as rosemary and garlic—not flowers. The smell was supposed to drive away any evil spirits eyeing the bridal party. Even the groom wore a few sprigs. Your groom, though, might sport white stephanotis, other blooms, or a flower from your bouquet in his lapel.

Why does the bride carry a handkerchief? Not all brides do, but if you choose to, it will be a lucky sign. Early farmers thought a bride's wedding-day tears were lucky and brought rain for their crops. Later, a crying bride meant that she'd never shed another tear about her marriage. Today's brides embroider their initials and wedding date on a lovely lace hanky, then pass it on to the next woman in the family to marry.

Why do bridesmaids and ushers dress alike? There's a reason why the entire wedding party dresses very much like the bride and groom. It was once common for bride, groom, and all their friends to walk together to the church. Afraid that someone—maybe a rejected suitor—would spot the happy couple and put a curse on them, the groom's friends wore clothes almost identical to his, and the women costumed themselves like the bride. These disguises tricked evil-wishers into letting the real bride and groom live happily ever after. The traditions of having beautifully dressed attendants is still with us. But today it's fine to vary the styles and colors of the bridesmaids' dresses.

Why something blue? The brides of ancient Israel wore a blue ribbon on the border of their fringed robes to denote modesty, fidelity, and love—ideals still associated with that color. Blue is also the color that represents the purity of the Virgin Mary. Because of its symbolic value, blue can be found on the bride's garter, the ribbon running through her slip, the border of her bridal handkerchief, and other small touches on her costume.

Why the trousseau? Derived from the French word *trousse*, meaning bundle, the trousseau originated as a bundle of clothing and personal possessions the bride carried with her to her new home. This was later expanded into a more generous dowry that enhanced the value of an unmarried daughter in the eyes of prospective suitors. Today, the trousseau encompasses all of the new things—for the household and for the couple themselves—that help make the transition to a new stage of life.

Why is the bride given away? She isn't always. In fact, nowadays, although many brides are escorted to the altar by their fathers, they are no longer "given away." In earlier times, when women were granted fewer personal rights, the bride was literally given to the groom in an arranged marriage. A vestige of that practice could be found in the question in the marriage service, "Who gives this woman to be married to this man?" The bride who keeps the "giving away" in her marriage service often sees it as symbolic of her parents' support for her union and their promise of continued trust and affection. A popular alternative found in ceremonies today is the question, "Who supports this man and this woman in this marriage?" Both parents might respond, "We do." Or, all parents and guests might join in the response.

Why is a glass broken in a Jewish wedding? One of the most well-known—and perhaps most misunderstood—Jewish wedding traditions is that of the groom's breaking of a glass. At the close of the ceremony, a wine glass is wrapped in a napkin or handkerchief and placed on the ground. The groom stamps down, smashing it not for good luck—as commonly believed—but as a reminder of the destruction of the Holy Temple in Jerusalem, and of other calamities that befell the Jewish people that should not be forgotten, even during this most joyous occasion. The breaking of the glass generally signifies the close of the marriage ceremony and is often greeted with shouts of *"Mazel Tov!"* or "Good Luck!" from guests.

Why a wedding cake? Cake has been a part of wedding celebrations since Roman times, when a thin loaf was broken over the bride's head at the close of the ceremony. The wheat from which it was made symbolized fertility; the crumbs were eagerly sought by guests as good luck charms. During the Middle Ages, it was traditional for the bride and groom to kiss over a pile of small cakes. When an imaginative baker decided to mass all these cakes together and cover them with frosting, the modern tiered wedding cake was born.

What is the groom's cake? The groom's cake is traditionally dark and solid, often a fruitcake with marzipan and white icing. But in modern times, the choice is up to the groom, and he often chooses a banana cake, chocolate pound cake, or other favorite. In America today, the groom's cake is either served at the reception, along with the white wedding cake, or cut ahead of time by the caterer and packed in small decorated boxes for the wedding guests to take home. This way, everyone can bring home part of the couple's good fortune! Tradition holds that single guests who put a sliver of groom's cake under their pillows that night will dream of their future spouses.

If you and your groom wish to save your groom's fruitcake for your first anniversary, soak it with liquor and store it in a sealed tin.

Why rice and old shoes? In the Orient, rice means, "May you always have a full pantry," and in other cultures, it's a symbol of fertility. Today, rice remains a token of a life of plenty. A red slipper thrown onto the roof of a house indicates that a honeymoon is in progress. Among early Hebrews, sandals were often exchanged as evidence of good faith in the sale of property. Today, throwing a shoe after the bride or tying shoes to the back of the couple's car (as is done in England) signifies recognition of the creation of a new family unit.

Why a honeymoon? In ancient marriages by capture, the groom kept his bride in hiding to prevent searching relatives from finding her. The term *honeymoon* has its origin in an early Teuton custom: couples drank a fermented honey drink, known as mead or metheglin, for thirty days after their wedding or until the moon waned. An intoxicant, it might have eased sexual inhibitions. Honey is an ancient symbol of life, health, and fertility; the couple's "month of sweetness" is a time alone—a month of happiness before taking up everyday responsibilities again.

Why is the bride carried over the threshold? The Roman bride, demonstrating her reluctance to leave her father's home, had to be dragged over the threshold to her new house. It was also believed that evil spirits hovered at the threshold of the new house, so the bride was lifted over to ensure her protection from them.

TRADITIONS AROUND THE WORLD

Along with these customs that have been woven into our American wedding heritage, you may want to personalize your celebration with customs from other countries, perhaps those of your and your fiancé's ancestors. Here are some ideas.

AFRICA: Some tribes still perform the ancient rite of binding the bride's and groom's wrists together with plaited grass. Show your new ties by holding hands as you take that walk back up the aisle together as husband and wife.

AUSTRIA: Brides crown their veils with myrtle, the flower of life. Learn the "language of flowers" and send a love message with your wedding flowers.

BELGIUM: The bride of long ago would stitch her name on her bridal-day handkerchief, frame it, and keep it till it was time for the next family bride to marry. Share this tradition with your attendants—embroider a handkerchief for each one of them to treasure and hand down to their families.

BERMUDA: Even today, islanders top off their tiered wedding cakes with a tiny tree sapling. The newlyweds plant the tree at the reception. Put your little tree in a place where you both can watch it grow along with your marriage.

CHINA: The color of love and joy in Old China—red—is the favorite choice for the bride's dress, candles, gift boxes, and her money envelopes. Tuck a red rosebud in your groom's lapel, wrap bridesmaids' gifts in red paper—for a touch of vivid color and for luck.

CZECHOSLOVAKIA: Brides in the countryside carry on a very old custom—wearing wreaths of rosemary woven for them on their wedding eve. Include a sprig in your bouquet for wisdom, love, and loyalty.

ENGLAND: The village bride and her wedding party always used to walk together to the church. Leading the procession: a small girl strewing blossoms along the road, so the bride's path through life would always be happy and flower-laden. Walk to your reception site if it's nearby; and if you've young friends or are parents marrying again, let the children head the parade.

FIJI: The groom presents the bride's father with a *tabua*—a whale's tooth, which is a symbol of status and wealth. Your groom might get to know your father better over lunch, or a game of tennis, just the two of them. They'll agree on their mutual affection for you.

FINLAND: Brides once wore golden crowns. After the wedding, unmarried women danced around the blindfolded bride. It was thought that whoever she crowned would marry next. Change your headpiece to a garland of flowers at your reception. If you choose the next bride-to-be the same way, you can save your bouquet as a memento.

FRANCE: As did newlyweds of days past, many couples drink the reception toast from an engraved two-handled cup (the *coupe de mariage*) which will be passed on to future generations. You might begin shopping now for the perfect silver cup to engrave with your initials so that you'll be sure to have it in time for a champagne toast at your reception.

GERMANY: Both bride and groom hold candles trimmed with flowers and ribbons. Planning a late afternoon or evening wedding? Then say your vows by candle-glow, too—save one of the tapers to relight for a romantic first-anniversary dinner.

GREECE: The *koumbaros*, traditionally the groom's godfather, is an honored guest who participates in the wedding ceremony. Today, the *koumbaros* is very often the best man, who assists in the "crowning" of the couple, and in the circling of the altar three times. Ask your other attendants to read scripture, hold candles, store your crowns in a special box after the ceremony.

HAWAII: Marry at a sacred place still popular with Hawaiian Americans like one of many natural caves feathered by giant ferns. Do the next best thing if you can't marry in Hawaii: Honeymoon there!

HOLLAND: Dutch families used to plan a party prior to the wedding. Bride and groom would sit on thrones under a canopy of fragrant evergreens—symbolizing everlasting love. One by one, the guests came up to offer their good wishes. Why don't you host an informal buffet or barbecue for all your out-of-town guests, or ask a friend to give a breakfast on the wedding morning. Introduce them all around so they'll get to know everyone before the wedding.

INDIA: The groom's brother sprinkles flower petals (to ward off evil) on the bridal couple at the end of the ceremony. After your ceremony is over—or before—have a special family member or friend hand a single flower to every guest.

IRAN: When this country was called Persia, the groom bought the wedding dress—ten yards of sheeting to wrap 'round and 'round his bride. Not your style? Then ask your groom to remember the old tradition with a token gift . . . a white wedding handkerchief to complete your wedding ensemble.

IRELAND: The traditional wedding cake of the Emerald Isle is not a delicate white cake but a heavy and rich fruitcake with golden raisins, ground almonds, cherries, and spice. In true Irish spirit, lace the recipe with brandy or bourbon.

ITALY: Wedding guests have for centuries tossed *confetti*—these are sugared almonds, not small pieces of paper!—at the new couple. Decorate your reception tables with pretty little boxes or bags brimming with almonds—your guests will love these favors that symbolize the sweet and bitter in life.

JAPAN: Bridal couples will take nine sips of *sake*, becoming husband and wife after the first sip. Borrow a Japanese reception tradition for your ceremony: After you and your groom drink from the wine cup, ask your parents and his to exchange sips to show the close new ties between your two families.

KOREA: The groom travels to the bride's house on a white pony, bearing fidelity symbols, a gray goose and its gander, fowl that mate for life. Your groom might travel to the church in stylish transportation, too—a horse and carriage or antique roadster.

LITHUANIA: The wedded couple are served a symbolic meal by their parents— wine for joy, salt for tears, and bread for work. Ask your parents and relatives to prepare festive ethnic dishes for the celebration.

MEXICO: Guests at many Mexican weddings love observing a reception tradition—they gather around the couple in a heart-shaped ring. Your guests might do the same as you whirl through your first dance together as husband and wife.

MOROCCO: Five days before the wedding, the bride has a ceremonial bath for ritual cleansing, then is painted with henna swirls on hands and feet, adorned with makeup and jewels by other women. Pamper yourself in the days ahead of your wedding with a facial, plenty of rest, and a beauty plan.

NORWAY: After a reindeer-kabob dinner lit by the midnight sun, certain nomadic tribes have always done what everyone at your wedding will do, if you plan a big reception with a band—dance the night away.

PHILIPPINES: A white silk cord is draped around the couple's shoulders to indicate their union. Signs of togetherness in your wedding might be lighting a Unity Candle, giving your groom a boutonniere from your corsage, sipping your first toast from each other's glass with arms interlocked.

POLAND: Many reception guests have customarily pinned money on the bride to buy a dance. Collect your pin money in a white satin purse. (You can make it or find one where you buy your dress.)

RUMANIA: Guests toss sweets and nuts at the new couple to wish them prosperity. Make up packets of birdseed for your guests to throw, a wedding feast for wrens and robins.

RUSSIA: Wedding guests don't only give presents—they get them! Favor your guests with tiny picture frames, bud vases, instant photos of themselves.

SCOTLAND: In olden times, a bridegroom traveled to the goldsmiths of Edinburgh to purchase a silver teaspoon, called a "Wedding Spune," engraved with the couple's initials and wedding date, to give to his bride. You and your groom might purchase something special to commemorate your day.

SPAIN: In certain regions long ago, the bride wore a black silk dress and mantilla, orange blossoms for the hair. For the groom: a tucked shirt hand-embroidered by the bride. Try a lacy white mantilla for your headpiece and gift your groom with a shirt to go with his formalwear, after hand-embroidering his initials on the cuff.

SWEDEN: To frighten away trolls (imaginary beings who were once thought to bring misfortune), bridesmaids carried bouquets of pungent herbs—and the groom sewed thyme into his clothes. You might include fragrant lavender in your bouquet.

SWITZERLAND: The junior bridesmaid leads the procession to the reception with handfuls of colored handkerchiefs for the guests. Whoever wants a handkerchief contributes a coin toward a first nest egg, so helpful for you two!

WALES: The bride gives her attendants cuttings of myrtle from her bouquet. Tell your bridesmaids that if their plants bloom—another wedding!

No matter what your heritage or faith, you'll certainly want to follow the ancient British wedding rhyme and wear "something old, something new, something borrowed, something blue, and a lucky penny in your shoe." More "old-country" traditions can be discovered by talking with your librarian, older relatives, or leaders of cultural associations.

RELIGIOUS CUSTOMS

Each religion has traditions associated with its liturgy. You can add significance to an interfaith ceremony by learning about the customs of each faith and incorporating something meaningful into your wedding service.

Jewish couples the world over, for instance, pledge a life together under a *huppah*, a canopy of embroidered cloth or flowers, to symbolize the home they will share. The couple may sign an elaborately embellished *ketubah*, or marriage contract, with the husband's promises to his wife, which is hung in a prominent place in the home. Toward the end of the service, the rabbi or various guests recite the seven marriage benedictions (See Chapter 9).

Before a Hindu wedding ceremony begins, a holy fire is lit to the fire god, Agni, who traditionally will bear witness to the wedding. Customs during the service are both religious and cultural. A tree is planted because of the ancient belief that plants and animals were representations of the gods, and this would insure their presence. The bride's father gives her hand to the groom, then sprinkles her with holy water to indicate that his ties with her are washed away. A *thali*, a gold ornament threaded on a yellow string, is tied on the bride's neck. She will wear it for all her married life, its three knots reminding her of her duty to serve her parents, husband, and sons. The ceremony concludes when the couple circle the holy fire three times, throwing offerings of rice and flowers into the air.

Many weddings are held before a Shinto shrine in Japan, even though a marriage is not considered a religious service. The ceremony brings the bride into the family of the bridegroom. Ancestors are honored in the ritual by bowing, ringing bells, and offering food before family ancestral shrines. The bride wears a ceremonial kimono. The nine sips of *sake* are the essence of the ceremony. There are no vows. Later, sips of *sake* are exchanged with the parents, both to honor them and to mark their formal acceptance of the marriage. A Shinto priest officiates.

Other customs, such as the public signing of the marriage certificate in the Quaker marriage service, the wearing of crowns in the Greek Orthodox ceremony, and the devotions to the Blessed Mother in the Roman Catholic liturgy are described more fully in Chapter 9.

AMERICAN HERITAGE

America has a rich heritage of regional wedding traditions. In many places, a wedding is a community event, in keeping with the centuries-old understanding of marriage as a public rite of passage.

The American Hopi Indian wedding, an early example, involved the whole tribal village. The groom's clan withheld approval of the marriage until the bride proved herself by grinding corn with his female relatives. As a sign of approval, the whole community spun cotton to weave a fine set of wedding garments, really blankets, which became the bride's treasured possessions. The couple's mothers performed a cleansing ritual—washing the couple's hair—to prepare them for marriage. Then the couple went to greet the rising sun, praying for a good life together, for children, and for faithfulness to each other. Many couples today participate in Engaged Encounter, or a number of other pre-marriage discussion and counseling programs through their church or synagogue, in order to begin marriage with that same dedication (for more information, see Chapter 4).

Many couples honor their heritage at wedding time, and since family reunions are a popular summer event, what better time for a wedding than when the whole family is gathered together! The reception might even be the traditional potluck buffet. Just be sure to include your spouse's family in all the fun activities.

The custom of "open church" is popular in small communities; it means everyone's invited. The congregation might prepare a wedding quilt for a priceless gift. The quilt can consist of commemorative squares, with each person embroidering or appliquéing a meaningful event or thought on a square, to be pieced together. Or it might recreate traditional quilting patterns—Bride's Quilt, Bridal Wreath, or Double Wedding Ring.

Some couples combine the excitement and sentiment of a national holiday with the joy of a wedding. A Fourth of July wedding could feature an outdoor tent, barbecue, corn on the cob, strawberry shortcake, horse and buggy, and, of course, fireworks. At Thanksgiving, lovely fall decorations, hymns such as "We Gather Together to Ask the Lord's Blessing," and parades (your processional from church to reception) can fit perfectly into a wedding ceremony.

A wedding held at an historic site—a turn-of-the-century mansion, a museum, or battlefield—gives a bride and groom an opportunity to recreate old times using replicas of the wedding costumes, accessories, and transportation of the period. And regional traditions may be honored with specific reception attire (Western tuxedos, string ties, and cowboy boots), wedding flowers (purple lilacs for New Hampshire), or music (jazz in New Orleans).

A family heirloom can play a cherished role in your wedding proceedings. You'll relive a chapter of family history when you cut your cake with great-grandmother's sterling silver cake knife. Some brides use a generations-old cut glass punch bowl, serve punch with an antique ladle, or adorn the wedding cake with either parents' cake topper.

Whatever customs and traditions you and your fiancé choose to incorporate, you'll enjoy the sense of continuity and family heritage they give your wedding celebration.

3
Pre-Wedding Parties

Y ou'll probably attend more parties during your engagement than at any other specific time in your life. Some, like the traditional bridesmaids' luncheon, you'll host yourself. But most, other people will give for you. You and your fiancé may be honored at anything from a picnic on stadium blankets to an elegant dinner with orchids and damask, over quiet cups of tea or high-spirited cocktails, at dawn near the beach or at midnight after the theater. Your only responsibilities are to show everyone how much you are enjoying yourself, and to follow up each event with a note of thanks, and flowers perhaps, to your hostess or host. You might also tactfully see to it that no guest is invited to so many parties that he or she ends up feeling pinched for time or money. And guard your own energy—especially the last week or two before the wedding—so you will be rested and relaxed on this most important day.

SHOWERS

Showers are parties with a purpose, given to help the couple outfit their new home or assemble a trousseau. A vestige of the age-old dowry, or wealth which a woman brought to her marriage, a shower traditionally is given by women who are good friends of the bride-to-be, sometimes by a relative, most often by the honor attendant or bridesmaids. Usually, relatives (your mother or sister, or his brother, for example) refrain from giving parties where presents are expected; otherwise, it might look as if they are asking for presents for you. But this is not a hard and fast rule either—in some parts of the country, showers are traditionally given by the immediate family. If you live in a community where this is common, follow local custom. Today, a married couple, even the best man, might host these parties. In fact, almost anyone who knows you may give a shower.

Increasingly, showers may be for the couple and not the bride-to-be alone, with the groom-to-be, his close friends, and the husbands or special dates of other guests also invited. This is becoming more and more popular because men are taking a greater interest in the home, and because it's so much fun! Now that men and women are hosting and attending showers, everyone's busy weekday schedule must be considered, and the weekend brunch has become a favorite party setting. The party may be almost any type, held at any time that's convenient for you and your host or hostess. Whenever or wherever, showers are almost always informal, with a light menu and the emphasis on your pleasure as you open your presents.

The host or hostess issues invitations by telephone, mail, or in person. People who do not know you may be left off the guest list, even though they may be friends of your or your fiancé's family. The usual guest list includes your honor attendant and bridesmaids, along with your and your fiancé's mothers, sisters, and other close relatives. (Showers given by co-workers, club members, or school friends mean only members of that group will probably be on hand.)

Usually those invited to a shower are only those invited to the wedding. But one exception would be a shower or "toasting" at your office or club, where the get-together is a break in the regular office routine and the gift may be an expression of affection in which everyone chips in. These participants need not be invited to the wedding. Your fiancé's colleagues may honor him in a similar way.

In the past, second-time brides didn't have showers. But now, they are very much a part of remarried wedding celebrations. The couple's children, co-workers, parents, and friends can gather to wish them well. Friends are often more creative with second-wedding gifts, selecting a costly chip-in gift such as a video recorder that suits the couple's life-style; or giving a new linen ensemble, or stocking a cabinet with exotic, as well as necessary, cooking ingredients. The older bride has probably already established her own home and her taste may be more sophisticated. Choose gifts with an eye to her style—lingerie, a gift certificate for a facial masque, a manicure set, the latest "entertaining" cookbook, a case of champagne.

Traditional shower activities include picture-taking (the hostess should be sure there is a camera on hand) and games. At some parties, a word game is cooked up by the hostess: A humorous paragraph is made up describing the wedding couple, with key words left out. Guests are asked to list certain types of words which are later read into the text ("When Richard _____ out of the bathroom, Jane was wearing _____"). Then the paragraph is read aloud with the words, suggested out of context, plugged into the blank spaces. At some parties, guests play charades using bridal or wedding superstitions ("Happy the bride the sun shines on"). Other games: a trivia quiz, using personal details from the bride's or groom's past; pin the boutonniere on the groom, using a blown-up photograph of your fiancé. Besides being fun, games are a great ice-breaker at a shower.

The best time for a shower is at least two weeks before the wedding. Those last two weeks will be hectic, so if the bride lives far away, hold the shower when she's in town for a dress-fitting or to get her marriage license. Occasionally there simply isn't time for a shower. One idea: friends gather anyway and bring unwrapped presents to show each other. Then, while exchanging stories about the bride ("Remember that ratty nightshirt she always wore in college? I hope she threw it out!"), and thoughts about the wedding, presents are wrapped (paper and trim provided by the hostess) and packed in a box to ship to her. So she won't feel left out, place a call to the bride-to-be and tell her how much you all miss her!

When several showers are planned, the guest list should be different for each so no one ends up having to buy several shower gifts, a wedding gift, and possibly a bridesmaid's outfit as well. In a small community, or when you know that many people are eager to honor you, it is considerate to suggest that people join together to host just one general shower instead of several small ones. Should yet another friend flatter you with the news she's planning a shower, though, remember she's already put a lot of thought into it. Thank her, and say something like, "You know Dorothy Murray and Sally Lowe? They're giving me a shower too—I'd love it if there could be one shower where I'd get to see all of you together before the wedding." The thoughtful bride-to-be who has planned a formal wedding also sees to it, if possible, that people not invited to the wedding are not put in the position of being asked to a shower. The shower is, after all, not just for guests to give presents, but for them to feel part of the wedding festivities.

SHOWER THEMES

Kitchen showers, bath showers, plant, book, or travel showers—the possibilities are endless. If you've something special in mind, let that "right person" know. Otherwise, trust the good judgment of your hostess to provide the theme.

Kitchen showers are probably the most popular because of the enormous range of paraphernalia every couple can use. Novice cooks—especially those who've never kept house on their own—need everything from pots and pans, small appliances and utensils, to wastebaskets, mops, brooms, and sponges. One variation on the kitchen theme has each guest bringing a favorite recipe along with one item needed for its preparation (e.g., a flour sifter with a cake recipe). If the hostess sends out uniform recipe cards in advance, she can assemble them all into one easy-to-use recipe box or notebook. Ask each guest to paste her picture on the recipe card. Some hostesses circulate a blank book (usually ahead of time) for guests to write in some advice, inspiration, or humorous remark about marriage.

For an around-the-clock shower, each guest is assigned an hour of the day, then brings a gift to match, enclosing a note telling why she chose it (7:00 P.M.

—"An apron for the chef, your husband!"). There are many possibilities: an alarm clock, coffee mugs, or newspaper subscription for the early morning hours, a casserole dish for suppertime, and so on.

A service shower is fun for "the couple who has everything." Guests pledge a way to help in the future—a catered dinner for two, an offer to paint the living room of that house they're redecorating, Saturday morning yard work.

An office shower suggests gifts for the busy career woman: a leather-bound weekly planner for the home, stationery, a dual-alarm clock, automatic coffeepot with timer, attaché case, or household hints books.

All-female showers are naturals for frilly lingerie, sewing accessories, closet or drawer organizers and sachets, and gift certificates for luxurious beauty treatments and products.

Showers for couples lend themselves to magazine subscriptions, his-and-her tools for household maintenance, plants, wines and liquor, books and records, sporting gear, and games.

It is the hostess's job to plan a party that complements both theme and guests: a pool party or backyard barbecue for a coed group; a champagne brunch or pastel-pretty luncheon for women only; a cocktail party, buffet, or hors d'oeuvres for a gathering that's both young and old.

Naturally your exuberant "thank-yous" contribute to the fun of the party, but you should follow up with notes to each guest. At one time, notes weren't considered necessary when you thanked someone in person. But now, with showers growing bigger and people getting busier, a personal note is the only way to make sure your sincere words of appreciation won't get lost in the crowd. If your fiancé attended the party, of course, he might write his own notes to those special friends of his you don't know as well.

Every shower guest brings a gift or participates in giving a group gift. And since gift-giving will always be an expression of individuality, the gifts will be as unique as your hometown, your heritage, or the shower theme. That is as it should be. But traditionally, shower gifts have been small and relatively inexpensive. If you list your preferences in a Wedding Gift Registry, it would be a courtesy to potential shower guests to include small items such as wooden spoons, mixing bowls, and bar tools, in addition to more expensive items such as a blender and toaster. An alternative is the joint or group gift, perhaps a vacuum cleaner or lacy nightgown and peignoir set, toward which all the guests contribute. The hostess collects the money and makes the purchase, seeing to it that in cases where incomes vary widely, no guest contributes more than he or she can afford. Or, all contribute anonymously to a gift certificate at a local store. The gift enclosure card lists everyone's name, but no dollar amounts. If you would prefer one major gift to many small ones, you might drop a discreet hint to the right person (your mother or honor attendant, perhaps).

BRIDESMAIDS' PARTIES

It is customary for the bridesmaids—individually or together—to entertain for the bride. While this isn't required, they may often want to host a shower or some other festivity. You may treat your bridesmaids to a party, of course—the traditional luncheon, an afternoon tea, or even a chili-and-beer supper held at your home or neighborhood pub. Again, it doesn't matter so much what kind of celebration it is; the important thing is that everyone feels comfortable enough to have a good time. Whoever is hosting, the bridesmaids' party is the perfect time to introduce out-of-town attendants, schedule final dress fittings, display your wedding gifts, and distribute your presents to your attendants. They may also take this opportunity to present their gifts to you.

There's a delightful tradition you might want to observe that goes along with any bridesmaids' party: Serve a pink cake for dessert with a ring, coin, or thimble baked inside. Legend says the maid whose slice of cake contains the trinket will be the next to wed. Just imagine the teasing and laughing if your little sister—the one who swears she'll never get married—ends up with the prize!

If the traditional luncheon isn't lively enough for your group, borrow from the gents and have a "last fling." This kind of bridesmaids' party ("bachelorette party") would not include your mother-in-law, or anyone else who might be made uncomfortable by your letting your hair down. Wedding friends these days are heading out to have some fun at a health spa, facial salon, fancy casino, or lively nightclub.

THE BACHELOR PARTY

The bachelor dinner is another optional custom, affording the groom-to-be and his attendants a chance to release their pre-wedding jitters. The bachelor dinner may be hosted by either your fiancé's friends or by the groom-to-be himself. Schedule it several nights to a week before the wedding—not the night before! Too many ushers and grooms have missed the wedding after a late night on the town. Some of the customary high spirits associated with this bachelor night have historic roots. It was once thought that bachelors needed to get philandering out of their system. Card playing or gambling was often part of the evening, the winnings going to the groom-to-be. Why? So he could afford another night out with the boys, once his wife got hold of his money! While some bachelor parties today carry on this tradition with visits to burlesque shows or casinos, others find close camaraderie on the softball field, with a rousing game followed by a keg of beer; others plan a day at the racetrack.

Because the ushers are gathered together, the groom-to-be may be tempted to pass out his gifts to them then. But if the evening is on the wild side, they might be lost, broken, and certainly not fully appreciated. The rehearsal dinner is a better choice for distributing the gifts.

At some point during a bachelor party, usually just after dinner, the groom-to-be proposes a champagne toast to his future bride. Traditionally each man then smashes his glass so it may never be used for a less worthy purpose. If the party is held at a restaurant or club, arrangements for following this custom should be made ahead of time!

OTHER PARTIES

Wedding work parties: Addressing invitations and announcements, working out the seating plan for the reception, and lettering the place cards don't have to be hard work. One way to lighten the load? Invite your wedding party and closest friends to enjoy a buffet supper and each other's company while getting these important jobs done.

Champagne and cake tasting: There are many decisions to be made before your wedding, but none so pleasant as which champagne and what type of cake to serve. This is a perfect excuse to round up your wedding party and close friends for a prenuptial "appreciation" night. (Most bakers will produce a small version of popular wedding cake recipes.) Make it fun with rating cards and blindfolded taste tests.

THE REHEARSAL DINNER

The wedding rehearsal is generally followed up with a dinner for members of the wedding party. In many locales, your fiancé's parents, or any other close relatives or friends, may also do the honors. All your attendants (except very young children), your and your fiancé's immediate families, and the ceremony official (with spouse, if any) usually attend, along with any out-of-town guests, family, and friends you or the host wish to invite.

This dinner may be held at a private home or in a restaurant, club, or hotel, and it may be as informal or as elegant as the host would like, as long as the upcoming wedding remains the main attraction. If it is a large group, you may want to use place cards. Arrange them so that those who do not know each other become acquainted before the wedding day. The rehearsal dinner for a weekend wedding may take the form of a welcoming party for all the guests who are gathering from near and far for the wedding the next day.

The dining and drinking have been known to go on for hours, but the rehearsal dinner should never be so lavish as to eclipse the actual wedding reception. If you've not already done so, pass out your attendants' gifts with a thank-you for everyone who has been supportive. At some point, the best man usually offers a toast to the couple. The groom-to-be may follow with a toast to you and your parents. You might, if you want, lift your glass to him and his parents next, with a toast such as, "To my future husband, and to his mother and father. They raised a man so special, I couldn't help but say yes." In this smaller setting, toasts will be longer than at the wedding reception, including vignettes and humor. Many people may join in the toasts, but if they go on too long, your fiancé should be prepared with a wrap-up thought that will bring the evening to a close and get everyone home early enough to feel rested and relaxed for the wedding.

THE WEDDING BREAKFAST

Hosted by a friend or neighbor in honor of all those who've come from out of town for the occasion, the wedding-day breakfast or brunch is a wonderful way to occupy and entertain guests who may feel in need of a warm welcome. Neither you nor your fiancé and your families are expected to attend, so you can take care of last-minute preparations. Therefore, you might suggest hosting such a breakfast to a relative or friend in town who has offered to help out with some aspect of the planning along the way.

AFTER THE WEDDING

Just because you and your groom have departed for your honeymoon does not mean everyone is ready to stop celebrating. Many families and/or friends host an "epilogue" brunch, lunch, or pool party the next day for guests who have traveled far to attend. It's a relaxed way to visit with distant family members, old friends, and to savor the wedding-day feelings.

4
Planning Your Wedding

A beautiful formal wedding—the kind most couples and their families dream of—takes six to ten months to plan, up to a year in big cities and their suburbs. Even the simplest and most intimate ceremony and reception require two to three months of planning. But before beginning, you'll need to decide when, where, and how you'll marry.

WHEN AND WHERE

To set the precise date and time of your ceremony, you'll want to consider certain religious observances and local customs, as well as the degree of formality you wish and the number of weddings being planned for the same time period. Some faiths, for example, do not allow formal weddings on certain days of the calendar. Others perform wedding ceremonies only during certain hours. Caterers, too, are frequently overbooked, so you must make sure your reception site will be available on the date you choose. June is the classic month for weddings, and very popular, as are August, September, and the winter holiday season. Incidentally, the earlier you begin your planning, the more time you will have to compare services and choose those best suited to your wedding budget.

Sit down with your fiancé and figure out some general priorities. For example, you may decide a church wedding is essential, or that you really want guests to have a sumptuous dinner. Some things to consider in coming up with your guidelines are: the approximate number of guests; activities (dancing, eating—buffet or seated meal?); budget limitations; location (near your home, your parents'?); time of year; time of day.

You'll probably have a wedding season in mind—Christmas, with the church bedecked with holly and pines and your bridesmaids in red plaid taffeta; or spring, when tulips are plentiful and pastels look so pretty. Each season has its virtues, and also its drawbacks. For instance, winter snowstorms can cause transportation problems; distant relatives have a harder time getting to the wedding. In summer, many friends may be on vacation just when you've planned your day. Choose whichever works best for you both (can you arrange to get your vacations together?) and for your families.

Next select several dates. You want to get married on the day you met—Valentine's Day, but it's a Wednesday? If it's a small wedding, you may choose a weekday without much concern about out-of-towners getting there; for a larger wedding, most couples choose Saturday or Sunday to avoid conflicts with other people's schedules.

Check your dates with an official of your church or synagogue. There may be other weddings scheduled for the day you've chosen or, because of a religious holiday, a wedding may not be allowed. Do be sure there's plenty of time before and after your ceremony hour—to allow for setting up flowers, cameras, assembling your wedding party, and clearing everyone out leisurely when it's all over. It can be beneficial to share a wedding day with someone else. Ask for the name of the other bride (who will marry before or after you) to see if you can cut costs by sharing flowers and special decorations.

Next, consider the time of day for your wedding. If yours is a busy church or synagogue, not every time may be available. Your choice may be influenced by where you live, what religion you practice, what wedding style you've selected. For example, in the South, evening weddings are popular, while afternoon celebrations are common in the Southwest. For Roman Catholic weddings, 11:00 A.M. or noon are usual times, while for Protestant weddings, afternoon and early evening are more common. For a formal wedding in which your groom and ushers wear "white tie," an evening hour is customary, while for semiformal attire, morning, early or late afternoon, or late evening weddings are scheduled.

It's customary for the ceremony to take place in your hometown, but today there are many other options open to you. If you and your fiancé live in a city far from both sets of parents, for example, it may make more sense to be married there among your mutual friends. A reception immediately following, and another party later near the home of your parents, will assure that no friends and relatives feel left out.

You may choose almost any location for your wedding—a small college chapel; a vast cathedral with spires and stained glass; stately and dignified judge's chambers; a glamorous old hotel ballroom; the home where you grew up; your grandmother's garden; even a public park or the grounds of some of the prettier new apartment or condominium developments. Your religious beliefs and the number of guests you expect are the main considerations in selecting a site. A civil ceremony at city hall meets all the legal requirements, but you'll be limited in the number of guests you can invite. A home or chapel is quite suitable for a small wedding, but a Catholic church is the best place to celebrate a nuptial mass. A Jewish wedding will be lovely in a synagogue, but in some areas large ceremonies are held in clubs or hotels.

You and your fiancé need not be active members of a congregation in order to have a religious wedding. Some churches or synagogues will rent all or part of their facilities for a fee. Do check with a church representative in advance, however, as some religions will not honor the marriage of people who are of different faiths, who are divorced, or who prefer not to attend special premarital discussions with the clergy. And not every church or synagogue will be receptive to a nonmember's wedding. When approaching an unfamiliar clergymember about the use of the sanctuary, you will have better rapport if you start off with the reasons why a religious wedding service is important to you rather than why you want to borrow the setting. Be prepared to field some comments about your lack of church involvement (if this applies to you), but also be open to the idea that sometimes a wedding can be the beginning of a couple's religious affiliation. You both should remember that a particular clergymember rarely speaks for the whole denomination. If it's not possible to hold your wedding in the sanctuary of your choice, or if personalities clash, try another place of worship rather than abandoning altogether the idea of a church wedding. (In the latter case, friends, a campus ministry group, or an ethical culture society may guide you to an appropriate house of worship.)

Picture yourself at an historic castle, by a waterfall, a wave-washed cliff, in a formal garden. A wedding held in an unusual site can be a fantasy come true. But there are special considerations for an event in an unfamiliar place for which you must allow. Ask: how to arrange access for the florist or caterer; if there is public parking; is there a telephone? For help in finding and using an unusual alternate site, either for the wedding itself or for the reception, see Chapter 10.

You may make unique wedding arrangements to deal with family or personal circumstances. A couple who met while working overseas may choose to marry there—with co-workers in attendance—then visit both families for a stateside reception party. If you've just discovered that being married before January first will save you a bundle on taxes, slip away to a state with a short waiting period for speedy nuptials. Later, reaffirm those vows in the setting of your choice with a party that includes everyone. Suppose your parents in Oregon had planned to come East for the wedding, but after a skiing accident, Dad can't make the trip. You can include your folks long-distance by videotaping the service and rushing it to Oregon by air express—where Mom and Dad can view it on the video cassette player/recorder you've rented for them. Again, look for more details about these and other practical weddings in Chapter 10.

While traditionally it's been the bride's prerogative to choose the wedding site and set the style and tone of the wedding, most wedding couples today make these important decisions together. Naturally, you'll also want to regard the wishes of your parents and his. And, while you two are making decisions about wedding plans, make some about the tasks you'll be working on together after you're married: painting the spare room, planting spring bulbs for years to come.

WHAT TYPE OF WEDDING

Once you and your fiancé decide on your wedding style, your other choices will be easier. Usually, all facets of a wedding keep the same tone, so that the wedding has a uniform point of view. Picture yourself in an ornate gown, with long cathedral train—wearing field flowers in your hair. The flower accessories just don't fit! Wedding style sets a pattern that will keep all the elements of your wedding consistent.

You have two main considerations—how traditional your wedding will be, and how formal.

A traditional wedding reflects society's accepted patterns. Usually, that's what you think of when someone says the word "wedding"—probably a religious setting, a clergymember, your families and guests gathered around, a white wedding dress, ushers and bridesmaids, food and drink, a tall tiered cake, and a shower of rice. What's traditional can change depending on your age, the area of the country in which you live, and what's in fashion the year you marry.

Yours can either be a traditional wedding—one that goes by the form prescribed by accepted etiquette; or nontraditional—one still perfectly acceptable (as long as it's in good taste), but outside of common practice.

Formality is the degree of decorum evident in your choice of invitations, flowers, decorations, wedding attire; the mood of your entertaining and wedding guests. There are four basic degrees of traditional wedding formality: very formal, formal, semiformal, and informal; there are also nontraditional weddings. Knowing which style you and your families prefer will help you plan an overall atmosphere where everyone feels relaxed and has a wonderful time. Garden weddings, military weddings, double weddings, and of course, weddings that are personalized in any way may be variations of the basic types. When you consider that you can have any of these four types expressed in a traditional or nontraditional ceremony, you can see just how much flexibility you have in deciding on *your* style.

You and your fiancé should not feel excluded from having a wedding of any style, even if your everyday life-styles are very different. In addition, it is important that everyone involved feels comfortable. If your father is against wearing white tie and tails, choose a formal style that's more compatible: a tuxedo or a daytime stroller.

Here are some elements usually, but not always, associated with:

A TRADITIONAL VERY FORMAL WEDDING:
A stately gown with a cathedral or chapel train and a veil for the bride.
Formal attire (white tie and tails in the evening, cutaways in the daytime, or contemporary black contoured long or short jackets, and wing-collared shirts) for the groom and men in the wedding party.
Four to twelve bridesmaids in floor-length dresses.
Long dresses for the mothers of the bride and groom.

A high noon, late afternoon, or evening ceremony.

200 or more guests.

Engraved or printed invitations, generally with the traditional wording, and separate reception invitations enclosed.

A large and lavish reception, usually with a seated meal.

A TRADITIONAL FORMAL WEDDING:

A long dress with a chapel or sweep train; a veil or veiled hat for the bride.

Formal clothes (traditional black tie in the evening, stroller jackets with striped trousers in the daytime, or contemporary colored formal suits) for the groom and his attendants.

Two to six bridesmaids, usually in long dresses.

Elegant long or street-length dresses for the mothers.

Ceremony at any hour of the day, perhaps personalized with a couple's own vows, songs, or readings.

At least 100 guests.

Engraved or printed invitations, with either traditional or personalized wordings (response cards may not be included).

A festive reception with food and beverages appropriate to the hour.

A TRADITIONAL SEMIFORMAL WEDDING:

An elaborate street-length or simple floor-length dress in white or pastel, a hat, hair flowers, or short veil for the bride.

Dark suits with four-in-hand ties, dinner jackets, or contemporary formal suits for the groom and his attendants, depending on the hour.

One or two bridal attendants in street-length or cocktail-length dresses.

Street-length or cocktail-length dresses for the mothers.

A morning, early afternoon, or late evening ceremony.

Fewer than 100 guests.

A single engraved or printed invitation to both the ceremony and reception.

An intimate reception with light refreshments.

A TRADITIONAL INFORMAL WEDDING:

Street clothes, often a lovely suit or jacketed dress, for the bride.

Business suits for the groom and best man.

A maid or matron of honor in street clothes; no bridesmaids.

A daytime ceremony anywhere, including city hall.

A guest list including relatives and close friends.

Fifty or fewer guests.

Handwritten or personal invitations to both the ceremony and the reception.

NONTRADITIONAL WEDDINGS:

Nontraditional weddings maintain the basic styles of formality, but sub-stitute or mix elements in surprising ways. Since nontraditional weddings do not fit a formula, each one is an original.

For example, a very formal wedding with the bride in a sleek satin floor-length gown, the groom and guests in white-tie formalwear, might be held at a glass-walled dining room high atop an urban skyscraper. After the 9 P.M. ceremony (with a panoramic city view as back-drop), the wedding party—bride, groom, two attendants, judge—and their twenty guests—may sit down to a five-course dinner. A month before, each might have received an engraved invitation, hand-delivered by a man in formal dress uniform. A piano player might entertain throughout the party. Nontraditional—but done very formally, with sophisticated flair.

Another example: An informal wedding might be held at the couple's college campus on Alumni Reunion Weekend. Six of the bride's sorority sisters and six of the groom's fraternity brothers might be attendants, even though there are just fifty ceremony guests. The bride might wear a white silk suit, her hat tied with veiling; while her bridesmaids wear their own favorite street-length dresses. The groom would look smashing in a white dinner jacket, while his attendants might wear dark suits, plain formal shirts, and college ties (provided by the groom). A traditional ceremony is personalized with readings and the "fraternity pin" (love) song. In keeping with the weekend reunion festivities, an open-house reception might be catered at the groom's fraternity house, serving hearty sandwiches, cheese, beer, champagne, and wedding cake to the 200 alumni who stop by to celebrate. The bride and groom might stay to enjoy the rest of the weekend activities. Nontraditional—informal—this wed-ding successfully blends elements of a more formal wedding.

Today, etiquette rules are not hard and fast. They're flexible enough to serve modern life-styles. You and your fiancé will be able to design a ceremony and reception that meet all your needs for privacy or personal expression, yet still look like the very special social occasion a wedding always is—whether yours is formal or informal, traditional or nontraditional.

WHAT TYPE OF RECEPTION

Whether your wedding is large or small, formal or not, it is customary for the reception to follow the ceremony and complement your wedding style. For exam-ple, you might serve a light luncheon or brunch after a morning wedding, cake and punch or cocktails and hors d'oeuvres following an afternoon ceremony. Late afternoon and evening weddings are often accompanied by dinner with dancing or a large cocktail/buffet party. A wedding cake and champagne and punch for toasting are the only reception traditions. Since it is most courteous to offer guests the kind of reception fare their appetites will anticipate at your chosen hour of the day, this guideline can give a clue to trimming costs. Serving only cake and punch to 300 guests will seem more natural at 3:00 P.M. than at 6:00 P.M.

You may hold your reception almost anywhere, from the church fellowship hall to your own home or backyard, to a private club, hotel, or restaurant. Adequate kitchen facilities, sufficient space for the comfort of all your guests, and accessible parking and transportation are the only limitations.

Ideally, of course, you'll invite all your guests to both the ceremony and the reception. But it is quite proper to follow an intimate family ceremony in the morning with a large reception for your friends that evening. You and your groom may later travel to multiple receptions in other parts of the country, to celebrate with several groups of friends and relatives. After all, the reception is a celebration of your marriage—a time to have fun!

VISITING YOUR CLERGY OR JUDGE

As soon as you've decided when and where you wish to marry, make an appointment to visit the person you would like to officiate—minister, priest, rabbi, or judge. This is not only the practical thing to do, it is the requirement in many religions.

Unless you are both members of the same church, you may have to show certificates of baptism or confirmation, and perhaps a letter attesting to your marital or religious status. If you are of different faiths, you may need to get a special dispensation and arrange to have religious instruction before your wedding.

In any case, you will have to confirm your ceremony date. Have several choices in mind, since it is often necessary to reserve your day and time several months in advance, and popular churches and halls may already be booked on your chosen date. Only when church or synagogue, clergymember, and reception site are all confirmed for your date is it safe to order invitations.

Depending upon your faith, you may be asked to sign a "Letter of Intention to Marry," or begin a "Preliminary Matrimonial Investigation," or complete an "Application to Marry." Usually this states your willingness to participate in counseling together with your clergymember. These sessions can be opportunities to strengthen your religious understanding of marriage.

Be prepared for this visit by asking what will be discussed beforehand. The clergymember's secretary may be able to help you when you call for an appointment. Most clergymembers are required to have this conference with you before they are able to perform your wedding. If a concerned official brings up a topic you feel is too personal to discuss, try to understand why it is being asked. A previous marriage, for instance, would probably be discussed (what went wrong, how you tried to resolve matters). The clergymember is not being intrusive; he or she is required to see that you are marrying in good faith, with your eyes open, after considering potential problems. If you and your fiancé should find yourselves in an awkward position, a polite response might be, "You brought up some good questions. Mark and I have been talking about this a lot. But this is something we prefer to resolve in private." Then steer the conversation back to a subject that is more comfortable for everyone.

You and your fiancé may want to pursue some issues raised here in future sessions of Engaged Encounter or other premarital counseling groups (see the Appendix for more information). Engaged Encounter offers couples a chance to clarify their feelings about money, sex, children, religion, family relations, goals, how to handle conflicts, and a host of other subjects that often crop up after marriage. You may discover some surprises about each other—he wishes he could work up the nerve to make a job change; you're envious of the time he spends with his friends—and come to an understanding of each other that will be part of your marriage for all the years to come.

You'll also want to go over the details of the wedding ceremony and clarify clergy preferences regarding music, photography, and decoration. Your clergymember will bring up practical matters, such as the requirement to use the church's flower urns, rules for when photographers can snap pictures, the best place for a soloist to stand, how an interfaith service progresses, and so on. If you would like to make any changes in the standard text, or to write your own ceremony, this is the time to discuss your wishes. Couples hoping to personalize the wedding service are often surprised that the clergymember is an enormous source of ideas—after all, he or she has attended many weddings. Do take advantage of this help.

Next, you'll want to speak with the sexton, verger, or church secretary as well. He or she can explain the fire laws governing evening candlelight ceremonies, for example, and tell you all about aisle carpets, prayer benches, canopies, and any other special equipment you might need. You can make arrangements for your rehearsal or for reserved parking spaces, too.

The next person to see is the church organist—to discuss your musical program, get advice and suggestions, and make sure the organist will be available for both your ceremony and rehearsal. If additional musicians or a soloist will perform, it may be smart to schedule extra rehearsals—to make sure the timing is perfect. (For some musical selections, see Chapter 14.)

LEGALITIES

Prenuptial agreements: There are situations in which a contract concerning expectations or property is very helpful. For instance: If you're in law school and he's working, you might agree that he will not accept a transfer until you graduate; if it's a second marriage for both of you and each of you has children and personal assets, your agreement might protect the rights of each partner's children; or, if your parents are giving you the family's valuable antiques, your agreement might specify that these heirlooms would remain in your family should you later divorce. A marriage contract may state whether or not you will have children; how you will handle savings and household tasks; whether or not you will keep your maiden name. It might define your role as wife or his as husband in an uncustomary way; for example, it may state that he will be a househusband, you the breadwinner. Such an agreement should be well thought out, reviewed by a lawyer, signed by you and your groom, plus witnesses, and notarized. Although these contracts have not been fully tested in court, clarifying how both of you feel about these important issues will start your marriage off right.

Ketubah: The traditional Jewish marriage contract or *ketubah* is the agreement that specifies the groom's responsibilities toward his bride, including that he "honor and cherish" her. It's one of the many old and beautiful Jewish customs you might make a part of your wedding. Originally, the *ketubah* also provided a financial settlement for the wife in case of divorce or widowhood. Now that section is only a token element of the agreement. Some rabbis allow a more "equalized" version of the *ketubah,* with the bride also pledging to assume responsibilities in the marriage. The *ketubah* is generally drawn up for Orthodox and Conservative Jews, but not for Reform Jews. It's signed by two witnesses before the ceremony (and sometimes the bride and groom) and is handed to the bride by the groom afterward for her safekeeping. After the wedding, the *ketubah* (which may be lavishly illustrated) may be handsomely framed and hung on the wall.

Marriage license: Each state sets its own requirements for blood tests, waiting time, age of consent, so do check with officials at your wedding location. You should ask how far ahead to apply for your license, and what hours the wedding license bureau is open. You may not have time to complete arrangements if you wait until the week of the wedding. You'll probably need to bring birth certificates, proof of citizenship if you were not born in the United States, identification, parental consent if you are underage, blood tests in most states (check to see how long before they expire). Finally, ask about fees, so you'll come prepared with a check or with enough cash. Since you'll both need to be present to apply, take time out from wedding plans for a quiet lunch together to mark the occasion.

Marriage certificate: Following your ceremony, your witnesses and the officiant (in some states, the bride and groom as well) will all sign the civil certificate. Some couples include the signing in their ceremony (a Quaker custom). Your church or synagogue may also issue its own certificate. This may be a page done in calligraphy, suitable for framing, or a lovely booklet for participants, and even guests to sign (the booklet may contain the words of your ceremony). In all cases, the signing makes a great picture—do alert your photographer. Your clergymember will file your marriage certificate with the proper authorities; you'll receive a copy some weeks later by mail.

Changing your name: Once married, you can choose to use your husband's surname, continue to use your maiden name, or combine the two to suit yourself. You should, however, record any name change on all legal documents and other important papers. Here are a few:

_____Driver's license
_____Car registration
_____Passport
_____Social Security card
_____Insurance policy
_____Will
_____Voter registration card
_____Checking account
_____Savings account
_____Credit cards
_____Stock certificates
_____Post office
_____Magazine subscriptions
_____Employee I.D. card
_____School I.D. card

Marriage Information

Source: Compiled by William E. Mariano, Council on Marriage Relations, Inc., 110 E. 42d St., New York, NY 10017 (as of Aug. 24, 1982)

Marriageable age, by states, for both males and females with and without consent of parents or guardians. But in most states, the court has authority to marry young couples below the ordinary age of consent, where due regard for their morals and welfare so requires. In many states, under special circumstances, blood test and waiting period may be waived.

| State | With consent | | Without consent | | Blood test* | | Wait for | Wait after |
	Men	Women	Men	Women	Required	Other state accepted	license	license
Alabama (b)	14	14	18	18	Yes	Yes	none	none
Alaska	16	16	18	18	Yes	No	3 days	none
Arizona	16 (i)	16	18	18	Yes	Yes	none	none
Arkansas	17	16 (j)	18	18	Yes	No	3 days	none
California	18 (i)	18	18	18	Yes (n)	Yes	none	none
Colorado	16	16	18	18	Yes (n)	...	none	none
Connecticut	16	16 (i)	18	18	Yes	Yes	4 days	none
Delaware	18	16 (o)	18	18	Yes	Yes	none	24 hrs. (c)
District of Columbia	16	16	18	18	Yes	Yes	3 days	none
Florida	18	18	18	18	Yes	Yes	3 days	none
Georgia	16	16	18	18	Yes	Yes	none (k)	none
Hawaii	16	16	18	18	Yes (n)	Yes	none	none
Idaho	16	16	18	18	Yes (n)	Yes	none (k)	none
Illinois (a)	16	16	18	18	Yes (p)	Yes	none	1 day
Indiana	17 (o)	17 (o)	18	18	Yes (p)	No	72 hours	none
Iowa	16 (o)	18 (o)	18	18	Yes	Yes	3 days	none
Kansas	14	12	18	18	Yes	Yes	3 days	none
Kentucky	— (o)	— (o)	18	18	Yes	No	none	72 hours
Louisiana (a)	18 (o)	16 (j)	18	16	Yes	No	5 days	none
Maine	16 (j)	16 (j)	18	18	No	No	5 days	none
Maryland	16	16	18	18	none	none	48 hours	none
Massachusetts	— (o)	— (o)	18	18	Yes	Yes	3 days	none

State	With consent		Without consent		Blood test*		Wait for license	Wait after license
	Men	Women	Men	Women	Required	Other state accepted		
Michigan (a)	18	16	18	18	Yes	No	3 days	none
Minnesota	16 (e)	16 (e)	18	18	none	...	5 days	none
Mississippi (b)	17 (q)	15 (q)	21	21	Yes	...	3 days	none
Missouri	15	15	18	18	none	Yes	3 days	none
Montana	15	15	18	18	Yes (n)	Yes	none	3 days
Nebraska	17	17	18	18	Yes (n)	Yes	2 days	none
Nevada	16	16	18	18	none	none	none	none
New Hampshire (a)	14 (e)	13 (e)	18	18	Yes	Yes	5 days	none
New Jersey (a)	—	12	18	18	Yes	Yes	72 hours	none
New Mexico	16	16	18	18	Yes	Yes	none	none
New York	16	14	18	18	Yes (p)	No	none	24 hrs. (g)
North Carolina (a)	16	16	18	18	Yes (p)	Yes	none	none
North Dakota (a)	16	16	18	18	Yes	...	none	none
Ohio (a)	18	16	18	18	Yes	Yes	5 days	none
Oklahoma	16	16	18	18	Yes	No	none (f)(h)	none
Oregon	17	17	18	18	Yes	No	3 days	none
Pennsylvania	16	16	18	18	Yes	Yes	3 days	none
Rhode Island (a) (b)	18	16	18	18	Yes (n)	No	none	none
South Carolina	16	14	18	18	none	none	24 hrs.	none
South Dakota	16	16	18	18	Yes	Yes	none	none
Tennessee (b)	16	16	18	18	Yes	Yes	3 days	none
Texas	14	14	18	18	Yes	Yes	none	none
Utah (a)	14	14	18	18	none	Yes	none	none
Vermont (a)	18	16	18	18	Yes	...	none	5 days
Virginia (a)	16	16	18	18	Yes	Yes (m)	none	none
Washington	17	17	18	18	(c)	...	3 days	none
West Virginia	18	16	18	18	Yes	No	3 days	none
Wisconsin	16	16	18	18	Yes	Yes	5 days	none
Wyoming	16	16	19	19	Yes	Yes	none	none
Puerto Rico	18	16	21	21	(f)	none	none	none
Virgin Islands	16	14	18	18	none	none	8 days	none

*Many states have additional special requirements; contact individual state. (a) Special laws applicable to nonresidents. (b) Special laws applicable to those under 21 years Ala., bond required if male is under 18, female under 18. (c) 24 hours if one or both parties resident of state. 96 hours if both parties are nonresidents. (d) None, but both must file affidavit. (e) Parental consent plus court's consent required. (f) None, but a medical certificate is required. (g) Marriage may not be solemnized within 10 days from date of blood test. (h) If either under 18, 72 hrs. (i) Statute provides for obtaining license with parental or court consent with no state minimum age. (j) Under 16, with parental and court consent. (k) If either under 18, wait 3 full days. (l) If under stated age court consent required. (m) Va. blood test form must be used. (n) Applicant must also supply a certificate of immunity against German measles (rubella). (o) If under 18, parental and/or court consent required. (p) Statement whether person is carrier of sickle-cell anemia may be required. (q) Both parents consent required for men age 17, women age 15, one parent's consent required for men 18-20 years, women ages 16-20 years.

SELECTING YOUR RINGS

Shopping together for an engagement ring and wedding rings assures that both you and your groom-to-be will be pleased with the choices. Wedding bands may be chosen to match the engagement ring or to be worn alone. The bride's rings may or may not match the groom's, but all rings should be bought with an eye to flattering the hands that will wear them. If you wish your rings engraved, you may decide on either the traditional inscription of the bride's maiden-name initials, the groom's initials, and the wedding date, in that order ("R.G.S. from J.R.B. 6 / 12 / 85"), or any other sentimental phrase that fits in the space available. If you plan a double-ring ceremony, your honor attendant will hold the groom's ring and the best man will hold yours, until they are exchanged during the ceremony.

SPECIAL PLANNING

Disabled persons: When a member of the wedding party is disabled, you can discreetly ease his or her possible discomfort with participating by keeping the focus on the wedding ceremony. Dress any person assisting a disabled attendant in the same attire as the rest of the wedding party. If anyone in your wedding party or attending your wedding has physical limitations, take special care to anticipate his or her needs.

Anyone in a wheelchair or walking with crutches will appreciate a parking place near the church or reception door and a ramp for easy access. Features to look for inside when selecting a reception site are rest rooms with wide stalls and grab bars, low elevator controls (and in Braille), and hallways and doorways wide enough for easy wheelchair passage.

Seat hard-of-hearing guests near the front of your church or synagogue, where they can read lips or follow a sign-language interpreter. Many worship centers have amplified earphones in the front pews. Ask the sexton to be sure they are turned on. The printed word can help, with signs pointing to REST ROOMS and EXITS, and a program that includes the words to prayers and hymns.

Rather than alter your party menu, order specially prepared plates for any guests with dietary restrictions due to food allergies, a diabetic condition, or low-salt needs.

Wedding consultant: A professional may be the answer to your needs if you and your mother are already very busy with work responsibilities. For a wedding in another state, when you cannot be on the scene; or for an at-home wedding and reception, where there are so many details to attend to, a wedding consultant is invaluable. Using a wedding consultant does not mean that you give up control of your own wedding. Rather, you add a very competent facilitator to your wedding staff. She or he will listen to your ideas and your fiancé's, make suggestions, research your options, and make all the arrangements. Wedding consultants specialize in putting everything together: coming up with an overall wedding plan that meets your tastes and budget, then making sure the plan is carried out smoothly. A wedding consultant might visit the dress salon and gift registry with you, handle the selection of bridesmaid dresses, invitations, flowers, caterer. On your wedding day she or he will be on hand to see that the tent is set up correctly, the cake is the same one ordered, the service personnel know what is expected. A consultant is thoroughly familiar with wedding etiquette, ready to deal with any emergency that comes along.

How to find one of these miracle workers? Ask friends for recommendations (see Appendix). Bridal salons may also provide leads. Ask florists, caterers, photographers, and check the Yellow Pages under "Wedding Supplies and Services." Discuss the fee—will it be a flat rate, a percentage of the total budget, or an hourly charge? Sign a contract specifying responsibilities and fees, and meet with the consultant regularly to discuss details and assess progress.

WHO PAYS FOR WHAT

The bride's family is traditionally responsible for the wedding ceremony and the cost of the reception as well. Today, sharing expenses is an option that's becoming more popular. You may want to contribute to your parents' overall budget, or pay for the wedding yourselves, which makes sense if you're old enough or financially secure enough to take this responsibility—or if you're marrying again. The fact that you're paying for your own wedding needn't change anything—your parents may still issue the invitations, still be host and hostess; and your fiancé's parents still be the honored guests. Decisions should be made with the feelings of both sets of parents in mind, no matter who pays the bills.

Your fiancé's family may be eager to help financially as a gesture of friendship and love. This is a celebration of two families coming together; therefore one family need not have the major burden. Also, attitudes about marriage are changing. A bride's parents are no longer thought to be "marrying off" a daughter. Your parents, however, may be very intent on paying for everything themselves, and may politely decline all offers to help, if they wish.

There are various ways to share expenses. You can split costs three ways. Remember, though, that conflicts do arise if one family has different ideas about the ideal wedding style ("What is a wedding without dancing?"). You and your fiancé should determine the wedding style and discuss your plans with both sets of parents before wedding expenses are mentioned—that way the style will already be established. Your fiancé's family might agree to cover some specific things, such as the flowers, music, and liquor. Then, bills would be sent directly to them, eliminating the need for handling money and for holding further discussions about costs between the families. Another alternative is for one family to pay for (and plan) the ceremony; the other, the reception.

There are no firm rules about wedding protocol when families are sharing expenses. Your mother would still head the receiving line, your father make a wedding toast. But you would probably want to highlight your groom's parents too. Both sets of parents' names might appear on the wedding invitations (see Chapter 5) and his father might be asked to say the blessing or give a toast too. When his family is giving the reception, they could mail a separate invitation to the reception; or, their name and address under "R.S.V.P." on the reception card would indicate their role:

Mr. and Mrs. Alan T. Jones
request the pleasure of your company
at the wedding reception of
Mary Elizabeth Harley
and their son
Gerald A. Jones

A reception card would read:

Reception
immediately following the ceremony
Forsgate Country Club
East Brunswick, New Jersey

R.S.V.P.
Mrs. Alan T. Jones
75 Fairview Avenue
West Orange, New Jersey 07052

It is probably best if the groom's parents who volunteer to handle some expenses not ask for special accommodations—more guests or an open bar, for instance. If the groom's parents would like to host a party for the couple after the wedding, this will give them the opportunity to entertain in the style familiar to them, their relatives, and friends. Traditionally, again, the costs are divided as outlined below.

The bride (or her family) pays for:
- Invitations, announcements, and enclosures.
- Wedding dress, veil, and accessories.
- Trousseau of clothes and lingerie.
- Bouquets or corsages for honor attendant, bridesmaids, and flower girl.
- Flowers for the ceremony and reception sites.
- Engagement and wedding photographs.
- Rental fee (if any) for the church.
- Fees for the sexton, organist, and soloist.
- Rental of aisle carpet, marquee, and other equipment.
- Transportation for the bridal party to the ceremony and reception sites.
- Groom's ring (or rings).
- Wedding gift for the groom.
- Gifts for bride's attendants.
- Hotel lodging (if necessary) for any out-of-town bridesmaids.
- Bride's personal writing paper.
- Complete reception, including all food, beverages, music, decorations, tent, gratuities, and professional services.

The groom (or his family) pays for:
- Bride's engagement and wedding rings.
- Marriage license.
- Ceremony official's fee (usually ranging from $10 to $100 for the clergy; for a judge, a suitable gift may be all that's necessary).

53

- Bride's flowers, including going-away corsage and bouquet (see below).
- Groom's boutonniere and those for his attendants.
- Wedding gift for the bride.
- Gifts for the best man and ushers.
- Hotel lodging (if necessary) for out-of-town ushers.
- Complete wedding trip.

Expenses that are optional or set by local custom:
- Bride's bouquet—traditionally a gift from the groom, but may be included in the bridal outfit supplied by her family.
- Flowers for mothers and grandmothers—usually provided by the groom, but the bride may buy those for her own mother and grandmothers.
- Attendants' dresses—usually bought by each bridesmaid, but the bride may provide them (if she chooses) as attendants' gifts.
- Bridesmaids' party—usually given by the bride, but may be given by her attendants or relatives.
- Bachelor party—given by the groom's attendants and friends in most parts of the country, but may also be given by the groom.
- Rehearsal dinner—given by the groom's family in most communities, but may also be hosted by relatives or friends of the bride.

WEDDING TIPPING

Tipping is a personal expression of gratitude for service given graciously and efficiently. Your wedding professionals usually try to make your day run as smoothly as possible. The figures given below are only guidelines.

WHOM TO TIP	HOW MUCH	WHEN, AND BY WHOM
Caterer, club manager, hotel banquet manager, bridal consultant.	Up to 15% for extra-special services only. The fee usually covers everything.	Reception hosts pay bill on receipt. Add any special tip to payment.
Waiters, waitresses, bartenders, table captains.	15% for servers; 1-2% for captains (often included in catering or club bill).	If included, reception hosts pay tips with bill. If not, right after the reception.
Powder room attendants, coat room attendants in hotels or clubs.	50¢ per guest, or arrange a flat fee with the hotel or club management.	If a flat fee, reception hosts pay it with bill. If not, right after the reception.
Florist, photographer, baker, musicians you hire, limousine driver.	15% for driver; others tipped only for extra-special service, up to 15%.	Ceremony hosts tip driver at reception site. Add other tips to bill payments.

Civil-ceremony officials (judge, justice of the peace, city clerk).	Usually a flat fee ($10 and up). Some judges cannot accept money. Ask when you apply.	Groom gives fee to best man who pays the official after ceremony.
Clergymembers who perform the ceremony (minister, rabbi, priest).	Usually a donation ($20 and up) depending on ceremony size. Ask secretary.	Groom gives donation to best man who pays after ceremony.
Ceremony assistants (altar boys, sextons, cantors, choir director, organists).	Sometimes covered by church fee, or ask clergymember what's customary ($5-$25), or gift.	Ceremony hosts pay church fee when billed; separate fees, tips after service.

These percentage figures show you the proportional amounts spent on weddings. These figures are based on a recent survey by *BRIDE'S* showing that in 1984, average wedding expenses totaled $6,009. Of all wedding costs, the expense that fluctuated the most was reception spending. The style of the reception—whether a seated dinner or a cocktail party—changed the cost considerably. The 33⅓% figure is based on an expenditure of $10 per person for 200 guests.

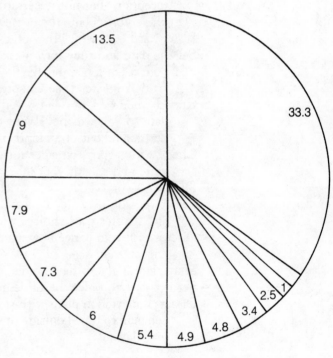

Reception	33.3%	Rehearsal dinner	4.9%
Rings	13.5%	Groom's and ushers' formalwear	4.8%
Bride's attire	9 %	Invitations	3.4%
Photography	7.9%	Attendants' gifts	2.5%
Bridesmaids' and mothers' attire	7.3%	Clergy, church	1 %
Music	6 %	Limousine	1 %
Flowers	5.4%		

BRIDE'S REMINDER LIST

A formal wedding takes months to plan. You may postpone or eliminate some of the usual preparations if you have a smaller wedding, but for a traditional large celebration, it is best to get everything done as soon as possible. The following reminder list is based on a six-month schedule. If you live in a metropolitan area, however, you may need to allow ten months to a year, and adjust the schedule accordingly.

SIX MONTHS before your wedding:

Buy (or begin) a wedding planning book or memory album.

Discuss wedding budget with your parents; if you'll share expenses, include your fiancé and his parents. Even if you won't divide costs, talk about the wedding style with everyone—everything from flowers and food to beverages and dancing.

Decide where your ceremony and reception will take place.

Determine the number of guests you can accommodate and start making out your guest list. Have your fiancé and his family start making out theirs. Guests invited to the ceremony should also be invited to the reception, but not necessarily vice versa.

Plan the color scheme for your ceremony and reception.

Visit your minister or other officiating authority with your fiancé.

Set the date and time for a wedding rehearsal.

Plan your reception and make the necessary reservations with the caterer, musicians, etc. (See Chapter 13.)

Choose your wedding dress, veil, and accessories, arranging a delivery date so you will have your complete outfit in time for your bridal portrait (about one month before the wedding).

Check with your newspaper for engagement announcement guidelines, write and submit your announcement with release date.

Shop with your fiancé for your engagement ring (his too).

Select your dinnerware, flatware, glassware, and other household items and register your choices with your favorite store.

Discuss with your fiancé how many attendants you will have and begin to choose them.

Start planning your new home and begin your household shopping.

Set the date to order the bridesmaids' dresses and headpieces.

Discuss honeymoon plans with your fiancé so reservations can be made. If you plan to travel outside the country, check on passports, visas, and inoculations.

THREE MONTHS before your wedding:

Complete your guest list and check it for duplication with your fiancé's.

Read Chapter 5 carefully, then order invitations and any announcements and enclosure cards, allowing at least four weeks for printing. Arrange to proofread them before giving the go-ahead for final printing.

Pick up invitation envelopes in advance and begin addressing them so they'll be ready for mailing as soon as the invitations are delivered.

Order your personal writing paper. (See the section on thank-you notes in Chapter 17.)

Discuss your wedding color scheme with your mother so she can choose her dress. She can then advise the groom's mother on length, color, and style for her dress.

Confirm delivery date of your dress, and if you haven't already, make the final selection of the bridesmaids' dresses.

Make appointments for fittings.

Begin shopping for your personal trousseau.

Engage a photographer or videographer to record your wedding day in pictures.

Arrange for your bridal portrait with a photographer other than the candid photographer, if you like.

Make an appointment for a gynecological examination; discuss birth control. Arrange for any tests you'll need for your marriage license.

Discuss ceremony details with organist, sexton, etc.

Firm up reception plans with the person in charge.

Visit your baker to discuss wedding cake options.

Consult with your florist and order flowers that are suitable to the wedding color scheme and season as well.

ONE MONTH before your wedding:

Mail your invitations, recording acceptances and regrets as they arrive. Send out maps and pew cards—if not included in the invitations. Begin addressing your announcements.

Check with your newspaper for directions on the wedding announcement, then prepare it accordingly.

Have the final fitting of your dress and headpiece.

Have your wedding portrait taken.

Choose and order the gifts for your attendants.

Select the groom's wedding ring (and yours, if a set) and wedding gift.

Arrange accommodations for relatives and attendants from out of town.

Plan the bridesmaids' party if you'll be giving it.

Discuss arrangements for the rehearsal dinner with the hosts.

Write thank-you notes for all gifts as they arrive.

Complete your trousseau purchases, including any luggage needed for the honeymoon.

TWO WEEKS before your wedding:

Make an appointment with your hairdresser for your wedding hairstyle.

Go with your fiancé for the marriage license.

Arrange transportation of the bridal party to the ceremony. A limousine is customary for the bride; private cars may be used for other members of the group.

Discuss details of the wedding and reception with your candid photographer. Fill out a list of "can't miss" shots.

Check on the delivery of all purchases for your new home.

Arrange to change your name, if you will be doing so, on insurance, bank, employee forms, etc.

Deliver your wedding announcement and photograph to the newspapers.

Remind each member of the wedding party about the date, time, and place of the wedding rehearsal.

ONE WEEK before your wedding:

Begin your honeymoon packing.

Make sure announcements are ready to mail on wedding day.

Give or go to the bridesmaids' party.

Present gifts to your maids at the bridesmaids' party or rehearsal dinner.

Give a final estimate of the number of reception guests to the caterer.

Check on final details with the florist, photographer, musicians, etc.

Arrange to move your wedding gifts and personal belongings to your new home.

Keep up with your thank-you notes.

GROOM'S REMINDER LIST

Today's groom shares responsibility for wedding planning with his bride, just as he participates fully in running the household after you're married. Therefore, it's important for you and your fiancé to discuss the wedding thoroughly and plan for it together from the very beginning, just as you will in your marriage.

Decide which jobs each of you will handle; which ones can be delegated to family members and friends. There are many ways to handle the division of duties: The groom might take full responsibility for the ceremony, the bride for the reception. He might take care of the reception music, you the food. Or, he might do any errands near his office while you look after stores and contacts near yours. Just be sure you talk to each other frequently.

The groom's reminder list represents the bare minimum of what the groom might do. These traditional duties are just a starting point for him today. Again a reminder that the list spans a six-month period, and should be adjusted if the wedding will take longer to plan.

SIX MONTHS before the wedding:

Order your bride's engagement and wedding rings.

If you'll be sharing wedding expenses, discuss this with your fiancée and all the parents involved.

Start making out your guest list.

Arrange a visit with the person who will be performing the ceremony.

Talk over with your fiancée how many ushers you'll need (about one for every fifty guests), and begin to select them.

Discuss honeymoon plans with your fiancée and start making transportation and accommodation reservations.

If you will be traveling abroad, be sure to update your passport, arrange for visas, and check on inoculations.

THREE MONTHS before the wedding:

Complete your family's guest list and give it to your fiancée, seeing that all addresses are complete and include zip codes.

Consult with your fiancée about the appropriate suits for you and all the men in the wedding party; order your wedding attire.

Decide on whom you want as your best man and ushers and invite them to participate.

Talk with the male attendants about their wedding attire.

Complete your honeymoon plans and purchase travel tickets.

Decide with your fiancée who will be responsible for the bride's bouquet and going-away corsage; check with her too on boutonnieres for men in the wedding party and the mothers' corsages.

ONE MONTH before the wedding:

Pick up the bride's wedding ring, checking the engraving carefully.

Arrange lodging for relatives and ushers from out of town.

Help plan the rehearsal dinner if your parents will be hosting it.

Select a gift for your bride.

Choose gifts for your attendants.

Make sure necessary documents—legal, medical, and religious—are all in order.

See that the ushers have ordered their attire.

Help your fiancée write thank-you notes.

TWO WEEKS before the wedding:

Make a date with your fiancée to get the marriage license. (This is the time to celebrate with a special date.)

Check on arrangements for the bachelor dinner, if you will be giving it.

Arrange with your best man for transportation from the reception site to the airport—or wherever you are planning to leave for your honeymoon destination.

Double-check all honeymoon reservations.

ONE WEEK before the wedding:

Remind your best man and ushers of the rehearsal time and place, and fill them in on rehearsal dinner details.

Present gifts to your attendants, at the rehearsal dinner perhaps.

Explain any special seating arrangements to the head usher.

Put the clergy's fee in a sealed envelope and give it to the best man—or give him the judge's gift. (In either case, the best man will deliver it on wedding day.)

Get your going-away clothes ready so you can change after the reception. Pack for your honeymoon.

Arrange to move belongings to your new home.

COOPERATIVE PLANNING

Working with others to create a memorable ceremony and reception is one of the major responsibilities of everyone involved. Yet disagreements, such as whether the menu should be lobster or prime ribs, whether the bride's limousine should be black or white, whether the invitations should be printed in block letters or script are bound to arise. Some disputes can be solved simply by looking up the answer among the pages in this book. Even so, etiquette is seldom a matter of right or wrong. The point is that the majority feel comfortable and happy. So if this book says one thing, and most of you would rather do another, choose what's right for you.

How to handle those situations when you can't agree? If you spend a little time to get to the bottom of the real issue, you'll often find a way to satisfy everyone's wishes at the same time. Take the mother who insists on a church wedding, while the daughter longs for a ceremony on the lawn of a country inn miles away. Then why not an intimate chapel service with a reception in the church court-yard or the family's own backyard? Incidentally, now that your fiancé is an active participant in wedding planning, you and he have a responsibility to keep communication channels open with your family and his (even more important today, when his family is likely contributing financially rather than being "honored guests"). You can seek advice when problems arise (the photographer you wanted is busy that day—what now?) or when plans change (you've decided to serve a chocolate pound cake instead of the banana nut cake you'd sampled). Your goal is to assure good feelings about each decision. And asking yourself "What difference will this make in ten years?" can help put your own preferences in perspective.

In the end, parents will do well to remember that no matter who pays the bills, it is the bride's and groom's wedding; and the couple should consider that the best thing for their marriage is to get relationships on all sides off to a warm and loving start.

5

Your Invitations and Announcements

Tradition has established guidelines for the wording, the paper, and the engraving or printing of wedding invitations and announcements. At the same time, many informal and original variations are now popular. Which is right for you? Think a moment about your wedding style. For a very formal wedding, the richness of a thick, creamy paper and "the honour of your presence" may seem most suitable. For a less formal celebration, parchment printed in pastel ink, perhaps carrying your favorite Bible verse, may appeal to you. The only thing that matters is that your guests receive your message with as much warmth and happiness as you have sent it.

THE GUEST LIST

After you and your family have settled on a budget and decided how many guests you wish to invite, ask your fiancé and his family to make up their list, letting them know how many guests you hope they will invite. Usually each family invites half the guests. Sometimes, however, one family will have a longer list—for instance, when only the groom's father and mother, brothers and sisters will be traveling to the bride's home city for the wedding. Another convenient way to divide the guest list is in thirds—the bride's parents provide one-third of the names; the groom's parents, one-third; the couple, one-third. Duplicates on the lists, and, eventually, regrets (as a rule of thumb, expect that at least three quarters of those invited will actually be able to attend) offer the opportunity to invite people who had to be eliminated on your original guest list. Mailing an invitation up to two and a half weeks before the wedding is perfectly acceptable, and that uncle downstate or former classmate away in graduate school will enjoy the invitation whenever it arrives. Incidentally, you must ask not only for names from your fiancé's family, but complete addresses with zip codes. If your fiancé's parents are divorced, the parent who raised him helps him draw up the list. But he should make sure that everyone to whom the wedding is important is invited—particularly his grandparents.

Do send invitations to your wedding official (and spouse), your fiancé's immediate family, the members of your wedding party and their parents (if you can), even though they've been invited informally. You need not invite companions for single friends on your list—the wedding may be a lot more interesting for everyone if unmarried people come without dates and mingle with one another! But if you wish to invite the friend or fiancé of a single guest, ask for the person's name and address and send a separate invitation (unless the couple live together, in which case you may mail a joint invitation, just as you would do to a married couple).

At the same time you draw up your invitation list, you should also put together your announcement list, including all those acquaintances (not invited to the wedding) with whom you wish to share the good news of your marriage. By all means, send an invitation to everyone you would like to have with you, even those you are sure will not be able to attend, if you won't be sending announcements. Old address and telephone books, alumni directories, Christmas card lists, and club rosters are all helpful in making sure no one is forgotten. Since neither an invitation nor an announcement requires a gift, you may send them to everyone who will want to share your happiness. (Remember, anyone receiving an invitation *may* come!)

Your fiancé's mother should receive three or four unsealed invitations—wedding mementos—as soon as they are ready. These may be accompanied by a note from you or your mother telling her when the others will be mailed. And, remember to tuck away some invitations for your mother and yourself as well.

PAPER AND PRINTING

While handwritten invitations may be sent for a small ceremony of fifty or fewer guests, for a larger wedding you'll undoubtedly want invitations done by your stationer. Traditionally, these are engraved, using a special process that "cuts" the letters into the paper (the letters can be felt, because they are raised). Today a wise couple learns something about other printing methods before making a choice. Thermography, a heat process fusing ink and powder, resembles engraving and is a less costly, attractive alternative. It is possible to reproduce calligraphy and hand-lettered Hebrew or Chinese characters with thermography. Your printer or stationer can advise you about other possibilities and show you samples from which to select. Formal printing is done with black, brown, or gray ink.

A classic, formal invitation is printed or engraved on the top page of a folded sheet of white or off-white paper and comes with two envelopes. The inner envelope, ungummed and unsealed, encloses the invitation (or announcement); the outer one is addressed and stamped.

The typeface you use is largely a matter of personal taste, but here are some examples of traditional looks:

Florentine Script

Venetian Script

Linear Modified Roman

SHADED ROMAN

Shaded Antique Roman

Park Avenue

Stuyvesant Script

Riviera Script

Of course, you may personalize your invitations and announcements as you wish, choosing translucent or shiny paper, a colored ink, even a border trim or a photograph of you and your groom. If colored ink is used in printing the invitations, that same color should be used to address the envelopes. Do ask someone with flawless handwriting to take on the task of addressing envelopes or writing out invitations individually.

Whatever look you have in mind for your invitations and announcements, you can order from a printer, a jeweler, a stationery or department store, or a bridal salon. Do so at least three months before the ceremony to allow plenty of time for printing, addressing, and mailing. Have the envelopes sent to you in advance (including some extras in case of mistakes). That way they'll be all addressed and ready to mail when the invitations arrive.

ADDRESSING

Make up a master list (if you put it on index cards, you'll have no trouble alphabetizing and eliminating duplications), seeing to it that all names and titles are spelled correctly. Address all invitations by hand in blue, blue-black, or black ink, never by typewriter. Remember, there is no need to do all the work yourself. Most couples today tackle this task together, turning addressing sessions into fun get-togethers with other members of the wedding party. Your bridesmaids are usually willing to help, as are your families. Consider, too, hiring a secretarial service or a specialist in calligraphy.

The outside envelope, the one to be sealed and stamped, is addressed to a married couple like this:

Mr. and Mrs. James Wallace McDermott
1088 Fielding Avenue
Metropolis, Ohio 12345

To a single person:

Miss Lucene Bedrosian
407 Kingsley Street, Apartment 4-B
Metropolis, Ohio 12345

The only abbreviations used are *Mr., Mrs., Ms.* (if it is preferred), *Jr.,* and *Dr.* Most elected officials are addressed as *The Honorable* (a judge, for instance); most clergy as *The Reverend* or *The Reverend Father,* or *Rabbi;* and high-ranking military personnel as *Commander, Colonel,* etc. Divorcées are either the very traditional *Mrs. Phillips Ross* (a combination of maiden and married surnames) or *Mrs. Joan Ross;* widows, *Mrs. Earl Johnson.* A single woman, even a child, is addressed as *Miss (or Ms.) Sandra Lightner;* a young boy, as *Master Jordan Sullivan.* Try to avoid nicknames or initials. Write out streets, cities, and states in full as well. And don't forget zip codes!

New situations may call for new forms of address. Once all women who were doctors, officers in the military, or the like went by their married names for social purposes. Now, some prefer their professional names and titles. Other wives may have retained their maiden names. In these cases, you may send one invitation to both husband and wife, putting her name above his on the envelope, as:

Dr. Sheila Vincente
Mr. David Vincente
1010 Maplewood Road
Metropolis, Ohio 12345

A married couple with different names or an unmarried couple living together receive joint invitations, with their names listed alphabetically, for instance:

Ms. Jane Adams
Mr. John Snyder
393 Atlantic Boulevard, Apartment 6-F
Metropolis, Ohio 12345

The unsealed inner envelope does not include first names or addresses, but reads simply:

Mr. and Mrs. McDermott
Dr. Vincente and Mr. Vincente
Ms. Adams and Mr. Snyder

If several members of a family are to be invited, avoid using the phrase "and family" because you want everyone who is invited to feel the invitation is especially for them. Instead, on the inner envelope only, include the name of each child invited, as:

Mr. and Mrs. McDermott
Elaine and Charles

Adult members of a family—everyone over eighteen—should receive separate invitations, whether they still live with their parents or not. You may, however, send one joint invitation to two brothers or sisters living together at another address. Two unrelated friends living together as roommates should each receive their own invitation. Each invited guest should receive a personal invitation to your wedding. Even if you've told your cousin to bring along her current boyfriend, it would not be correct to address the invitation to *Miss Sheila Hoffmann and Guest*. Give her a call and get his exact name and address so you can send him an invitation of his own.

MAILING

The larger, more formal invitation is first folded across the middle of the engraved double sheet, then slipped into the inner envelope with the folded side down. On opening, the guest should first see the names of the wedding sponsors—usually the bride's parents. The less formal, and more popular, invitation is not folded again, but is placed in the envelope as is, with the engraved side facing up.

Extra enclosures—pew cards, reception cards, at-home cards, maps—may be placed next to the engraving or be inserted in one fold of the invitation or announcement. Tissues placed over the lettering to prevent smudging while the ink dries are usually tossed away, but may be left in place for convenience. However, if they are not inserted by the printer, there is no need to add them.

The unsealed inner envelope is placed in the outer envelope so that the guest's name immediately comes to view when the outside envelope is opened.

Mail invitations four to six weeks before the wedding; two months ahead is courteous if you will marry during the holiday season, when friends and relatives will be juggling many commitments on their calendars.

Do allow people time to consider your invitation and to word their replies. Depending on the formality of your invitation, they will respond with formal written acceptances or regrets, with informal notes, even phone calls or response cards (if you've chosen to send them). It's two weeks until the wedding, and you still haven't heard? Then a member of your family may call and check: "We are all looking forward to seeing you at Rachel's wedding on the twenty-third, Mr. Goldberg. Will you be able to join us?" When each invitation is accounted for, tell your caterer how many guests to expect.

Formal announcements—as beautiful as classic invitations and intended for those who will not be asked to the wedding—should be mailed the day of the wedding or immediately afterward. Ask a bridesmaid or your sister to do this, or you and your groom can stop by the post office yourselves on your way out of town.

Do include a return address on invitations and announcements both. Once it was standard to emboss the return address colorlessly on the envelope flap. Now, however, the U.S. Post Office encourages that all return addresses appear in the upper left-hand corner of the envelope front to expedite mail handling. Talk to your printer and local post office officials if there is any question about your return address. And, if your invitations are handwritten, do follow the suggested form and write the return address on the front of the envelope.

WORDING YOUR INVITATIONS

Parents of the bride usually issue the invitations and announcements, whether or not she still shares their home. If your parents are no longer living, your guardian, closest relatives, or family friends may sponsor your wedding and issue the invitations. If your parents are divorced, the one who raised you customarily issues the invitations and announcements. Are you confused about the wording? It helps to remember that the names at the top of a wedding invitation refer to those sponsoring the wedding, not to those paying for it. Even if you and your fiancé will be paying, your parents can still be considered sponsors and should feel proud to see their names on the first line. Whenever debating between one wording for an invitation or announcement and another, remember that a name is very special, very important to a person.

On formal invitations, all names are spelled out in full without nicknames. Spell out numbers, including those in short addresses, and *Junior,* if space permits. The date is written, *Saturday the sixth of July,* with the year spelled out on the following line. (You may, if you wish, omit the year from invitations.) The time is indicated as *four o'clock* or *half after four o'clock.* If there are churches with similar names in the same city, and many of your guests are unfamiliar with the location, the street address should be indicated beneath the name of the ceremony site. The state may or may not be included, depending again on how many of your guests are familiar with the area.

The honour of your presence is the wording always used for a religious ceremony, but use *the pleasure of your company* for the reception. You may bid a reply to a reception invitation with *R.S.V.P., Please respond, Kindly respond,* or *The favour of a reply is requested.* (*Honour* and *favour* are always spelled with a *u.*) You may also specify a response date. Traditionally, the bride's surname is not listed, unless it is different from that of her parents. "Mr." before the groom's name may be omitted.

No matter how carefully you scrutinized your copy before giving it to the printer, request a proof of your invitation and study every detail. Check the time, spelling of words and names, address of the church, date, punctuation. Mistakes in the final prints add unnecessary confusion and expense.

When the bride's family is sponsoring the wedding, the typical invitation reads:

> *Mr. and Mrs. Charles Andrew Jones*
> *request the honour of your presence*
> *at the marriage of their daughter*
> *Mary Lynn*
> *to*
> *Mr. Edward Robins Hill*
> *Saturday, the sixth of May*
> *at four o'clock*
> *All Saints Church*
> *Barton, Texas*

The formal reception card to accompany this invitation would read:

> *Mr. and Mrs. Charles Andrew Jones*
> *request the pleasure of your company*
> *Saturday, the sixth of May*
> *at five o'clock*
> *Glen Oaks Country Club*
> *R.S.V.P.*
> *Sixty-two Laurel Lane*
> *Barton, Texas 12345*

The reception card may also take this simplified form:

> *Reception*
> *immediately following the ceremony*
> *Glen Oaks Country Club*
> *Kindly respond*
> *Sixty-two Laurel Lane*
> *Barton, Texas 12345*

If all guests are to be invited to both the ceremony and a reception that takes place right after, a combined invitation may be sent without separate enclosure cards. This very popular form reads:

Mr. and Mrs. Charles Andrew Jones
request the honour of your presence
at the marriage of their daughter
Mary Lynn
to
Mr. Edward Robins Hill
Saturday, the sixth of May
at four o'clock
All Saints Church
Barton, Texas
and afterwards at
Glen Oaks Country Club

Please respond
62 Laurel Lane
Barton, Texas 12345

If the reception has a larger guest list than the ceremony, invitations are issued to the reception with ceremony cards enclosed. The invitation reads:

Mr. and Mrs. Charles Andrew Jones
request the pleasure of your company
at the wedding reception of their daughter
Mary Lynn
and
Mr. Edward Robins Hill
Saturday, the sixth of May
at five o'clock
Glen Oaks Country Club
Barton, Texas

Please respond
62 Laurel Lane
Barton, Texas 12345

The ceremony card reads:

Mr. and Mrs. Charles Andrew Jones
request the honour of your presence
Saturday, the sixth of May
at four o'clock
All Saints Church
Barton, Texas

The ceremony card may also take this simplified form:

Ceremony
at four o'clock
All Saints Church

A similar reception invitation that includes the names of the groom's parents might read:

Mr. and Mrs. Charles Andrew Jones
request the pleasure of your company
at the wedding reception of their daughter
Mary Lynn
and
Mr. Edward Robins Hill
son of
Mr. and Mrs. Donald Lawrence Hill
Saturday, the sixth of May
etc.

Another form for the longer reception invitation indicating joint sponsorship is common. However, it does not spell out the relationships of parents to the bride and groom quite so clearly. And some couples may not be comfortable with the word "children." Others may think the wording has a particularly warm sound. The invitation reads:

Mr. and Mrs. Charles Andrew Jones
and
Mr. and Mrs. Donald Lawrence Hill
request the pleasure of your company
at the wedding reception of their children
Mary Lynn
and
Edward Robins
Saturday, the sixth of May
etc.

Should there be too few guests invited to the ceremony to warrant special cards, tuck in a plain or printed informal note card with the simple handwritten message, "Ceremony at four o'clock, All Saints Church."

To include both sets of parents, follow the form shown earlier in this chapter.

For a small, informal wedding, or one planned in a hurry, printed invitations are not necessary. Instead, your parents may send handwritten notes with an R.S.V.P. address, or they may invite guests personally at least two weeks before the ceremony. Such a note might read:

Dear Rose,

Judith and Michael are to be married at half past three on Sunday, the fifth of September, in the chapel of Temple Emanuel here in Green Heights. It will be a small wedding with a reception afterward at our house. You know how much we all want you to be with us on that day.

Affectionately,
Ruth

It is more gracious to write notes, but it is all right, too, for you or your parents to telephone your invitations. If you make the call you might say, "Mother and Dad wanted you to be with us . . ." so that guests know your family is hosting the wedding.

SPECIAL INVITATIONS

Widowed parents: A deceased parent is mentioned in wedding announcements in the newspaper, but not included on the invitation for two reasons: First, an invitation is issued to share an occasion together; second, a wedding is a happy time and this would strike a note of sadness. If one of your parents has died, the wedding invitation takes the following form, unless the widow or widower has remarried. A widow would send an invitation reading:

Mrs. Robert Kowolsky
requests the honour of your presence
at the marriage of her daughter
Theresa Louise
etc.

A widower would substitute the phrase "his daughter."

When the bride's mother has remarried, the following wording is used:

Mr. and Mrs. Ricardo Rojas
request the honour of your presence
at the marriage of Mrs. Rojas's daughter
[or, if the bride is close to her stepfather, their daughter]
Angela Madelena Mendoza
etc.

When a remarried father sponsors the wedding, this wording is used:

Mr. and Mrs. Victor Mendoza
request the honour of your presence
at the marriage of Mr. Mendoza's daughter
[or, if the bride is close to her stepmother, their daughter]
Angela Madelena
etc.

Divorced parents: When the parents of the bride are divorced, the wedding invitation is usually issued by the parent who raised the bride. If she or he has remarried, the invitation would be worded just as for widowed parents who've remarried (see above).

If your mother issues the invitations, and she has not remarried, she may use either the traditional divorcée's combination of her maiden and married surnames (Mrs. Collins Anderson) or drop the "Mrs." altogether (Sarah Collins Anderson). If she ordinarily goes by her first, middle, and married surname (Mrs. Sarah Beth Anderson), that too is now considered acceptable. The rest of the invitation is worded as for a widowed parent.

If your divorced father is sponsoring the wedding, then the invitation carries his full name and the phrase "his daughter."

When divorced parents are still very friendly, they may wish to send a joint invitation to their daughter's wedding. Generally they avoid "Mr. and Mrs." since that is no longer the case, and list their names—remarried or not—separately, as:

Sarah Collins Anderson
and
Steven Randolph Anderson
request the honour of your presence
at the marriage of their daughter
Abigail Blake
to
Christopher Howard Geist
etc.

Notice in this case that the "Mr." can also be omitted from the groom's name to keep the look of the invitation consistent.

Sometimes the daughter of divorced parents would like both to be acknowledged equally at her wedding, but they are not entirely comfortable with their names appearing together. Then the solution might be for one parent to issue the wedding invitations and the other the reception invitations—mailed in the same outer envelope, of course.

Is your groom the one with divorced parents? The same guidelines apply, and the samples here can be adapted accordingly.

A single parent, divorced or widowed, may sponsor the wedding with someone else—a live-in partner, grandparents, or an aunt. The form for such an invitation would list the names of sponsors separately and designate which person is the parent, as follows:

Mrs. Estelle Mahoney
and
Mr. Stephen J. Barkley
request the honour of your presence
at the marriage of Mrs. Mahoney's daughter
Ellen Victoria
etc.

Sponsors other than parents of the bride: If the bride is being sponsored by other relatives, words such as "his sister," "her sister," "his," "her," or "their niece" are substituted for the phrase "their daughter" to indicate the relationship. Close friends may also sponsor the bride (see wording, below). Then the invitation gives the bride's full name, with "Miss" before it:

Mr. and Mrs. George Anthony Donato
request the honour of your presence
at the marriage of
Miss Cheryl Diane Callas
to
Mr. Arnold Lee Gregory
etc.

The bride's surname: In several instances the bride's surname would appear on the invitations.

The bride has a professional title:

Mr. and Mrs. George W. Harvey
request the honour of your presence
at the marriage of
Dr. Stephanie R. Harvey
to
Dr. Alan G. Anderson

The bride has been previously married:

Mr. and Mrs. George W. Harvey
request the honour of your presence
at the marriage of
Ms. Stephanie Harvey Millsap
to
Mr. G. Allen Montclair

The bride's mother has remarried:

Mr. and Mrs. Albert G. Sutton
request the honour of your presence
at the marriage of Mrs. Sutton's daughter
Stephanie R. Harvey

Sponsorship by the couple themselves: When the bride has no sponsor—no family or close friends nearby—and she and her fiancé have been on their own for a while—they may prefer to issue their own invitations. Such an invitation reads:

The honour of your presence
is requested at the marriage of
Miss Margaret Jean Murphy
to
Mr. Leo Stanley Stark
Saturday, the fifth of November
at eleven o'clock
St. Cecilia's Church
South Bay, California

The invitation might include the simplified reception card shown earlier in this chapter, or a card saying:

The pleasure of your company is requested
Saturday, the fifth of November
at half after eleven o'clock
The Waterside
South Bay, California
R.S.V.P.
1600 Ocean Parkway, Apartment 12-L
South Bay, California 12345

Second marriages: Whether the bride has been widowed or divorced, formal invitations to her wedding may be issued. Her wedding may be hosted by those close to her or by her and her fiancé themselves. There are lovely options in wording (see them in Chapter 11).

Double weddings: Most often a double wedding involves two sisters. The invitation to the occasion would read:

Mr. and Mrs. Nicholas Pappas
request the honour of your presence
at the marriage of their daughters
Katherine Denise
to

Mr. Milton Zara
and
Christine Eugenia
to
Mr. Matthew Hercules
at half after seven o'clock, the first of August
St. Barbara Greek Orthodox Church
Inport, Connecticut

When the brides are not sisters, separate invitations may be sent by each family, or they may mail a joint invitation:

Mr. and Mrs. Samuel Catt Saulsberry
and
Mr. and Mrs. Gaylord Rogers
request the honour of your presence
at the marriage of their daughters
Susan Ann Saulsberry
to
Mr. Bruce Raymond Harnett
and
Brenda Lou Rogers
to
Mr. Randolph Sloan Lincoln
etc.

Personalized invitations: Couples and their parents today, especially those who wish to share religious feelings with their guests, may choose to send invitations worded in other than the classic manner. An experienced printer can suggest complementary paper—a scroll of parchment, perhaps, or a prettily decorated pastel. Or, of course, the invitations may be written by hand. If composing your own wording, do remember to include the basics that are so frequently forgotten on personalized invitations: sponsor's names; ceremony site, date, time; reception site, date, time; address, if any, for replies. Just so long as your invitation is easy for guests to follow, you may adapt any traditional guidelines as you see fit, for instance, substituting numerals for complete spellings (7 P.M. for seven o'clock).

As with any touch used to personalize a wedding, some guests may comment adversely. It is likely that this will be minimal if you take care to make the invitation warm but not effusive, concise rather than long, and in keeping with the mood of the entire celebration—not ultraformal. One invitation to a semi-formal wedding:

Warner and Pamela Simpson
and
William and Mary Marcus
invite you
to share in the joy
of the marriage
uniting our children
Nicole and Jerry
at the First Baptist Church
607 Lincoln Avenue
New Petersburg
Saturday, the thirtieth of August, 1985
at 4 P.M.
Worship with us, witness their vows
and
join us afterward at
the Church Fellowship Hall.
If you are unable to attend, we ask your
presence in thought and in prayer.

R.S.V.P.
(301) 223-1234

SPECIAL ENCLOSURES

Enclosures are printed on the same quality paper and in the same style as the invitation itself.

At-home cards: At-home cards may be enclosed with formal invitations but are more often used with announcements (see the section later in this chapter). What are they? Small cards that let everyone know your new address and the date you will be ready to receive mail—and visitors—there. A typical at-home card reads:

At home
after the twenty-sixth of August
1413 Fountain Avenue
Atlanta, Georgia 12345

When enclosed with announcements, they may also take this form:

Mr. and Mrs. John Simon Eagle
after the tenth of April
1035 Fifth Avenue, Apartment 9-B
New York, New York 12345

If the bride plans to retain her maiden or professional name, the at-home card is the perfect place to announce that, as:

> *Dr. Mary Ann Janacek*
> *Mr. John Simon Eagle*
> *after the tenth of April*
> etc.

Name cards: This is an efficient way for the working woman to inform her colleagues of her intention to retain her maiden name or adopt a hyphenated one:

> *Kirsten Andrews and Roger Sullivan*
> *wish to announce that they will be*
> *adopting the surname Andrews-Sullivan*
> *following their marriage*
> *June 16, 1985*

Ceremony cards: When there is any chance that uninvited persons may try to attend the ceremony or when the wedding is held in a public or historic place such as a museum, a mansion, or a yacht, engraved cards may be enclosed with invitations to be presented at the door for admittance. These would read:

> *Please present this card*
> *The First Congregational Church*
> *Saturday, the twelfth of March*

Pew cards: Special seating arrangements for relatives and for very close friends are indicated with these cards. They are best sent after the acceptance has been received to ensure the correct number of reserved seats. But they too may be enclosed with the invitation. There are several forms, the simplest being a handwritten note from the bride's parents. A more elaborate form reads:

> *Please present this card*
> *The First Congregational Church*
> *Saturday, the twelfth of March*
> *Pew number 9*

General reservations may also be indicated by the phrase "within the ribbons"—in which case pretty satin ribbons or bows decorate the last pew of the reserved section, and all special guests are escorted to seats in front of this pew. The phrase may appear on either the admission or pew cards (above) in the lower left-hand corner instead of the special pew number. However, general reservations are used only for very large, very formal weddings.

Reception response cards: To send them or not is a question to consider carefully. Traditionally they are avoided for very formal weddings. But reception response cards are gaining acceptability in many areas and may be enclosed with invitations, as long as this is welcomed as a convenience among the majority of your guests. Others look forward to observing the courteous custom of a personal reply (see Chapter 18 for wording). It is up to you to decide. If you do enclose response cards, they must be at least 3 × 5 inches and the return envelopes should already be stamped and addressed. The following form seems to be the clearest and easiest for guests, who circle the correct answer or cross out the response which does not apply:

Miss Lorraine Doyle
accepts
regrets
Saturday, July second
Court Hotel
Charlottesville

Another form used frequently asks the guests to fill in his or her name and add the word "not" if the invitation must be declined. It reads simply:

_____*will*_____*attend.*

Rain cards: If your invitation is for a garden wedding and outdoor reception, bad weather will throw everything into chaos unless guests have some idea of what to do. A rain card saves all those last-minute telephone calls by telling them just what to do:

In case of rain
the wedding and reception
will be held in
Myers Park Methodist Church
424 River Road
one o'clock in the afternoon

Travel cards: If you have chartered a bus to ferry your urban wedding guests to your country inn reception; or, if you've arranged for picking up the tab for parking and gratuities at a nearby garage, a travel card is useful. Have the necessary information printed on a card that will also serve as an admission pass:

A special bus will leave
St. Mary's Parish Hall
at three o'clock in the afternoon
and arrive back in Washington

at eight o'clock in the evening.
Please present this card to the driver.

Parking provided
McKenzie Parking Garage
2018 Main Street
Gratuities included
Please present this card to the parking attendant.

Maps: More frequently, these are being enclosed in formal invitations, saving guests the trouble of requiring directions to the ceremony site at the time of response and requiring another mailing. After the ceremony, ushers take on the responsibility of seeing that guests have their instructions and transportation to the reception. The maps, of course, should be drawn and printed in as beautiful and professional a manner as the invitation itself. (Be prepared with extras, in case guests misplace them.)

MILITARY AND OTHER TITLES

Traditionally, the bride's last name and title of "Miss," "Ms.," or "Mrs." (for certain second-time brides) are omitted on the formal invitation, while the groom's full name is used, preceded by "Mr." Perhaps, though, the bride and groom wish their names to be in the same form. In this case, they may leave off titles and both use their first, middle, and last names.

If the bride's father, the groom, or the groom's father (when his name appears on the invitation) are clergymen, physicians, high elected officials, or members of the armed forces on active duty, they may go by their professional titles. A clergyman's full title—The Reverend, The Most Reverend, Rabbi—is spelled out before his name. The name of a medical doctor is preceded by "Dr." instead of "Mr." When the bride or her mother is a physician, judge, or member of the clergy, the title has customarily been dropped, although it now may be included along with her complete name (i.e., Mr. John Smith and The Honorable Jane Smith; Mr. John Smith and Dr. Jane Smith). The titles of senators and judges, and other high officials, may be used, but those of lesser officials are usually omitted.

Military titles and social invitations are subject to changing regulations and should always be verified with the commanding officer. Even so, the title of the bride's father is usually spelled out before his name. The groom's title appears before his name only if he holds a rank equivalent to or higher than captain in the Army or commander in the Navy. If he occupies a lesser rank, it may be listed with his branch of service, as follows:

Jeffrey Ronald Sherman
Lieutenant, United States Army

If the groom is an enlisted man, his branch of service may be shown without mention of his rank. In either case, the title "Mr." is omitted. Reserve officers do not use military titles unless they are on active duty. A bride in the military service follows the same guidelines as the groom—or she may do without her title in favor of the familiar first-name form.

The use of titles in forms of address varies with rank, denomination or religion, and sex. Here are some titles you may need to know for addressing invitations, making introductions, or writing out place cards.

PERSONAGE	ADDRESS INVITATION	INTRODUCTION	NAME CARD
Clergymember, Protestant (no degree)	The Reverend Paul Jones	Mr. Jones	Mr. Jones
Clergymember, Protestant (with degree)	The Reverend Doctor Paul Jones	Dr. Jones	Dr. Jones
Clergymember, R. Catholic	The Reverend Paul Jones	Father Jones	Father Jones
Orthodox Priest	The Very Reverend George Kontos	Father Kontos	Father Kontos
Bishop	The Most Reverend Daniel Bell, Bishop of Texas (R. Catholic)	Your Excellency, Bishop Bell	Bishop Bell
	The Right Reverend John Smith, Bishop of Detroit (Episcopal)	Bishop Smith	Bishop Smith
Vicar General	The Right Reverend Monsignor Robert Macdonald	Monsignor Macdonald	Monsignor Macdonald
Rabbi	Rabbi Nathan Ziff, D.D.	Rabbi Ziff or Doctor Ziff	Rabbi Ziff or Doctor Ziff
Cantor	Cantor David Levy	Cantor Levy	Cantor Levy
Professor	Martin S. Severino, Ph.D. or Professor Martin Severino	Dr. Severino or Professor Severino	Dr. Severino or Professor Severino
Judge	The Honorable Walter Reynolds	Judge Reynolds	Judge Reynolds or Mr. Justice Reynolds
Dean	Dean Samuel Brandon or Samuel Brandon, Ph. D.	Dean Brandon or Doctor Brandon	Dean Brandon or Doctor Brandon
Lawyer	Mr. Alfred Standish or Alfred Standish, Esq.	Mr. Standish	Mr. Standish
Mayor	The Honorable Patricia Kelly, Mayor of Middletown	Madam Mayor or Mayor Kelly	Mayor Kelly or Ms. Kelly
Army Officer	Captain Leslie Wainwright, U.S. Army	Captain Wainwright	Captain Wainwright
Navy Officer	Lieutenant Commander William G. Smith, U.S. Navy	Lieutenant Commander Smith	Lieutenant Commander Smith
Physician	Marcella D. Hopkins, M.D.	Doctor Hopkins	Doctor Hopkins

INVITATIONS IN A HURRY

If you're getting married quickly—and that may mean six weeks or one week from now—you will not have time to get invitations printed and in the mail. You may send handwritten notes, telegrams, mailgrams, or even telephone your invitations. You will probably need to enlist friends to help get the news out. The important thing to remember is to include all the information your guests need. Since you'll not be able to avail yourself of printed invitations (which include an incredible amount of information in a small space), you will have to tell your guests who's getting married, where, when, what kind of service, location of the reception, where to respond, and where to send gifts (a return address).

RECALLING INVITATIONS

If a formal wedding is postponed or canceled after the invitations have gone out, all invited guests must be notified as soon as possible. When time permits, this is best done with printed cards, rush-ordered from the stationer. If there has been a death in the family, the card would read:

Mrs. Gerald Timothy Allen
regrets that the death of
Mr. Allen
obliges her to recall the invitations
to the wedding of her daughter
Saturday, the third of February

An invitation recalled in this manner indicates only that the wedding will not take place as originally planned. When a death or serious illness in the family means a large wedding would be inappropriate, the marriage may still take place as a small family ceremony. The couple may wear their formal wedding attire, but they usually have honor attendants only.

If the wedding is postponed and a new date set, you may send out new printed invitations to your guests. Such a notification would read:

Mr. and Mrs. Stuart Dean Jefferson
announce that the marriage of their daughter
Virginia
to
Mr. Frank Martin Gallagher
has been postponed from
Saturday, the fourth of October
until
Saturday, the eighteenth of October
at four o'clock
Grace Episcopal Church
Wilfordshire

If the wedding is canceled, invitations should be recalled promptly with an engraved or printed card reading:

Mr. and Mrs. Warren Troy Peterson
announce that the marriage of
their daughter
Ellen
to
Henry Karl Schneider
will not take place

If time is short, invitations may be recalled by personal notes, telegrams, or telephone calls. Notes should be patterned after the cards, and signed by the person who issued the invitations. Calls should be made in the name of the bride's parents. Reasons other than a death or illness in the family are not usually mentioned.

WORDING YOUR ANNOUNCEMENTS

Announcements are problem-solvers. Usually not mailed to anyone who has been invited to the wedding, they can go out after an intimate ceremony for family only, after an elopement, or a wedding so far away many people could not attend. One instance in which announcements might be sent to wedding guests would be when a small group of twenty to twenty-five were invited to the ceremony by telephone. Your announcement, after the wedding, would be a lovely memento.

Business associates with whom the couple work day to day might also receive announcements. (Remember, no one on the announcement list need feel obliged to send you a gift.) With time and budget on the minds of more and more couples and parents, sending announcements is an old wedding custom that makes good sense today.

Printing and paper for announcements are the same as for invitations. Announcements should be addressed just as wedding invitations are and, whenever possible, mailed out immediately after the ceremony. A typical announcement reads:

Mr. and Mrs. Peter Young Chow
have the honour of announcing
the marriage of their daughter
Annette Elizabeth
and
Mr. Leonard Park Ling
on Friday, the tenth of July

one thousand nine hundred and eighty-five
Our Redeemer Lutheran Church
Seattle, Washington

The bride's parents may also "have the honour to announce a marriage" or simply "announce the marriage." The date, year, and city in which the marriage took place are always included. It is optional, however, to mention the actual ceremony site.

When the bride or her parents are divorced or widowed, the wording is varied in the same way as it is for invitations. If you have no parents or close relatives to issue the announcements, you and your groom may issue your own. This is also an option for mature couples or those who have been previously married. Such an announcement would read:

Miss Deborah Schwartz
[Deborah Suzanne Schwartz, Mrs. Meyer Schwartz, Dr. Deborah Schwartz, etc.]
and
Mr. Eric Davis Fisher
announce their marriage
Friday, the twenty-seventh of November
One thousand nine hundred and eighty-five
Chicago, Illinois

POST-WEDDING PARTIES

Occasionally someone will host a party for the newlywed couple after the wedding has occurred. Complete with receiving line and formal dress, the party will call for invitations that are equally formal. Such an occasion would be when the groom's grandparents want everyone in their hometown to see their grandson grown and married, and to meet his wife. It might not be a time for gift-giving but for good wishes. And the invitation would read:

Mr. and Mrs. Albert Hughes Hudson
request the pleasure of your company
at a reception in honour of
Mr. and Mrs. Theodore Russell Hudson
Sunday, the fourteenth of January
at four o'clock
Castle Mountain Inn
Woodtown, Vermont

R.S.V.P.
263 Spruce Road
Woodtown, Vermont 12345

If the party is to be almost like a second wedding reception for close friends and relatives in another part of the country and hosted by parents of the couple or the couple themselves, reception cards like those shown earlier in this chapter may be enclosed with announcements. Or formal reception invitations, if it's a very large party, may be sent. Handwritten notes are always appropriate.

REAFFIRMATION OF VOWS

Whether they have eloped, married in city hall, or come to the point of celebrating a very special wedding anniversary, many couples are asking others to witness a ceremony where they will speak their marriage vows once again. A service will be designed with them by the official involved, and could take place in a house of worship or at home. (More information about reaffirmation ceremonies will be found in Chapter 20.) A possible invitation for this ceremony would read as follows:

The honour of your presence
is requested at the reaffirmation
of the wedding vows of
Mr. and Mrs. Walter Aldrich VerderMay
Saturday, the eighth of June
at three o'clock
Christian Reformed Church
Amsterdam, Michigan
and afterward at a reception in
the church parlour

WEDDING ANNIVERSARIES

If it is to be a formal celebration for more than fifty persons, formal invitations are appropriate. Typical would be a party given by a daughter and her husband for her parents. The invitation could read:

Mr. and Mrs. Joshua Spiegel
request the pleasure of your company
at a reception to honour
the thirtieth wedding anniversary
of her parents
Mr. and Mrs. Morris Weidman
the evening of Wednesday, the second of August
half after eight o'clock
1614 Greatfalls Avenue
Minneapolis, Minnesota 12345
Kindly reply

UNUSUAL INVITATIONS

Wedding invitations can come packaged as surprises. A gorilla-gram, printed balloon, baby-picture postcard, or billboard invitation would not be the best choice for a formal wedding, however. These "fun" invitations are more appropriate for informal weddings and even then, most couples opt for a more sophisticated style. Creative ideas are great: Pull out all the stops for your first at-home party, but do steer clear of wedding invitations that will embarrass you later.

KEEPING TRACK

As soon as your invitations are out, you'll begin getting telephone calls and notes from guests saying "they can hardly wait." In the excitement, don't forget to start a system of recording who's coming, who sends regrets. Some brides use 3 × 5 file cards, ledgers (perhaps *BRIDE'S Wedding Planner*), or even a computer system. In most cases, a simple notebook will do for this, with additional space to describe any gift received and a notation of when a thank-you note is sent.

Even though wedding invitations have a greater rate of response than party invitations, there will still be some who neglect to let you know whether or not they will attend. What to do? Simply call them up and ask. After all, most receptions require an accurate head count. Your hotel banquet manager or caterer will give you a deadline.

OTHER PRINTING NEEDS

Thank-you notes: While you're at the stationer's, choose formal thank-you note paper for both of you, since your groom will be writing many of the thank-yous. For your formal notes, subtle shades of pearl gray, ecru, or white are better choices than strong designer colors. For the groom, tan, white, or gray are most popular. Your names, monograms, and addresses can be engraved in a contrasting color. Stationery monograms, by the way, do not combine a couple's initials as a linen monogram might. Since only one person will sign the note, print just one person's monogram.

Your note paper may be engraved with your new address only, in which case you could both use it after the wedding. City and state names are printed out in full with no abbreviations. A street number of twenty or under may be spelled out or shown as numerals. Before ordering your stationery, be sure to become familiar with changing postal regulations (location of return address, size of envelope).

Stationery imprinted with your married name or initials is never used until after the wedding.

Wedding programs: Besides being a wonderful memento of your wedding, a program is extremely helpful in guiding your guests through the ceremony. It gives vital information: date, time, and place of the ceremony; the names of clergy or judge who participate; the members of the wedding party; organist, soloist, choir members; parents of the bride and groom. In a program, guests can find a translation of prayers in another language, an explanation of customs from different cultures. Your program also preserves your original vows, special greetings you worked so hard to create.

Your printer will show you quality paper, coordinated with your wedding colors. A program might be an elaborate booklet, printed with a cover sketch; a calligraphy-inscribed scroll, rolled up and tied with a ribbon; or a pre-printed wedding bulletin with your wedding service photocopied inside (bulletin covers are available from religious supply houses).

6

The Wedding Party

A wedding is as much for family and friends as for the bride and groom themselves. A wedding can be as small as five people—the bride, groom, two witnesses, and an officiant. But because it is a social rite, usually a larger community assembles to witness and participate. Traditionally, certain roles have been established, but today individual circumstances, the size of the wedding, the age of the wedding couple, may cause these roles to shift.

A wedding party is aptly named. After all, the people you invite to be your attendants—from the pal from your fiancé's old neighborhood to the new friend who'll soon be your sister-in-law—are people who will make your wedding the best party of your lives.

THE BRIDE

You have a great many things to do before that very special day. The ultimate responsibility for everyone's comfort and for a smoothly run event is yours and your groom's. After discussing budget with your family (and with your groom's, perhaps), you and he will be able to decide how elaborate a wedding and reception you'll have, and where it will take place. Once the decisions have been made and you make them known, parents, relatives, friends, and co-workers will begin volunteering to handle some of the tasks, and of course, you will delegate others. It is even more important, when the bride has other responsibilities—work or school—to seek help from friends or professionals (such as a wedding consultant). But it will still be up to you both to see that the plans are carried out.

One of the most pleasant privileges of being a bride is choosing your attendants. It is also your prerogative to find the dresses they will wear. It is considerate, however, to let them make the final selection from about three styles you like. It's doubly thoughtful to shop with an eye to your maids' budgets, their prospects for wearing their dresses again, and their taste in clothing. Your bridesmaids will look prettiest when they feel pretty—you'll want an outfit to flatter your former roommate who is still trying to fill out as much as your little sister who is forever on a diet.

To show your appreciation to your attendants, give each one a small gift—a pendant or silver picture frame perhaps, engraved with her initials and the wedding date—as a memento. You may entertain for your bridesmaids as well, but this is not required.

Another optional custom you'll probably want to follow is that of exchanging gifts with your groom. Almost anything you know he'd like, from a new tennis racquet to a leather briefcase, would be suitable.

The last (but certainly not least) of your responsibilities is the acknowledging of your wedding gifts. You must write a personal note of appreciation for every gift you receive. Your groom might help, especially if presents come addressed to you both, or arrive from people only he knows. The notes need not be long, but they should be sincere and mailed promptly. The best policy is to write a few each day so that you won't get behind. (For more details on thank-you notes, see Chapter 17.)

Even if you are working or going to school full time, you can prepare in a way that will leave you relaxed and able to enjoy your wedding day fully, and ready to leave for your honeymoon with a sense of satisfaction about how well things went.

THE GROOM

Today's groom expects to be included in wedding planning. At the outset, decide together what tasks he can best accomplish. Then turn these jobs over to him completely.

Your groom's first responsibility is to see that his family's guest list is compiled, with no more names on it than you and your family have agreed upon. He may compare the services of caterers, photographers, and other professionals with you, and you will visit the ceremony official together. On his own, he is privileged to choose his best man and ushers and may entertain them if he likes. He makes sure his attendants are informed about proper dress for the wedding and presents each of them with a small gift, perhaps an initialed belt buckle or key ring.

You may pick out your wedding ring with him, but your groom buys it and has it engraved, just as you do with the ring he will wear. He may give you a special wedding gift as well. The groom assumes responsibility for getting the marriage license and any other necessary documents. (For information on legalities, see Chapter 4.)

Once you decide together where to honeymoon, your groom can handle all the arrangements, and traditionally he pays for this. He's the person who may check on available hotels for out-of-town guests, find out how much the musicians charge for overtime, oversee all contracts, and research the best champagne.

On wedding day, your groom's primary concern is the proverbial "getting to the church on time," although his best man will assist him in this, as well as everything else. The groom accepts the congratulations of the guests in the receiving line, responds to all toasts, then thanks all those who have made the day so special. Finally, the two of you depart for your honeymoon haven.

THE MAID OR MATRON OF HONOR

Your maid or matron of honor should be someone who is very close to you, perhaps your sister, or a dear friend, favorite cousin, or roommate. You needn't ask your fiancé's sister to be your honor attendant unless she also happens to be especially close.

If you have two sisters or best friends, you may ask both to be honor attendants, dividing the official duties between them. Ask one to hold your bouquet during the ceremony, for example, the other to present you with your groom's ring. Let them decide between themselves who will precede you down the aisle, stand beside your groom in the receiving line, and sit at his left at the bridal table. They could always walk side by side in the processional; or, reverse roles for the processional and recessional. There is no rule about who precedes you. An honor attendant may be single or married, young or old, male or female. The matron of honor is a married woman; the maid of honor is a single woman; the maiden of honor is a child. Women have served as Best Person for the groom; men have stood as Best Person for the bride. Mothers and fathers can serve as honor attendants for either the bride or groom.

The honor attendant has no definite pre-wedding responsibilities, but is expected to assist the bride wherever she can. She might help address the invitations, or take charge of recording and displaying your wedding gifts. When you cry, "Oh, I'll never get it all done!" she's the one who will lend moral support.

If you have several bridesmaids, your honor attendant might arrange to have their outfits fitted, see that each is dressed perfectly to the last detail, and make certain they're at the church on time. She assembles her own wedding outfit, paying for everything except the flowers. She attends all pre-wedding parties and may give one herself. At a home wedding, the honor attendant may be the person who greets the ceremony official and shows him or her where to change clothes.

It's fun to pick out those special friends you want to honor as members of your wedding party, but remember—it's a special favor to you that they take on the responsibility, the added expense and time that their participation involves. Do invite each friend in a personal way, letting her know you really want *her*.

Remember, too, she may have to rearrange her vacation time, so give her plenty of notice.

It's best to be forthright about what expenses are involved. While it's not customary to pay for an attendant's dress, hotel accommodations, or travel expenses, you might decide to make it your gift—say so when you invite her. And try to distribute duties among the bridesmaids so that no one person has too much to do.

The honor attendant is usually one of the two witnesses required by law to sign the marriage certificate. The witness, who needs to be old enough to sign a legal document, and the maid or matron of honor, do not have to be the same person. So, if your "best friend" breaks her leg and would feel awkward being in your wedding party, you could still designate her your witness. She would then be the one who signs your marriage certificate. A second-time bride might choose to have her young daughter as her honor attendant, then designate someone of age to be the legal witness.

Your honor attendant precedes you and your father down the aisle, arranges your train and veil, and holds your bouquet during the ceremony. She also passes you the groom's ring. (For safekeeping up until this point, she may wear it on her middle finger or thumb, or carry it in a hidden pocket or dainty bag.) The honor attendant stands next to the groom in the receiving line and sits on his left at the bride's table. Once the receiving line disperses, she is free to enjoy the reception as an honored guest, but she may take time out to help you freshen up now and then and, finally, to change—before she hugs you one last time prior to your departure.

THE BEST MAN

This indispensable role is usually filled by the groom's most trustworthy friend or relative. His brother, cousin, best friend, even his father—all are appropriate choices.

The duties of the best man are many and varied. He is chief of staff at the wedding, toastmaster at the reception, and personal aide and advisor to the groom, checking on such things as bills for the flowers, accommodations for out-of-town ushers, along with the groom if need be. It's the best man's responsibility to see that the groom is properly outfitted and at the church in time for the ceremony, and that the ceremony official is paid (along with any altar boys that should be remembered). The best man takes charge of the marriage license (which he signs as a witness) and the bride's wedding ring, producing each at the proper time. He may also supervise the ushers, making sure that all are uniformly dressed, thoroughly briefed, and at the ceremony site at the appointed hour.

Although the best man does not participate in the receiving line, he does have a number of reception responsibilities. He sits to the right of the bride and proposes the first toast to the new couple, usually a wish for health, happiness, and prosperity. After the toasts, he collects any congratulatory telegrams and reads them aloud if the bride and groom wish. He helps see that the reception goes as it should, and that no practical jokes are played on the couple. The best man is the one who'll make sure, for example, that the windshield of the honeymoon car isn't so painted up or covered with paper streamers that the driver won't have a safe view.

Another of the best man's duties is to help the newlyweds get off on their honeymoon. He assists the groom into his going-away clothes and with any last-minute packing. He also takes charge of the luggage, making sure it is locked in the honeymoon car or checked ahead at the station or airport. When you and your groom leave the reception at last, the best man will escort you to your car or drive you off. Then, as you make your departure, he will hand over the keys, tickets, and baggage checks given to him for safekeeping.

The first business day after the wedding, the best man (or one of the ushers in his place) might also see to it that all the men's rental clothes are returned to the formalwear store, and that any gifts of money received at the wedding are deposited in the appropriate bank accounts. Any of the best man's duties may be assigned to one of the ushers, except holding the ring during the ceremony and offering the first toast.

THE BRIDESMAIDS

The number of bridesmaids you'll have in your ceremony depends on its size and style, ranging from none at a small informal wedding to as many as twelve for a large formal one. Don't worry about having an equal number of male and female attendants. Your clergymember will arrange the aesthetics of the procession and altar line-up, even if numbers do not match up. Again, it is the bride's prerogative to choose her attendants from among her friends and relatives. Custom dictates that they will be close to her age. If you have young sisters or cousins between the ages of nine and fourteen, they may participate as junior bridesmaids (they walk first in the procession, need no partners in the recessional, and have no specific duties). It is nice to ask at least one relative of the groom—his sister or a favorite cousin, perhaps—to be a bridesmaid, but not necessary.

Today, pregnancy does not automatically rule out an honor attendant's participation in the wedding ceremony as long as both the bride and the mother-to-be feel comfortable about this. Pregnancy, with its promise of new life, can be a joyful addition to a wedding celebration. But, you two friends might want to consider questions such as: "How pregnant will she be by my wedding date?" "What style of dress can all the bridesmaids wear to blend with her maternity needs?" If your wedding is close to her due date, you may both worry that she won't make it. Then, too, her pregnant condition may make her self-conscious about her appearance. If she chooses not to participate, or you prefer that she doesn't, do ask her to read a passage instead, or sit up front with your family.

Incidentally, you may feel free to invite only the woman of a married couple to be in your wedding. And if both husband and wife participate, they need not be paired in the recession nor be seated side by side at the reception. Mingling and meeting new people is one of the things that makes a wedding so much fun for everybody!

Bridesmaids have no particular pre-wedding responsibilities, yet they usually offer to run errands, address envelopes, and help the bride in any way they can. They are invited to all the pre-wedding parties and may give one if they wish. Bridesmaids assemble their own wedding outfits, paying for them as well (although you may assume this expense). Unless you are having all the flowers delivered directly to the ceremony site, they pick up their bouquets at your home an hour or so before the ceremony. Bridesmaids always take part in the wedding procession and usually stand at the bride's side during the ceremony. They may all greet guests in the receiving line or take turns if you prefer. They sit alternately with the ushers at the bride's table. They take part in all the reception festivities and, if unmarried, are usually in the front ranks when the bride tosses her flowers. Since your wedding gown should be properly cared for after you depart for your honeymoon destination, you may ask one of your bridesmaids to do this.

THE USHERS

Ushers seat the guests at the wedding ceremony and act as escorts for the bridesmaids. While it makes it easier if bridesmaids and ushers balance out, it isn't necessary. A junior bridesmaid needs no escort. To avoid seating delays, there should be at least one usher for every fifty guests.

Your groom might ask his brothers, future brothers-in-law, cousins, and married or single best friends to act in this capacity. He should also include any brothers or close relatives of yours who are adult enough to handle the job.

The ushers usually attend all the pre-wedding parties the groom goes to and may give one if they wish. They provide their own wedding clothes, renting the proper formal attire if they do not own it. Boutonnieres are provided by the groom, and gloves and neckwear too, when these are not included in the rental package. The groom may also gift his ushers with shirts or some other accessory. Renting from one source, of course, assures the most coordinated look for the men. To be sure there are no problems, ask your best man or one of the male attendants to see that all formal wear is returned on time.

Ushers arrive at the ceremony site forty-five minutes to an hour before the ceremony time, and assemble near the entrance. As guests arrive, an usher steps forward and offers his right arm to each woman. If she does not present a pew card and he does not know her, he asks if she is a friend of the bride or of the groom, then seats her accordingly. This usually means bride's guests on the left, groom's on the right; the opposite in Jewish services. When one side has many more guests than the other, the usher may also explain, "We will all be sitting together today, so everyone will have a clear view." Late-arriving guests are shown to the best available seats on the side with more room.

When a man and a woman arrive together, traditionally the woman takes the usher's arm, and the man follows them down the aisle. What to do if several women appear together? Seat the eldest first. Unless he is elderly and in need of assistance, a man alone may simply be accompanied to his seat by an usher. A new alternative for informal ceremonies is simply for the usher to lead people to their seats, after saying something like, "Please follow me." All the groomsmen are expected to make polite conversation (in low tones, of course) with guests as they walk unhurriedly down the aisle: "Lovely day for a wedding, isn't it, Mrs. Lane?" "I'm glad you could fly in, Uncle Mort—can't wait to hear the toast you've got in mind this time."

The groom usually designates a head usher to supervise special seating arrangements. For instance, if either the bride or groom has divorced parents who must be seated separately, a definite seating plan should be worked out and the ushers informed ahead of time (see Chapter 8). If one of the ushers is the brother of the bride or groom, he will probably escort his own mother to her place. Otherwise, the head usher assumes responsibility for the mothers. Should an aisle carpet or pew ribbons be used, the groom appoints two ushers to take care of unrolling them.

Ushers participate in both the procession and the recessional, returning to escort mothers and honored elderly or disabled guests from the church first. Next, two ushers loosen the pew ribbons, then pause at the side of each facing pew, signaling guests to file out row by row, from front to back. In addition, the ushers should be prepared to direct guests to parking and rest room facilities as well as to the reception site. They make certain the ceremony site is cleared of all belongings of the wedding party before leaving for the reception themselves.

Ushers do not stand in the receiving line, but they do sit at the bridal table. They often propose toasts to the bride and groom, dance with the bridesmaids. Throughout most of the reception, however, they simply circulate and make sure that all the guests—especially the bridesmaids—have a wonderful time.

What do you do if, because of illness, a bridesmaid or usher drops out of the wedding party at the last minute? Luckily, this seldom happens. But when it does, you have two choices: Find a replacement who fits the outfit and wants to help, even though you could not ask him or her to participate long ago; or go ahead without the original attendant (remember, you don't need balanced pairs). In either case, do send along flowers and special souvenirs of the wedding to let the person know he or she has been with you in thought on your special day.

CHILD ATTENDANTS

Children can add a great deal of charm to a wedding ceremony. And if you are marrying a second time, their being a part of the wedding will make them feel that much more a part of your marriage (see Chapter 11). But very young children who are not with you every day, not often dressed up, or never in a crowd may behave unpredictably. This is why one or two children between the ages of four and eight may be all you need to invite to your ceremony. If you don't know any children well enough, it may be preferable not to invite them to participate.

At the reception, young children need physical supervision. A teenager might supervise an area with snacks and activities to hold their interest. A gift from you and your fiancé will let children in your wedding party know how glad you are to have them participate. You'll find delightful possibilities for gifts—a teddy bear dressed as a bride; colorful watches; tickets to the circus or a baseball game; an engraved locket with the child's name and your wedding date.

A maiden of honor may be designated from among the junior bridesmaids if there are no adult attendants. It is a common, and quite beautiful, European custom to have all child attendants, especially in Britain or France. The junior bridesmaids precede the maiden of honor in the procession.

The flower girl is the most popular child attendant. She may walk alone, with the ring bearer, or with another flower girl about the same height, but she always comes immediately before the bride in the procession. Traditionally, flower girls carried baskets of loose rose petals to strew in the bride's path. But the possibility of someone slipping on the petals is very real. So today, most flower girls carry a basket of posies, a tiny nosegay, or a flower-covered muff. In any case, see that the girl's flower arrangement is the same front and back so they will look pretty no matter how she holds them.

The ring bearer, who can as easily be a girl as a boy nowadays, balances a white pillow with a fake ring tied to the center with ribbons or stitched down lightly with satin thread. (The best man keeps the bride's real ring tucked safely in his pocket; the honor attendant keeps the groom's real ring slipped on her finger or thumb, or in a special pocket or purse.) After the ceremony, the cushion is turned upside down so the dummy ring doesn't show. Although he or she may be paired with a flower girl, the ring bearer usually walks alone in the procession, immediately preceding the flower girl (if there is one) or the bride.

Pages or train bearers always walk in pairs and are about the same height. They are generally little boys, but girls, too, may serve in this capacity. You will not need pages, of course, unless your dress has a very long train for them to carry.

Candle lighters are common in some parts of the country. The candles are left unlit until just before the mother of the bride is seated. Two boys from either family, wearing dress clothes, step forward to light them.

Young child attendants may attend the rehearsal so they can practice their parts. They need not go to pre-wedding parties but will enjoy showing off their fancy clothes and dancing with the grown-ups at the reception. During the ceremony, you may choose to have a child attendant slip into your parents' pew and sit down, rather than risk having him or her fidget through the ceremony at the altar.

THE BRIDE'S MOTHER

Your mother helps you compile the guest list, arrange the details of the ceremony and reception, and select your wedding outfit and trousseau, if you like. (It is your choice, not a necessity, that she accompany you to shop for your dress, and go along when you and your groom select items for your household.) Your mother may also keep track of your gifts, seeing that they are attractively displayed in a safe spot. It's your mother's responsibility to keep your father and the groom's parents posted on the progress of the wedding plans. She should inform your fiancé's mother of her choice of wedding attire so that their dresses will be of the same length and similar in style.

If you will be traveling to your parents' hometown just for the wedding, you are probably counting on your mother to do most of the on-site planning. Purchase two identical wedding notebooks and make plenty of long-distance phone calls to stay in touch.

Your mother is the official hostess for your wedding, unless you are serving in that capacity yourself, or some other arrangement has been made. She is privileged to sit in the very first pew on the bride's side of the aisle. She is the last person to be escorted to her seat before the wedding and the first to be ushered out after it is over. As hostess for the reception, she greets all the guests at the head of the receiving line, sits in a place of honor at the parents' table, makes sure everyone is having a good time, and is on hand to say good-bye to guests.

THE BRIDE'S FATHER

Your father rides to the ceremony with you in the limousine and escorts you down the aisle. After giving you away, or offering his support or blessing (as you choose), he joins your mother in the first row. As the official host of the reception, he usually mingles with the guests, getting the party going, instead of standing in the receiving line. He also keeps an eye on the bar and champagne supply; dances with you (after your groom does), even if it is not his favorite activity; and usually makes a short toast or welcoming speech. He's the last person to leave the reception, and the one who bids the guests good-bye.

When you are ready to leave the reception, you should take a few moments alone with both your mother and father for a hug, a kiss, and a "thank you for all you've done."

Since your father's part is a prominent one, it is important that his attire blend with that of your groom and the other men in the wedding party.

If your father is not living, you may ask your brother, uncle, or other male relative, a close family friend, or an usher to escort you down the aisle, and then serve as your mother's escort for the reception festivities. Your mother may also walk you down the aisle if you feel closer to her than any male relative or friend.

Your parents are divorced? Your father may still escort you down the aisle and give you his blessing. Instead of sitting in the first pew with your mother, however, he would sit in the third row on the bride's side of the aisle. If you are close to both your father and your stepfather, you choose who escorts you, but find a way to honor the other. Would it work for both of them to walk you up the aisle? Additional options for smoothing over the awkwardness of remarried parents are covered in Chapter 8.

THE GROOM'S PARENTS

Although the role played by the groom's parents is smaller than that of your parents, they should be treated with equal respect. Your fiancé's mother should be invited to all the showers, and both of his parents should be included in the rehearsal dinner, if they will not be giving it themselves. Your fiancé's parents contribute to the guest list for the wedding and reception, and may or may not offer to share expenses. They consult with your parents on the proper wedding attire and dress accordingly. The groom's parents are honored guests at the ceremony and are seated, just before your mother, in the first pew on the groom's side of the aisle. The groom's mother always stands in the receiving line to meet the guests, but his father's participation is optional.

If the groom's parents are paying for the reception or sharing wedding expenses, but are not sole sponsors of the wedding, their roles would remain the same. But as sponsors of the wedding, they would become more visible. The groom's father would oversee reception service; his mother, preside as first greeter in the receiving line; and both be near the door for good-byes. Before you leave the reception, your groom will want a few quiet minutes with his parents, just as you have had.

SPECIAL MEMBERS OF THE WEDDING

If your wedding party is not large enough to include all of your favorite relatives and friends, or if you have brothers and sisters who are not old enough to participate as attendants, you may include them in other ways. Young girls or boys, for example, might distribute Mass books or *yarmulkes*, give out wedding programs, or serve as acolytes at the ceremony; at the reception, they might take charge of the guest book, pass out groom's cake or packets of rice, or help with refreshments. An uncle might read the Scripture or another piece of prose; family members join in "sentence prayers"—each adding a line to continue the prayer.

Occasionally, someone in the wedding must use crutches or a wheelchair. If your groom or either of your parents is in this situation, he or she can still play a traditional role in the service, with some modifications to make entering or leaving the site of the ceremony as comfortable as possible. With other friends and relatives, think of the individual circumstances and the duties to be performed.

The feeling of being a part of the festivities and the aura of hope and happiness that only a bride and a groom can confer is a gift you will be giving your wedding party—and all your family and friends.

7
Guide to Wedding Clothes

Your dress sets the style of your wedding, and everyone else is outfitted accordingly. You may fall in love with a certain dress and plan your wedding around it. It could be regal satin, graced with a mantilla to the floor—so stately, it belongs at a very formal ceremony. Or it could be a wide-skirted cotton banded in pastel, suggesting a semiformal occasion outdoors. You might also, of course, decide the mood of the wedding, the time and place first, then shop for the prettiest and most appropriate look. A spectacular wedding ensemble fits together harmoniously. When one element of your bridal attire is out of place, attention is drawn to that detail and away from your total appearance. Styles of wedding dress change as do other fashions, but the pleasure of wearing a special and beautiful costume draws brides year after year to the traditional long dress and veil in one of the many and varied shadings of white and ivory.

THE BRIDE

Very formal weddings: You'll look magnificent in a breathtaking dress of satin, lace, peau de soie, or another equally formal fabric. It will most likely be an elegant new design with a long train, perhaps cathedral- or chapel-length. In some cases, it may be an heirloom dress worn with pride by generations of brides in your family; or one you've purchased from a bridal manufacturer (antique lace is now incorporated into the design of gowns and headpieces for an "heirloom look"). Very formal wedding dresses are almost always worn with a full-length veil and headpiece embellished with lace, beading, silk flowers, or even fur. You'll probably carry an elaborate bouquet of flowers or a flower-trimmed prayer book and wear simple shoes to match your dress. Gloves enhance the formality of a short-sleeved or sleeveless look.

Formal weddings: You'll look every inch a bride in a traditional, floor-length wedding dress, most likely with a chapel or sweep train. A formal wedding dress is a little less elaborate than that worn in a very formal wedding and will probably be accompanied by a veil or mantilla flowing to the hem, but shorter veils—shoulder-length or fingertip-length, for instance; hats are also lovely. If the sleeves of your dress are less than full-length, you may wear gloves in white kid, lace, or fabric to match your dress. Your bouquet may be simpler than one you'd carry at a very formal wedding, but your shoes and all other accessories are the same.

Semiformal weddings: You'll be a radiant bride wearing an elegant short dress or a simple floor-length dress without a train. Picture a gossamer chiffon, flowing jersey, lace from neckline to hem. Your accessories, including your flowers, are simpler than those for a formal wedding. With a street-length dress, a short veil is best; with a long dress, you may choose a longer veil. Hats, or flowers worn through the hair, are also lovely.

Informal weddings: You'll look elegant in a becoming street-length outfit appropriate to the season. Perhaps a suit or jacketed dress is the most polished look. It may be in white or any color except black. Accessories include flowers to wear instead of to carry.

Remarriage and reaffirmation: Any of the four traditional formal wedding styles is suitable for a second marriage or a reaffirmation of vows, except that a veil is omitted, as it is traditionally a symbol of virginity (unless a reaffirming bride is wearing her original wedding gown, which has a train). For specific clothing suggestions, see Chapters 11 and 20.

SHOPPING FOR YOUR GOWN

Choosing a wedding gown is a unique experience, one you might share with a friend or your mother, lest you become overwhelmed by all the decisions. As you become aware of what styles are available—and there are many—you'll begin to narrow down your own preferences. The following terms will keep coming up as you visit bridal salons and look at wedding gown advertisements. The brief descriptions accompanying them will help you put a name to the look you hope to achieve. In today's diverse bridal market, you should have no trouble finding a romantic look that suits your height, weight, and body type—in short, a dress that's perfect for *you*.

SILHOUETTES
Ballgown—appealing off-the-shoulder bodice nipping into a natural waist with lavish, full skirt.

Basque—natural waist with V-front . . . a full skirt.

Empire—small, scooped bodice gathering at high waist, a slender yet graceful skirt.

Princess—slim-fitting style, with vertical seams flowing from shoulders down to hem of flared skirt.

Sheath—narrow, body-hugging style without a waist.

LENGTHS AND TRAINS

Street length—hem just covering knees.

Intermission length—hem falling slightly below or midway between the knee and ankle.

Ballet length—hem swirling to ankles.

Floor length—hem fully skimming the floor.

Sweep train—shortest train, barely sweeping the floor.

Court train—a train extending one foot longer than the sweep train.

Chapel train—most popular of all bridal trains—trailing about one-and-one-third yards.

Cathedral train—worn at very formal weddings—cascading two-and-one-half yards.

Extended cathedral train—unfolding more than three yards (reminiscent of Princess Diana's voluminous train).

FABRICS

Brocade—heavy fabric with interwoven, raised design.

Chiffon—delicately sheer . . . a simple weave—often of silk or rayon—with a soft or stiff finish.

Eyelet—open-weave embroidery used for decorations.

Moiré—silk taffeta that is patterned to glisten like water when illuminated.

Organza—sheer, crisply textured fabric, almost transparent.

Silk-faced satin—brimming with body, with an antique sheen.

Slipper satin—light, soft . . . a more closely woven fabric.

Taffeta—smooth, glossy . . . a finely textured fabric with body.

Tulle—tiny-meshed net of silk, cotton, or synthetics.

Polyester may also be used for dresses, alone or blended with natural fibers, such as polyorganza or polychiffon.

LACE

Alençon—originated in Alençon, France; a pretty, delicate, yet durable design, outlined with cord on net ground.

Chantilly—from Chantilly, France; graceful floral sprays on fine lace background, outlined with silk threads.

Schiffli—machine-made, delicate floral embroidery.

Venise—heavy, raised-floral design, first made in Venice.

NECKLINES

High—collar just brushing the chin.

Off-the-shoulder—gracefully hovering above bustline, sometimes attached to a sheer net yoke and high collar.

Boat (or Bateau)—gently following curve of the collarbone; high in front and back, opening wide at sides, ending in shoulder seams.

Queen Anne—rising high at the nape (back) of neck, then sculpting low to outline a bare yoke.

Sabrina—a high scoop neck.

Square—shaped like half of a square.

Sweetheart—shaped like the top half of a heart.

SLEEVES

Bishop—fuller in the lower forearm, then gathered at wrist into a wide cuff.

Dolman—extending from an armhole so large it creates a cape-like effect, often fitted at wrist.

Leg-of-mutton (or Gigot)—full, loose, rounded from shoulder to slightly below elbow, then shaped to the arm.

Melon—extravagantly rounded from shoulder to elbow.

Puff—gathered into gentle puff near shoulders.

HEADPIECES

Coronet—crescent resting high on crown of the head.

Floral wreath—circlet of flowers that can nestle on top of the head or at mid-forehead.

Half hat—small hat covering half, or less than half, of crown.

Juliet cap—cap, ornately festooned with pearls and jewels, that snugly hugs the crown.

Mantilla—lace-trimmed netting usually secured to an elegant comb, gently framing the face.

Picture hat—ornamented hat with a very large brim.

Tiara—crown, usually encrusted with crystals, pearls, or lace, resting high atop the head.

Toque—small, close-fitting hat without a brim.

Upturned picture hat—picture hat with brim tilting up to one side.

Except for the mantilla, veiling is usually attached to all of these headpieces.

VEILS

Blusher—loose veil worn forward over face or back over the headpiece; often attached to longer, three-tiered veil.

Fly-away—multi-layers that brush the shoulders, usually worn with an informal, ankle-length dress or a style with too-pretty-to-hide details in back.

Birdcage—falling just below chin, gently shirred at the sides, and usually attached to hats.

Chapel length—cascading about two-and-one-third yards from head-piece.

Cathedral length—flowing about three-and-one-half yards from head-piece, usually worn with cathedral train.

Ballet (or waltz) length—falling to the ankles.

Fingertip—most popular length, gracefully touching the fingertips.

Most veils are made of nylon or silk material called illusion. Embellishments often include poufs, which are small gathers of veiling on the crown of a headpiece. Wreaths often have flowing ribbons called streamers, tied into "love knots."

PRESERVING YOUR DRESS

A bride marrying today may look ahead to a time when she might renew or reaffirm her vows (see Chapter 20). And remember that certain fabrics and finishes—no matter how well they are preserved—can never look as beautiful as they did on wedding day. Your dress and veil should be cared for by a professional dry cleaner immediately after your wedding. Point out any beverages spilled on the dress—they may be invisible at first but can stain later. Any protective shields or bra inserts should be removed and discarded. Once processed, your dress is wrapped in tissue paper (to protect against any hard creases and to puff up the sleeves, bodice), then packed in a box with a clear plastic window inset. That box is wrapped in plastic (to guard against inadvertent moisture), then placed in a brown cardboard box. Store your gown in a cool, dry place (your attic would be too hot; your basement, too damp). After a year, and occasionally after that, take it out, inspect for any slow-to-emerge stains (return to the dry cleaner if you find any), and enjoy the happy memories. Rewrap just as carefully as before when you put it away again.

ACCESSORIES

Jewelry: Because a wedding gown is so spectacular, most brides wear very little jewelry. You may choose small earrings—diamonds, gemstones, gold, or pearl. Dainty seed pearls dangling from a gold chain give a delicate effect. If your groom has given you a gift of jewelry, or some beloved relative has given you jewelry for good luck, you can wear it with your wedding gown providing it's simple (for example, a string of pearls), or with your going-away outfit if it's dramatic (for example, a lotus blossom necklace). You may wear a classic gold chain or a diamond drop necklace with your wedding dress; a strand of pearls or gemstones twisted around your upswept hair.

You may move your engagement ring to your right hand until after the ceremony, when you'll return it to your left hand. Avoid wearing any ring on your right hand for the receiving line; it may prove painful when you shake hands many times with all your guests.

Lingerie: You're sure to have a visit from your aunt, your groom's mother, your former roommate while dressing for the wedding or changing to honeymoon clothes. That's one reason your underclothing should be as glamorous as your gown. Fine lingerie will enhance the overall line of your wedding dress and give you that inner confidence that's so important for public occasions. When you are buying your gown, the bridal shop consultant will tell you what sort of slip your dress requires. A petticoat made from a firm fabric (nylon taffeta, for instance) would add body to a flouncy skirt on a wedding dress; while a soft, body-hugging liner would smooth the lines on a sheath silhouette. Undergarments should be chosen with a critical eye—a sheer, blousy bodice may call for a pretty camisole; a clinging fabric may need special attention to stockings and slip to preserve the formality of the look down to the last detail. Whatever style, your petticoat should be white under any shade of white, nude under pastel, and the same length as your wedding dress.

Even though your bra may be trimmed in lace, no part of it should show above the lines of the bodice. Do secure your straps in place at the shoulders, and check that the shape conforms to your dress.

Stockings can be plain, patterned, or embroidered. Designers have given hosiery a fancy new look—with wedding bells, pin dots, tiny flowers gracing tights or stockings. But don't go overboard: Choose a neutral shade that's harmonious with your gown, such as an off-white, pale ivory, or sheer white.

The bride's garter: The garter, an optional accessory, is worn just below the bride's knee. Why? For luck—it's often the "something blue" of the wedding verse; to preserve a tradition—it all started in old England, when the guests would invade the bridal chamber and steal the bride's and groom's stockings. By the fourteenth century, only the bride's garter was prized; it was a portent of the next to marry, and all the male guests would race to grab it. Before long, the bride or her groom began tossing the garter to the male guests in self-defense. At your reception, the garter should be thrown right after the bride's bouquet. Your groom will slide the garter from your leg, turn his back to the crowd, and toss it over his head. Buy your garter at your bridal salon, wear your mother's, or make one yourself with lace, satin, or a sentimental ribbon (perhaps a piece of blue ribbon that your groom's mother saved from his baby sweater).

Shoes: You'll want your shoes to be as lovely as the rest of your outfit. White is the most popular shade for shoes, in an assortment of materials—lace-covered, fabric, leather, satin. Shoes may also be dyed to match a special shade, or you may prefer to wear silver, gold, or a pastel color. A medium heel is a good choice—so you'll walk steadily down the aisle. Be sure to scuff the soles of new shoes to avoid slipping. Flat-heeled shoes are classic enough to go with any style wedding dress—and great if you don't want your shoes to add much height. Ballet slippers look pretty with satin ribbon in a criss-cross pattern up the leg. Both are available at regular shoe or dance supply stores.

Other accessories: These can be blended into the bride's attire and become lasting mementos. An embroidered parasol or lace fan at a summer wedding, or a leather-bound prayer book with a sprig of herbs or flowers tied to it are treasures to keep. If you wear lace gloves, remove them before you receive your wedding ring, or have them made so that the ring finger is uncovered. Gauntlets, which leave fingers exposed, may remain in place. An heirloom handkerchief (your "something old") can be carried or worked into your floral bouquet by the florist.

THE GROOM, MALE ATTENDANTS, FATHERS

Clothes for the groom and other men in the wedding party follow a traditional pattern as well. Yet you and your groom may also find styles that are somewhat different from the traditional in the wider range that exists today. New colors and fabrics are acceptable, as long as they complement the style of your dress.

Very formal weddings: The groom and other men in the wedding party wear formal clothes, which they usually rent. Everyone, including your fathers, dresses alike, but the neckwear and boutonnieres may be varied slightly to distinguish the groom and best man from the other men. (Your groom's boutonniere might be a white rose or another flower to match your bouquet; theirs, carnations, perhaps.) For ceremonies beginning before six o'clock in the evening, formal daytime wear consists of a handsome black or oxford gray cutaway coat, gray-and-black striped trousers, gray waistcoat, and formal white shirt with a wing collar. Accessories include a striped silk ascot with a pearl or gold stickpin, gray gloves, black shoes, and black socks. Ushers sometimes wear starched, turned-down collars with striped four-in-hand ties in place of the wing collars and ascots worn by the groom and best man. Gray spats and black silk top hats are an optional part of this distinguished ensemble.

Men who want a more contemporary look may wear colored, contoured long or short jackets, usually with wing-collared shirts.

After six o'clock, correct dress for your groom and his attendants is the ultra-sophisticated formal attire known as "white tie": a black tailcoat and matching satin-trimmed trousers, a white piqué waistcoat and a stiff-front shirt with a wing collar and French cuffs. Accessories include studs, a white piqué bow tie, white gloves, black patent leather pumps, and long black socks. A black silk top hat is optional for all but the most formal weddings. At a Jewish wedding (all but Reform services), the men all wear hats (*yarmulkes*, fedoras, or top hats when very formal) throughout the ceremony. Otherwise, hats are only worn out-of-doors. A groom may distinguish himself from his groomsmen with accessories in several ways besides wearing a different boutonniere. He alone wears a top hat, for instance, or a cummerbund, gloves, or ruby studs.

The proper attire for the groom at a military wedding is the full-dress uniform of his branch of service. His attendants would also wear full-dress uniform if they are in the service, or formalwear suitable for the style and hour of the ceremony.

If your groom is wearing national costume, he should wear the most formal version. A groom of Scottish descent wears his own clan tartan with either a daytime or evening jacket. As with a military wedding, only those men eligible to wear a specialized formal outfit do so; the others wear traditional formalwear.

Once, only the father of the bride dressed to match the other men in the wedding (because he escorts his daughter down the aisle, he is an official member of the wedding party). The father of the groom chose the same attire as a guest. Today, however, both fathers generally take their cues from the groomsmen, highlighting their honored roles and lending a uniform look to the occasion. In the event that contemporary suits are the choice, the fathers may want to wear an elegant business suit, if this makes them feel more comfortable.

Formal weddings: The groom, fathers, and other men in your wedding party dress according to the season and the hour of the ceremony. For a formal daytime wedding, the traditional attire includes a black or oxford gray sack coat or stroller (styled like a regular suit jacket and just as comfortable), striped trousers, gray waistcoat, and white shirt with a turned-down collar and French cuffs, plus a striped four-in-hand tie, gray gloves, black shoes, and black socks. The accompanying homburg may be omitted, except where required in a Jewish ceremony.

For a formal ceremony beginning after six o'clock, the men wear "black tie": a black or charcoal gray dinner jacket with matching trousers, white pleated-front shirt with a turned-down collar and French cuffs, and a black vest or cummerbund. Black shoes, socks, and bow tie are the traditional accessories, along with chamois or gray gloves. For a summer wedding, your groom and his men could opt for white dinner jackets, wear a cummerbund in place of a vest, and leave off the gloves.

When the men wish a more contemporary look, this usually means it will be a formal, rather than very formal, wedding. They may wear formal suits in neutral or dark colors, dress shirts, bow ties, and vests or cummerbunds. And to indicate his role, the groom may want to wear a different—but harmonizing—suit or jacket altogether. He may wear a double-breasted tuxedo or tails, while the best man and ushers wear single-breasted tuxedos of the same shade.

Confused about which formal suit is right if the ceremony will begin before six, the reception after? Always select the look according to the time of the ceremony.

Semiformal weddings: The groom and his attendants traditionally wear solid dark suits in the day, with plain white shirts, four-in-hand ties, and black shoes with long socks. It is not necessary for their ties to match, but an overall effect should be achieved—rather than a mix of bright paisley or colorful stripes, somewhat similar club ties, perhaps. For a summer wedding, the men may look cool and crisp in white linen jackets with oxford gray trousers or dark blue jackets with gray or white flannel trousers. They may prefer dinner jackets or contemporary formal suits with dress shirts, bow ties, vests or cummerbunds, especially in the evening. Is it an evening wedding? Then black tie appropriate to the season is also a good-looking possibility.

Informal weddings: Even when the wedding is nontraditional, or very simple, jackets and neckwear for the men dignify the occasion. Your groom's choice can be a three-piece business suit or a maroon velvet jacket (worn with a paisley print necktie or an ascot), so long as it is in the same mood as your attire.

HONOR ATTENDANTS AND BRIDESMAIDS

Proper dress varies with the hour and the season, but your wedding party will look most striking coming down the aisle and standing in the receiving line if the clothes are similar. Bridesmaids and honor attendants should wear dresses that complement your own and are of the same length and formality. You can shop for bridesmaids' dresses with your honor attendant, choosing her dress first, then narrowing the selection to about three you find appropriate. Let the bridesmaids make the final decision, since they are, most likely, buying their own dresses.

Very formal weddings: The bridesmaids and your honor attendant wear elegant floor-length dresses in harmony with the feeling of your own dress. If you'll be in a classically rich silk, with an exquisitely rolled piping tracing empire lines, for example, think about silk—similarly unadorned—for your attendants. Or if you have decided on a look that is sculpted low in the bodice, theirs might drape low in the back. The bridesmaids usually wear identical dresses, but your honor attendant may be identified by a different shade, a contrasting color (deep rose instead of pink), or, for a more subtle distinction, the same dress as the bridesmaids'—with contrasting trim or accessories. Floral wreaths and ribbon headbands, lace hats and wisps of veiling, and three-cornered scarves all make attractive headpieces, as long as they match or harmonize with the dresses. The bridesmaids in a very formal wedding almost always wear gloves to complement short or sleeveless looks. Wrist-length white gloves are always correct and frequently the most attractive. Bridesmaids' shoes should be simple and match the mood and color of their dresses. Attendants' jewelry is always uniform (a gift from the bride, perhaps) and usually light and delicate looking.

Formal weddings: The bridesmaids and honor attendants dress much the same as for a very formal wedding, in floor-length dresses, with complementary headpieces and shoes. Gloves are optional for a formal wedding, and the style of dress is usually a little less ornate than for a very formal ceremony. They may, for example, carry parasols with summery styles. If your wedding is very small or early in the day, street-length or cocktail-length dresses are a possibility.

In shopping, you may find bridesmaids' dresses that are made to match your own. This can be an enormous help in creating a unified look for the wedding party. A formal wedding does, however, allow you to choose a slightly less elaborate mood for them if it means they will then be able to wear their dresses again.

Semiformal weddings: The honor attendant and bridesmaids, if any, wear street-length or very simple long dresses in harmony with that of the bride. One colorful look would be identical long (or short) flowered (or solid-hued) skirts, with blouses of different shades.

Shoes and jewelry should complement their dresses. Gloves and hats or flowers for their hair are optional. Attendants at a semiformal wedding may carry small bouquets or wear flowers at their collars, waists, or wrists.

Informal weddings: There may be just one honor attendant, who would dress in a style similar to that of the bride. She can select her own dress, perhaps one she already owns, or purchase a new one that will be versatile after the wedding. Even one attendant is honored with flowers.

CHILDREN

It will take very little effort to dress your child attendants adorably—they're already so cute! When choosing clothes, remember that a child will perform better if he or she is happy with the way he or she looks. If you've insisted on a silk cummerbund that your four-year-old nephew thinks is "stupid," he'll probably take it off during the ceremony.

Very formal or formal weddings: If a junior bridesmaid wears an adaptation of the bridesmaids' dresses, hers should be styled along more youthful lines (no low-cut necklines). Her dress, in that case, would be of the same color and, if possible, the same fabric as those of your other attendants. The flowers and headpieces should match as well. A teenage junior bridesmaid usually dresses like the older bridesmaids.

There are other choices. The young lady may dress in a facsimile of the bride's dress (same leg-of-mutton sleeves, lace ruffle at the neckline), but hers would be made of a tiny floral print, rather than white, and accented with a bright silk sash to match the flowers. A child's innocence is more poignant in distinctly childlike fashions, such as a white organza pinafore over a forest-green velvet dress. Little girls look charming with flowers or ribbons in their hair. For shoes, ballet slippers or flat black (or white) patent leathers are safest, but trim them with bows, flowers, or buckles. She can carry a flower pomander of white crysanthemums and yellow roses on a satin ribbon. As long as she does not scatter any petals (that are slippery), she may carry them in the traditional basket. But a dainty old-fashioned nosegay or flower muff may be easier for her to handle.

Ring bearers (or boy pages) will be charming in the satin and velvet suits once traditional. Or, if the little boys don't feel comfortable in unfamiliar clothes, they might wear dark blue Eton suits, white shorts, and white or blue knee socks. For a summer wedding, a young boy might appear in a white linen suit with white knee socks and white shoes. If the style of the men is contemporary wedding dress, young boys may be outfitted in matching formal suits, especially if they're likely to be better behaved sporting long pants and jacket "just like Daddy's."

Semiformal or informal weddings: Children seldom participate in either semiformal or informal weddings unless they are children of the bride and groom. If yours is a remarriage, your children's role is important. Everyone in the family should feel "extra-special" on your wedding day. Your children can wear their best "special occasion" outfits, or be treated to new ones. There is no need (and it would be very impractical) for your children's clothes to match; although two boys can have matching neckties, two girls, identical bouquets or lacy stockings.

MOTHERS OF THE BRIDE AND GROOM

The mothers of the bride and groom are on display as much as any member of the wedding party. They are the last seated, greet each guest in the receiving line, and dance with the groom at the reception. Their dresses should be dignified yet stylish, flattering to figure and personality.

Very formal weddings: The mothers of the bride and groom always wear elegant floor-length dinner or evening dresses to a very formal wedding. The styles may be less formal for a daytime wedding than for an evening ceremony, but the length remains the same. Almost any flattering color, except all-black or all-white, is appropriate, but rather than match the wedding party, the color should be one that blends with that of the bride's attendants. The mothers may wear small hats or veils, simple shoes and gloves, and carry or wear flowers, as long as their looks are similarly accessorized.

If they take part in the ceremony, as in the Jewish service, the mothers entrust their handbags and wraps to a seated family member. Traditionally, the mother of the bride selects her outfit first, then describes it to the mother of the groom, so she can choose hers. The mother of the bride must give the mother of the groom ample time to shop. Today it's more likely that the mothers will talk about the wedding style and agree on a "look" and complementary colors before either shops. It's fine if both mothers end up with pink dresses, as long as it isn't the same pink dress! One mother may choose to wear a dress she already owns, the other agree to look for one of a harmonizing hue. It's most important that the dresses reflect the same degree of formality.

Formal weddings: To a formal evening wedding, the mothers of the bride and groom usually wear long dinner dresses; to daytime ceremonies, street-length or cocktail-length outfits. Either is correct as long as both mothers dress similarly. It is courteous to keep in mind that the mothers set the style for the guests—the mothers may choose to appear in the kinds of outfits they know their guests will feel comfortable in for the occasion.

Small hats or veils were once customary at a church ceremony but are now often optional, unless they are expected of all women in the house of worship (Orthodox or Conservative Jewish). They are unnecessary when the wedding takes place at another location. Guidelines for other accessories are the same as those for mothers at a very formal wedding.

Semiformal or informal weddings: The mothers wear dresses similar to the honor attendants, most likely elegant street-length dresses.

Having something very special—and probably new—helps make a wedding the celebration it is. In addition to choosing clothes with care, the people involved should allow a day or two off in the final week of planning to rest and relax. That way the bride and everyone—from mothers to bridesmaids—will be assured of hearing the time-honored compliment, "You look beautiful!"

8

Your Wedding Ceremony

This is the big moment, one of the richest experiences the two of you will ever share. Like many couples today, you'll want your ceremony to be steeped in tradition, to convey the importance of this step called marriage; but full of personal touches that show the unique quality of your love. To ensure you'll have the beautiful ceremony you want, make an appointment to speak to your minister, priest, rabbi, or judge as soon as possible. Discuss the significance of the vows you'll recite; what, if any, individual changes or additions you'd like (a meaningful prayer or poem, a musical interlude, perhaps the exchange of vows you've written yourselves); and what each of you would like your ceremony to express about yourselves, your families, and the marriage you plan.

YOUR REHEARSAL

Here is your chance to practice for the "real thing," an opportunity for you and your groom and all the members of the wedding, including musicians, ushers, and clergy, to smooth out all the last-minute details.

The officiant is in charge of the rehearsal and is a pro at previewing everyone's role. The time to discuss ideas for the ceremony is at the premarriage conference with your clergymember, not at the rehearsal when everyone is excited. If you take the time to go over your plans with parents and honor attendants ahead of time, there will be no surprises or hurt feelings erupting during the rehearsal ("But I thought you would surely use the 'Wedding March' for the processional . . ."). Superstition once held that the bride-to-be have a stand-in at the rehearsal, but nowadays the clergy urge her to participate so she'll feel confident on wedding day.

The marriage service will not be read in full at the rehearsal, but you'll go over any special variations you've requested, to pick up the cues for your responses, and to outline the roles of the honor attendant and the best man. This is the time to make certain anyone who must do something unique—light a candle to symbolize the joining of families, start the "kiss of peace" among guests—does a run-through of his or her part.

The clergy (or wedding consultant, if you have one) can brief the ushers on the procedure for seating guests and give instructions to those with special duties, such as spreading the aisle canvas or pew ribbons. It helps, of course, if the best man has familiarized himself with these details ahead of time. "Where can people get a drink of water?" and "When do we seat the groom's mother?" are the kinds of questions that are likely to come up.

Incidentally, it may be a good idea to take along dummy bouquets—perhaps made from gift-ribbon bows from your shower. This way, you and your attendants can practice passing your flowers, as well as trying the turns necessary at the altar. As one whose actions will be interpreted as signals to guests, your mother will want to know at what points the clergy will say such things as "All rise."

A rehearsal for a ceremony of any size is reassuring for everyone involved, but some clergymembers do not schedule one for a small ceremony or one being held in a public place, such as a hotel. In that case, everyone assembles a little earlier and brief instructions are given before the ceremony begins.

Afterward, you will probably all celebrate with a rehearsal dinner or some get-together—to graciously welcome out-of-town guests and allow time to relax with family and friends—perhaps hosted by your fiancé's family. Many couples believe that the rehearsal and dinner must be the night before the ceremony. If possible, schedule your rehearsal two nights before the ceremony, so the party can continue as long as everyone wishes, without worry about having to hurry home to get a good night's rest. Not possible? At least make certain you and your fiancé leave on time.

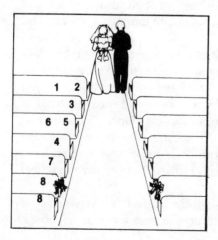

AT THE CHURCH . . .
1. Bride's mother 2. Bride's father 3. Bride's brothers and sisters 4. Grandparents 5. Special guests 6. Bride's guests (if bride's parents are divorced, follow seating order shown here for groom) 7. Groom's mother (if divorced) 8. Mother's husband (or companion) 9. Brothers, sisters 10. Groom's father (if divorced) 11. Father's wife 12. Grandparents 13. Special guests 14. Groom's guests.
Several front pews on each side of the aisle are reserved for the family—marked by floral markers. A warm touch is for the groom's parents to greet guests at the church door.

SEATING FOR THE CEREMONY

In a Christian wedding, the left side of the church as you face the altar is reserved for the bride's family and friends, the right side for the groom's. In Conservative and Orthodox Jewish weddings, it is the reverse. (If one family will be having many more guests than the other, everyone may sit together.) Your parents sit in the first pews on their respective sides, grandparents in the second pews to ensure they'll get the best view—along the aisle. You may wish to reserve additional pews on each side for other close relatives and friends.

When the bride's or groom's parents are divorced, individual circumstances determine the seating. For instance, if neither has remarried and they are amicable, it is perfectly all right for them to sit side by side in the front pew. Otherwise, your father should sit in the third pew with his wife, if he has remarried. All of these directions assume that your mother has been the custodial parent, but today that role is as likely to be filled by your father. If you have been raised by your father, seat him, with his family, in the first pew. Your mother would then sit in the third pew.

The most important thing is that everyone—including the bride—feels comfortable and happy with the arrangements.

The section reserved for family is often marked with flowers or ribbons; pew cards or "within the ribbons" cards may be sent to those guests you wish to honor with these special seats. All other guests are seated from front to back as they enter the church. Late-arriving guests should slip into the back rows, as no one should be seated after the bride's mother.

CEREMONY TIMETABLE

Study this sample countdown based on a large formal wedding taking place about fifteen minutes from the bride's house. Adapt it to your own situation, allowing plenty of time—even if traffic is heavy—to arrive at the church relaxed and ready.

Two hours before the ceremony: You, your mother, and your attendants begin dressing. If you're getting ready at the ceremony site, plan to arrive there at least an hour and a half before the ceremony.

One hour before the ceremony: Any bridesmaids who've dressed elsewhere gather at your house to pick up their flowers and pose for pictures.

Forty-five minutes before the ceremony: The ushers arrive at the ceremony site and pin on their boutonnieres. They distribute Mass books and wedding programs, pick up seating plans from the head usher, then gather near the entrance to wait for guests to arrive.

Thirty minutes before the ceremony: The organist starts to play the prelude while the ushers escort guests to their seats. Your mother and attendants leave for the church.

Twenty minutes before the ceremony: The groom and his best man arrive. The clergy makes certain the marriage license is on hand, receives the fee from the best man, and issues any last-minute instructions. Meanwhile, you and your father leave for the church.

Ten minutes before the ceremony: Your attendants arrive at the church, followed by your mother, the groom's parents, and other close members of your families. The bridal party and the parents wait in the vestibule while the other relatives are seated.

Five minutes before the ceremony: The groom's mother is escorted to her seat. The groom's father follows a few feet behind the usher, then takes his seat beside his wife. You and your father arrive and, if possible, park at a back entrance where you won't be seen by late-arriving guests (you want to surprise everyone!). As your mother—the last person seated by an usher—starts down the aisle, you and your father join the wedding party in the vestibule.

One minute before the ceremony: Two ushers walk in step to the front of the aisle to lay the aisle ribbons and canvas, if either is used. They then return to the vestibule and take their places in the procession.

Ceremony time: The minister, priest, or rabbi takes his place, followed by the groom and the best man. The procession begins, and all turn to watch the bride enter.

In some areas and within some families, the groom's parents will be in front of the church to greet the guests. Especially if a small informal ceremony is held at a site other than a church, the couple as well as both sets of parents may mingle with guests before the actual start of the service. People in this situation are urged to draw up a suitable timetable of pre-ceremony details.

TRANSPORTATION

A note about the cars. A fleet of chauffeur-driven limousines—probably rented—is part of what can make a wedding ultra-elegant. There is one for the bride and her father, one for the mother of the bride and the bride's attendants, one for the groom's parents, and one or two for the groom and his attendants. The limousines appear at their various pick-up points ten minutes before departure time. When a single chauffeured car is hired, it carries the bride and her father to the church, waits outside until the bride and groom dash out from the ceremony, then takes them on to the reception. Brides do arrive at the church by other means than limousine—horse and carriage, a walking procession, a bridal van (which brings the attendants as well, equipped with makeup mirrors). Friends who are not members of the wedding party can also provide transportation using their own cars; being relieved of the responsibility of maneuvering through heavy traffic means the mother of the groom, for instance, will arrive feeling relaxed and fresh. Do be sure that the car assigned to the bride is big enough to handle a voluminous dress and train. And, it's a thoughtful gesture to ask those friends with cars to be sure that all guests have a ride from the ceremony to the reception site. The friend who taxied from train to church may find himself or herself stranded after the service. Remember, all drivers should be given money for a car wash and a full tank of gas, complete instructions with addresses and phone numbers of all the people they are to pick up, and perhaps a special gift of thanks.

THE PROCESSION

In the Protestant service, the ushers enter from the back of the church first, in pairs, with the shortest of them leading. The bridesmaids (junior bridesmaids, if you have any, go first) follow individually, when there are fewer than four; otherwise, they are often paired much like the ushers or with the ushers. Instead of the old-fashioned "hesitation step," they may walk slowly and naturally along with the music. If there is an odd usher or maid, the shortest attendant leads off alone. The honor attendant comes next, then the ring bearer, then the flower girl. Now the bride and her father enter, with the pages, if any, carrying the bride's train behind her. As you wait for this moment, remember it is a sensitive—and proud—time for your father; a loving squeeze of his hand may mean a lot to him.

Catholic brides and grooms frequently observe the same procedure, but they may forego the traditional procession and be met at the church door by the priest.

All Jewish processions—Orthodox, Conservative, and Reform—vary according to local custom and to the preferences of the family. In the simplest service, the ushers lead the procession in pairs, followed by the bridesmaids in pairs. Then come the groom and his best man, the honor attendant, the flower girl, and the bride on her father's right. The groom's parents and the bride's mother may join in the procession.

The most elaborate Jewish ceremony is led by the rabbi and cantor, followed by the couple's grandparents, the ushers, the bridesmaids, the best man, the groom and his parents, the bride's honor attendant, her flower girl, and the bride with her parents. Your rabbi will tell you how he prefers to organize the procession, taking into account the local customs and the amount of space available for the wedding party.

Some Christian couples have borrowed from Jewish custom and included parents and grandparents in the processional. It's a happy way of showing family support for the marriage. And, there are a number of variations for the procession. At a remarriage, the couple's children—his and hers—may process ahead of the wedding couple, who come in together. To some this is a strong way of saying "This wedding is an important step for all of us."

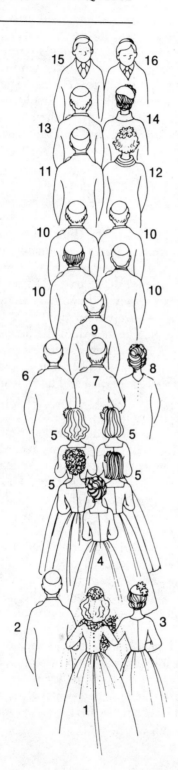

TRADITIONAL JEWISH PROCESSION:
1. Bride 2. Father of the bride 3. Mother of the bride 4. Honor attendant 5. Bridesmaids 6. Father of the groom 7. Groom 8. Mother of the groom 9. Best man 10. Ushers 11. Groom's grandfather 12. Groom's grandmother 13. Bride's grandfather 14. Bride's grandmother 15. Cantor 16. Rabbi. Note: If a flower girl and ring bearer participate, they immediately precede the bride and her parents.

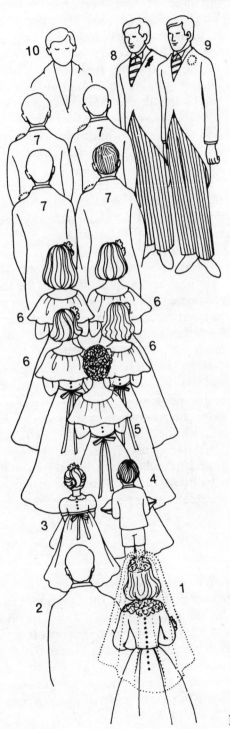

CHRISTIAN PROCESSION: 1. Bride 2. Father of the bride 3. Flower girl 4. Ring bearer 5. Honor attendant 6. Bridesmaids 7. Ushers 8. Groom 9. Best man 10. Wedding officiant.

115

Another option is for the bride to be escorted by one of her children. You may, of course, process alone, but it's nice to have someone you love by your side. When a marriage takes place during a worship service (such as during a Roman Catholic mass, or a Quaker meeting), the bride and groom could be seated at the front of the sanctuary and come forward at the proper time.

If your father has died, you may ask your stepfather, brother, uncle, other close relative, a family friend, or an usher to escort you. Your mother may also walk you to the altar if she feels comfortable with this idea. Your stepfather (should you feel close to him) or your mother may give you away as well. Ask your mother if she would prefer to simply nod or say "I do" from her seat in the first pew, or if she would like the best man to escort her to your side at the appropriate moment in the ceremony.

If someone takes the place of your absent father, he then joins your mother in the front pew. If your father is a widower and you have asked an aunt or your grandmother to take your mother's place, she would sit in the front pew with your father.

If your own parents are divorced, you may be faced with a dilemma. Should your father or stepfather be the one to walk you down the aisle? There is no one right answer. Each family—and the feelings of all family members do need to be considered—weighs its own situation. If you've remained close to your father, you will probably want him to fill the traditional role. There's no need for your stepfather to be left out, though. He can do a special reading during the ceremony, or propose a toast at the reception.

If the church has two center aisles, you may use the left aisle for the procession and the right aisle for the recession, or close off the second aisle entirely. When both aisles are used, the bride's relatives and friends sit on both sides of the left aisle, the groom's on both sides of the right aisle. The parents sit in the center section; the bride's on the left, the groom's on the right.

Civil ceremonies are usually quite small, with the bride preceded by one attendant and escorted into the room by her father. For a large civil ceremony in a ballroom or other formal setting, choose the procession format that seems suitable to your needs and to the ceremony setting.

ALTAR PROCEDURES

When the bridal party reaches the first row of seats, they traditionally form one of two arrangements: the ushers turn to the right to create a diagonal line behind the groom and best man, while the bridesmaids assemble in a similar line on the left side; or each pair of attendants separates at the altar, with one pair going to each side. Ushers and bridesmaids may stand side by side, or the bridesmaids may stand one step in front of the ushers. Another contemporary variation is for the bridesmaids and ushers to gather in a semicircle around the bride and groom, facing the congregation. Children may stand at the altar through the ceremony, but they're frequently happier if allowed to slide into the second or third pew with their parents. In some churches, particularly those with a modern freestanding altar, the priest stands with his back to the guests and the wedding party faces the congregation. Remember, your clergymember is used to conducting services in this space and will have a good sense of what works best.

CHRISTIAN CEREMONY AT THE ALTAR: 1. Bride 2. Father of the bride 3. Flower girl 4. Ring bearer 5. Honor attendant 6. Bridesmaids 7. Ushers 8. Groom 9. Best man 10. Wedding official. Note: The father of the bride takes his seat following the giving-away.

In the Protestant service, you leave your father's arm and take one step forward as you reach the head of the aisle. The groom comes forward to join you on your right. The honor attendant and best man take their positions on either side of the bride and groom, while the other attendants turn toward the altar. Your father remains standing one step behind and to your left until the minister asks, "Who gives this woman to be married?" He replies, "I do" or "Her mother and I do," then takes his seat next to your mother in the first pew. As a contemporary alternative to the giving-away, the minister might ask, "Who blesses this marriage?" Both your and your groom's parents reply, "We, their parents, do." The minister may also ask, "Who supports them in this marriage?" and the whole congregation and wedding party would respond, "We do."

In Catholic ceremonies, where the bride is not actually given away, your father places your hand in your groom's, pauses to give you a kiss, or sometimes to lift your veil, and joins your mother as soon as you have reached the altar.

The Jewish ceremony is performed under a pretty wedding canopy, a *huppah*, which in Hebrew means "a covering." Symbolic of the ancient bridal chamber of consummation, and also representing a home to nomadic tribes, it's made of silk, satin, brocade, velvet, greenery and flowers, or even a prayer shawl spread across the top of the four slender poles. In a synagogue, the *huppah* is placed on the pulpit. Holding the poles aloft is a task assigned to honored friends or relatives.

117

JEWISH WEDDING: 1. Bride 2. Father of the bride 3. Mother of the bride 4. Honor attendant 5. Bridesmaids 6. Groom 7. Father of the groom 8. Mother of the groom 9. Best man 10. Ushers 11. Rabbi. Note: Grandparents of the bride and groom may take their seats after the procession; the cantor takes his appropriate place.

In the Jewish ceremony, all the parents may remain standing throughout.

In any faith, if you've written your own vows and carefully selected readings to be used in your service, you'll want the congregation to hear what is said. It will help if anyone speaking—you, your groom saying vows or exchanging rings, a member of the wedding party saying a prayer—turns at a slight angle toward the congregation. Ask your clergymember if the synagogue has amplification; if not, would you be allowed to rent a portable system? A wedding program, with all parts written out, allows guests to follow along despite poor acoustics.

Usually members of the weding party are not required to be of the same faith as the bride and groom. However, anyone accepting an invitation to take part in a wedding is agreeing to participate fully. That may mean kneeling, praying aloud, singing hymns, and observing customs of the faith (such as wearing a *yarmulke*). Anyone who feels uncomfortable in a religious service should excuse himself when first asked.

If you are required to kneel or climb steps during the ceremony, your groom will take your arm to help you up and down. Then, when the ceremony is over and the official has congratulated the two of you, your groom or honor attendant lifts your face veil (if you are wearing one and if your father did not lift it earlier) for the custom kiss. (It is not mandatory that you kiss, but it is a long-loved custom that says it's time to celebrate! And, it ensures that no one breaks the tradition of your groom being the very first to kiss you, his wife!) The honor attendant puts your bouquet in your right hand and arranges your train as you turn to face your guests for the recession—with a smile.

THE RECESSION

When the organist sounds the happy signal, you take your groom's right arm and start up the aisle together. Your attendants, starting with the children, quickly fall into step behind you: the honor attendant on the right arm of the best man, each of the bridesmaids on the arm of an usher (an usher may escort two bridesmaids if bridesmaids outnumber ushers), and extra ushers walking together at the end.

On reaching the vestibule, the ushers you've designated in advance return to escort the mothers and honored guests from the church and to roll up any pew ribbons. Some newlyweds prefer to have their attendants precede them out of the church, and they stop at each pew, greeting guests as they exit.

You, your groom, and your honor attendants will probably join the clergy in his or her chambers to sign the marriage license, although this may be incorporated into your ceremony, as it is in a Quaker wedding. The marriage certificate may be set on a table off to the side. Just before the close of the service, the bride, groom, witnesses and clergymember step over to sign it.

You and the wedding party may wish to return to the church to pose for photographs as well. In the meantime, guests may wait in front of the church

RECESSIONAL: 1. Bride 2. Groom 3. Flower girl 4. Ring bearer 5. Honor attendant 6. Best man 7. Bridesmaids 8. Ushers.

for you to appear—to receive their hugs, and their applause, or the ushers delegated to do so will direct guests to the reception site.

If the marriage license has been signed (by all but the legal officiant) prior to the ceremony—perhaps at the rehearsal dinner—you would be wise to form a receiving line immediately after the ceremony, in the vestibule or in front of the church. Receiving lines are the time when guests can tell the bride and groom how happy they feel, and wish them well.

This official greeting can be handled more quickly at the church. Or, you and the bridesmaids may dash immediately into your waiting cars—and off to the reception! There, you'll have time to pose for pictures, freshen your makeup, and form the receiving line before guests arrive. The ushers stay at the church to see that it is cleared of guests and any of their belongings before they head on to the reception.

SEMIFORMAL WEDDINGS

Most formal wedding procedures also apply to the smaller, semiformal wedding. With fewer guests, you may omit the pew ribbons and aisle carpet, especially since you probably will not be wearing a dress with a train. (For details on semiformal, home garden weddings, see Chapter 10.)

INFORMAL WEDDINGS

An intimate, informal wedding may be held at home, in a small chapel, a judge's chambers, or your favorite restaurant or club. Guests may be welcomed and directed to the wedding area by your mother, your honor attendant, or by another close friend or relative. You and your groom may enjoy mingling before the ceremony or you may wait in another room, where your best friends may come to help you make sure your hair is just right and that you haven't forgotten anything. At ceremony time, the two of you, your honor attendant, and the best man take your places before the ceremony officiant. Your groom or your father may escort you, if you wish. After the ceremony and the traditional kiss, you simply turn to greet your guests and receive their heartfelt good wishes.

Informal or formal, your ceremony will no doubt remind all your guests of their own marriage vows or their sentiments regarding family and friendships. In this way, your wedding can be rich with meaning for everyone.

9
Religious Rituals

While American marriage ceremonies share many similarities, there are differences among religions. And even within the same faith, local customs may influence the style of the wedding. It is important, therefore, to discuss the details of your ceremony with the proper church officials as soon as possible. If you and your fiancé are regular church members, you'll want to explore the relationship of the service—and the church itself—to the family you are now forming. If you are not members, you may wish to make certain that the practices of the church in which you hope to marry reflect your personal beliefs. Here is a brief guide to the wedding ceremonies of major American religions today.

PROTESTANT WEDDINGS

Almost all Protestant churches use the standard ("Dearly Beloved . . .") wedding service, and most require the congregation to stand during part of the ceremony. Although there are no laws which prohibit marriage on particular days of the year, many of the Protestant clergy are reluctant to perform wedding ceremonies on Sundays and religious holidays. Rules about music vary, but prior approval of a church authority may be required for the use of secular music, especially any modern popular songs you may have in mind. There are no specific rules on attire, but bare-backed or strapless dresses may need a little jacket or wrap until reception time. (Many dresses for brides, bridesmaids, and mothers come with cover-ups for this very reason.) The following variations can be found among some of the Protestant faiths.

Episcopal: The Episcopal church usually discourages formal weddings during Lent. Often, too, at least one party to the marriage must have been baptized, and a number of premarital meetings with the priest may be required. The remarriage of divorced persons is customarily allowed, but the divorced party will be asked to discuss the previous marriage with the clergymember. Dispensations are sometimes needed. The clergymember is trying to determine if both parties are marrying freely and if there are issues lingering from the first marriage that will spill over into the second. A Nuptial Mass similar to the Catholic ceremony may be part of a wedding in the "High" or Anglo-Catholic branch of the Episcopal church.

Quaker: A Quaker wedding requires prior approval (which may take up to three months) from the monthly meeting of the Society of Friends. The marriage itself usually takes place during a meeting of worship where those in attendance meditate quietly. The bridal couple may enter the meeting together and join the circle of Friends already seated. A traditional procession, comprised of the couple, their parents, honor attendant, and the committee members, is another option. But, there would be no music. The bridal party would then take seats on benches facing the meeting.

After the traditional Quaker silence, the bride and groom rise, join hands, and say their vows. The groom speaks his promises first, then the bride. The bride is not given away nor does a third person pronounce them married, for the Friends believe that only God can create such a union.

Further details of the Quaker wedding are usually worked out in advance between the couple and an appointed group of meeting members. It is this group that oversees the vows during the wedding. In a typical wedding, the marriage certificate is brought to the couple to sign after they have shared their vows. The certificate is then read aloud by a member of the meeting. The meeting may continue until the bride and groom feel ready to leave. All guests sign the marriage certificate before departing, which is a custom couples marrying in the Quaker faith may particularly treasure.

A Quaker couple today may design a highly personalized service with attendants, flowers, musical solos, or readings; however, the wedding remains a simple one—very much in the Quaker tradition. Neither a bridal party nor the exchange of rings is necessary at a Quaker wedding, but both are commonly seen today. Bridesmaids dress quite simply. In some areas of the country, the meeting will have a pastor, who naturally would take part in the ceremony and in the prewedding discussions.

Christian Scientist: Readers of the Christian Science faith are not ordained and may not perform marriages. When members of the faith marry, the ceremony may be performed by any minister ordained in another denomination or by proper legal authority. Readers and members of the Christian Scientist congregation can be a helpful source for finding those willing to officiate and to create an especially meaningful service for the bride and groom.

Mormon: The Church of Jesus Christ of Latter-Day Saints recognizes two kinds of marriage. The first is for the faithful deemed fit for marriage by members of the Holy Priesthood; this wedding takes place in a temple of the church. Such couples are wed "for time and eternity" (instead of "until death do you part"). Their children are believed to belong to them for all eternity as well. The second is a civil ceremony performed by bishops of the church or other legal authorities. These couples are sometimes rewed in a temple at a later date. A Mormon and a non-Mormon may be wed in such a civil ceremony.

ROMAN CATHOLIC WEDDINGS

When both the bride and the groom are Catholic, the banns (intentions to marry) are published in the parish churches of both. These announcements may be made from the pulpit at the principal Masses on three consecutive Sundays before the wedding, or published in the church calendar or bulletin. The purpose of the banns is to make sure that each party is free to marry. The banns are not usually proclaimed for an interfaith marriage, nor for the marriage of an older couple. The non-Catholic party to a mixed marriage need not be baptized, but must be free to marry in a Catholic church, which means the Catholic party will first have to obtain a dispensation by the bishop of the diocese. It is easily secured these days, and the priest who will marry you will most likely handle the procedure. Couples who will marry in the Catholic church generally are required to attend a series of pre-wedding sessions before they receive permission for the wedding. The couple may be asked to bring as many practical issues—money management, for example—to the surface as spiritual issues, and they may find this kind of communication invaluable to their relationship. The marriage of divorced persons is usually not allowed in the Church, unless the previous marriage has been declared null before a Church court.

A Catholic bride must have the permission of her own pastor to be married in another parish. The officiating priest will need proof of baptism for baptized persons and evidence of freedom to marry. Catholic weddings are rarely conducted outside the church, although mixed marriages are sometimes performed in the church of the non-Catholic. In such cases, a Roman Catholic priest may officiate along with the non-Catholic minister, pronouncing a prayer or blessing over the couple. An interfaith wedding with two clergymembers officiating may also be held in a Roman Catholic parish, in which case the priest would officiate at the exchange of vows and the guest minister assist in other ways. The host clergymember is always the principal.

The procession for a Catholic wedding may follow the procedures for a Protestant ceremony, except that the bride is not given away. Her father, or another person she chooses, escorts her to the steps of the altar where her groom and the priest are waiting. There are many options open to the couple in the new marriage rites. Each couple may discuss these with the priest before the wedding. Many couples at this point exchange a greeting with the priest and with the bride's father. Then in a gesture of both recognizing the groom and "handing over" responsibility to him, the father places his daughter's hand in the groom's hand. He may lift his daughter's veil and kiss her before taking his seat beside his wife.

Some couples choose to be greeted at the vestibule door by the priest, then led by him to the altar. Many of the traditional wedding marches are not allowed in some Catholic dioceses since, as opera themes, they are deemed secular rather than religious. (See Chapter 14 for alternatives and consult the officiating priest.)

While Catholic marriages may be performed and Nuptial Masses celebrated during Lent and Advent, the decoration of the church and the style of the wedding may be somewhat restricted. A profusion of gaily colored flowers, for instance, may be discouraged in favor of the more subtle beauty of white ones.

A Nuptial Mass may be arranged for almost any Catholic wedding, with the brief wedding ceremony being incorporated into the Mass. Non-Catholics at a Nuptial Mass (including the bride or groom if it is a mixed marriage) do not take Communion. Mass books, which may be imprinted with the names of the bridal couple and the date of the ceremony, are often distributed to guests so they may follow the ritual of the Mass. Non-Catholic guests needn't give the responses, but they may kneel (or sit quietly while others kneel) and stand at the proper times in the ceremony.

A custom seen less frequently today than a decade ago is an act of devotion performed by the bride to honor Mary, the Blessed Mother. The bride dedicates her flowers to Mary, the patroness of family life, either during or following the marriage ceremony, with a prayer for her own new family.

Incidentally, altar boys should be given a tip or gift—the best man can pass it along. (See Chapter 17 for gift suggestions for children.)

EASTERN ORTHODOX WEDDINGS

The churches of the Eastern Rite, including Greek and Russian Orthodox, are similar in some ways to the Catholic Church. Mixed marriages are allowed, but the non-Orthodox party to the marriage must be a baptized Christian. Eastern Rite churches permit the remarriage of those who've received religious decrees of annulment following a civil divorce. The banns of marriage may be proclaimed but are not necessary.

Orthodox weddings usually take place in the afternoon or early evening and may not be solemnized in church during any season of fasting, on the eve of certain holy days, during the week after Easter, or in the two weeks after Christmas. They seldom include the Divine Liturgy, as the marriage itself is a long ceremony rich with symbolism and pageantry. Traditionally, the only music allowed in an Orthodox church is that of an unaccompanied choir and the singing of the ancient Byzantine and Russian chants. Organs are now used, however, in some Greek American churches.

The standard wedding procession in which the bride's father gives her away is customary in the Greek Orthodox ceremony. In the Russian Orthodox ceremony, the wedding party is met at the vestibule door by the priest, and the bride is given away before the procession proceeds. The size of the wedding party and its arrangement are matters of personal taste and local custom, with the honor attendant and best man frequently having somewhat more complex duties during the ceremony, such as holding the crowns above the bride's and groom's heads. Traditionally, a Greek Orthodox bride wears a face veil, but a Russian Orthodox bride need not. The guests at a Russian Orthodox wedding usually remain standing during the ceremony, but in Greek churches in America, they are often allowed to sit during the less sacred parts of the service.

An Orthodox wedding begins with a betrothal ritual, usually at the front or center of the church. This includes the blessing and exchange of the rings, which are customarily worn by both bride and groom on their right hands. The rings are exchanged between bride and groom three times to signify the Holy Trinity. Many rituals are repeated three times for this same reason.

At the close of the betrothal ritual, the bride and groom move up the center aisle of the church to positions before the altar screen or iconostasis to begin the Order of Marriage. Two crowns are placed on the heads of the bride and groom and exchanged three times in the Greek ceremony. In the Russian ceremony, the honor attendant and the best man hold the crowns above the couple's heads. The crowning of the wedding couple, the bridegroom first, followed by the bride, signifies their "coronation" into a new family realm. After the Gospel is read, a cup of wine is shared three times by the bride and groom to symbolize the joys and the sorrows they will share in marriage. Afterward, in the Greek ceremony, the wine is also drunk by the best man.

The *koumbaros*, or sponsor, is an important figure in the wedding. Traditionally it was the groom's godfather, but any person who will continue a significant relationship with the couple may perform the function of introducing them into the married state. The bride, groom, and *koumbaros* are then led around a ceremonial table three times with their hands bound. At the close of the ceremony, the congregation joins in singing "God Grant Them Many Years."

After the recessional in a Greek church, friends of the family often stand on the church steps and distribute festive packets of candy to the other guests. This has the same significance as the shower of rice tradition originated among the Chinese: "May you always enjoy a life of plenty."

JEWISH WEDDINGS

No single set of rules applies to all Jewish weddings, for there are differences among the Orthodox, Conservative, and Reform branches of the faith. Individual rabbis and synagogues are also likely to have their own interpretations of the marriage ceremony, so verification of all guidelines and procedures with the

125

officiating rabbi before plans are finalized is wise. Rabbis, as a rule, will not perform mixed marriages, and Orthodox and Conservative rabbis do not recognize any divorces except those granted by religious decree. Reform clergy, however, often recognize civil divorces.

Jewish weddings may take place at any time except on the Sabbath (from sundown on Friday to sundown on Saturday), on Holy Days, during a three-week period in midsummer, and during almost all of Passover and Shabuoth. Most weddings are celebrated on Saturday evening after sundown or on Sunday. A Jewish wedding may occur almost anywhere, and many are not performed in synagogues or temples: It is more usual in some localities for the ceremony to take place at a club, hotel, or catering hall where the centuries-old splendor of the wedding feast and dancing may follow. Conventional wedding attire, including a face veil for the bride if she is Orthodox, is generally worn. In a pre-wedding ritual, she is "veiled" by the groom as a sign that she is, indeed, his betrothed. In Conservative and Orthodox ceremonies both, all the men—including those in the wedding party—cover their heads with either *yarmulkes* or silk top hats.

In Jewish tradition, the bride and groom may not see each other before the "veiling" (if there is one) just before the ceremony, yet the bride and her attendants may wait, in all their finery, in a separate room where they sometimes receive guests beforehand. At the appropriate time, the bride's family will be seated on the right side of the hall or temple, the groom's family on the left, before any other guests are shown to their places.

The order of the procession and positions during the ceremony are set by local custom, with Orthodox and Conservative processions usually including the groom and both sets of parents (see Chapter 8). The ushers walk down the aisle first, followed by the bridesmaids, then the ring bearer. Sometimes the ushers and maids form a guard of honor through which the rest of the wedding party will pass.

Jewish marriages are traditionally performed under a *huppah,* a heavily ornamented canopy symbolizing the ancient bridal chamber of consummation, shelter from the open sky in nomadic times, and today, the home the couple will live in together. The *huppah* may also be embellished with—or woven entirely of—fresh flowers. It is usually placed in front of an attractive background at one end of the room or in front of the Ark in a temple. The procession walks toward the canopy, with each person taking a prescribed position under or near it.

The bride stands on the groom's right under the canopy, and the rabbi faces them. It is also customary for the honor attendants to be under the *huppah*—the bride's attendant on her right, the groom's best man on his left. When space permits, the parents sometimes gather alongside or directly behind their children under the *huppah.* The bridesmaids and ushers usually line up in single file on either side of the canopy (see the illustration in Chapter 8).

During the wedding ceremony, the rabbi stands next to a small table covered in white and set with cups of ritual wine and a glass, frequently wrapped in white silk or a napkin. The service begins with a betrothal ceremony, then an introductory blessing. Next, the groom sips from the glass of wine and passes it to the bride. After the couple have spoken their vows, the groom places a plain gold band on the bride's right index finger in the Conservative and Orthodox ceremonies, on her left ring finger in the Reform ceremony. Conservative and Orthodox rabbis now read the *ketubah*, or traditional marriage contract. How much of the service is conducted in English, how much in Hebrew may vary. But all Jewish ceremonies end with the traditional Seven Blessings, the last of which includes the ritual crushing of the wine glass beneath the groom's heel (as a reminder that in marriage there are times of sorrow amidst the joy), an address by the rabbi to the couple, and closing benediction. At that, *"Mazel tov!"* will sound from all the corners of the room, as guests call out their best wishes to the bride and groom.

The order of the recession may differ, but it is always led by the bride and groom. They are usually followed by the bride's parents, the groom's parents, the maid or matron of honor on the best man's arm, then the rabbi, with pairs of bridesmaids and ushers bringing up the rear.

In a Reform wedding, the procession, recession, and other ceremony details are similar to those used in the Protestant service, including the use of the traditional wedding marches. There may be a double ring ceremony, and the marriage may or may not be performed under a *huppah*.

The wedding feast is traditionally very important to a Jewish wedding. It usually includes a marriage grace or blessing at some point in the dining. The receiving line and other details are similar to those for any kind of reception.

THE INTERFAITH WEDDING

When the bride and groom are of different faiths, it is possible for them to be married in a ceremony that combines the rituals of both faiths. The interfaith wedding, sometimes known as the ecumenical service among Christian groups, can take several forms, depending on your own wishes and those of the clergy involved. The ceremony can be performed almost entirely by the official of one faith, with the other one giving a short blessing at the end. For example, the couple might be married by a Catholic priest according to the ritual of the Mass, and have a rabbi present to offer the Hebrew Seven Blessings after the vows are exchanged. Or, the service can be divided equally between the two faiths, with a minister and priest, perhaps, alternating religious readings and then joining together for the exchange of vows and the ring ceremony.

It is doubly important when considering an interfaith ceremony to begin your plans early. First, check to make sure that your own clergy agree to participate. More and more clergy are willing to take part in this type of service, but there are individuals who prefer not to.

It is important for you to remember that even if the ceremony is ecumenical, the clergymember of the church or synagogue where you will be married is the host. He or she is in charge of arrangements and has the final approval of the service. The host clergymember, not yourselves, officially invites the other clergy to participate. You, of course, could pave the way by finding out if both are willing.

Also keep in mind, for both religions, the days of the calendar when marriages may not be permitted. In planning the actual ceremony, work closely with the clergy to be sure that the final service is one that is both acceptable and meaningful to everyone present.

An interfaith ceremony is a symbolic demonstration of your determination to let your differences enrich each other's lives. Your ceremony sets a positive tone of cooperation, not just for yourselves, but also for family and friends. Each partner should feel that his or her religion is respected equally. If your faiths have distinctive symbols, intertwine them on your wedding invitation or program. You might emphasize symbols that each faith shares—candles, flowers, wine, and bread are used in many religions. Use prayers and music from each church in customary language, but also include opportunities to pray and sing in unison. Communication is so important. Do explain the reasons for traditions to everyone. And find ways for members of each family to participate meaningfully in the service. Compromise is possible once you determine what's most important to each of you. For example, if being married under a *huppah* is essential to your groom, yet including your Methodist minister is a must for you, consider a garden wedding where your minister and his rabbi can officiate together under a flower-bedecked *huppah*.

THE RELIGIOUS WEDDING PERSONALIZED

Almost all religions allow certain variations in their ceremonies; many even have several services from which you might choose. You and your fiancé should discuss the standard vows. Is this what you want your wedding to express? If your wish changes—and they can be accomplished with dignity—alterations in the wedding service can greatly enrich this day in your memory. (Some of the classic additions to the wedding service are mentioned briefly in Chapter 8.) A special rose given to each mother after the giving away, a scripture selection read by his father, a poem spoken by a bridesmaid, a hymn sung by guests—these are the kinds of ideas the clergy may also be able to suggest. In trying to involve your guests, do consider the sensitivities of your own family and friends. Asking them to renew their vows aloud may sound like a wonderful thing, but they may not feel comfortable doing so. They may also be somewhat embarrassed if your vows become very personal or go on at length (an hour for your total ceremony is probably the upper limit).

Your clergymember will suggest appropriate scripture selections, but you may have favorites of your own. Themes of love, family, human relationships, joy, and new beginnings are all suitable for weddings, and easily found in a Bible concordance that lists verses by subject. For your interfaith ceremony, you might emphasize what you have in common. Then, at a Jewish/Protestant wedding, you might use only scripture from the Old Testament. To demonstrate your respect for each other's faith, have your sister read scripture from his faith; his brother, a passage from yours.

Wedding readings, known as secular scripture, are an expression of your own personal ideas. Do consult with your clergymember about your choices. A passage from the fields of philosophy, psychology, or religion may speak of the quality of relationships, the meaning of love, the value of marriage. Look in anthologies under "love" and "marriage" themes for ideas.

Poetry speaks the language of love so beautifully. Choose old favorites, such as the work of Elizabeth Barrett Browning, Shakespeare, Kahlil Gibran; or more modern poems, those written by Robert Graves, e.e. cummings, Rainer Maria Rilke.

There may be a passage from a novel, play, or even children's story that particularly appeals to you. Share that with your wedding guests in your cere-mony. Song lyrics can be quite moving when read rather than sung. Sentimental, poignant, thought-provoking lyrics abound. Once your listening antennae are up, you'll find many possibilities.

The wedding ceremony may seem brief (and sometimes it is, in fact, made too brief by a bride's or groom's reluctance to be in front of an audience), but the ritual, the symbolism, the tradition create a connection that has lasted for centuries among all those who have married and will continue on in the future. It is this realization that can touch everyone at your ceremony in a quiet and marvelous way. Do remember, when planning your ceremony, that this wedding ritual belongs to your wedding assemblage, as well as yourselves, and all of you will savor its beauty.

10
Special Weddings

Marry in the warm and comfortable setting of home, amidst the splendor of a military service, or outdoors under an open sky. You may choose the special setting and touches of individuality that will make your wedding most significant to you and your fiancé. The following are classic variations to the traditional ceremony you may want to think about.

THE MILITARY WEDDING

The flourish of a military wedding with its famous arch of sabers (swords in the Navy) appeals to many brides who marry commissioned officers on active duty. The arch, under which the bride and groom walk at the end of the ceremony, is formed by the groom's fellow officers, who also serve as ushers.

A groom in any branch of military service, whether an officer or not, may be married in uniform, but swords and sabers are carried only by officers in full dress uniform (blue in winter, white in summer). Do you wish to have your brothers or other close friends who are not officers in the military participate? If so, they wear traditional formal attire. As a rule, however, your father is the only man in the procession in civilian clothes, unless he is also in the military. Instead of boutonnieres, military decorations are worn by men in uniform.

Since full dress military uniforms are very formal, you might complement the men with the utmost in elegance—a long dress of satin, velvet, or lace with flowing train and veil. Dress your bridesmaids and honor attendant in equally formal long dresses, perhaps matching the colors of your groom's academy. Mothers and wedding guests may dress as they would for any other formal wedding at the same hour and season.

Many military weddings take place at military chapels, including those at the Army, Navy, and Air Force academies, but other locations are acceptable.

Decorations usually include the American flag and the standards of the groom's unit, in addition to flowers. Do verify all your plans, of course, with the proper military authorities.

Invitations and announcements differ only in that the groom's rank and service are indicated. If your fiancé is a junior officer (below the rank of Army or Air Force Captain or Naval Commander), his title appears under his name, followed by the branch of service on the same line. "Mr." is never used to address or refer to an officer on active duty. (See Chapter 5 for further details on the use of military titles.)

The military procession follows standard procedures, but the recession is dramatized by the traditional arch of steel. With the splendid regalia of the men's uniforms and the flash of metal in the sun, this is truly a memorable sight for guests. The arch may be formed outside the church, in front of the chapel—or both—depending on church rules, the branch of service, and personal preference. The head usher usually issues the commands, starting with "Center face," the signal to form two facing lines. When the order "Arch sabers" (or "Draw swords") is given, each usher raises his saber in his right hand, cutting edge on top. After you and your groom have passed under the arch, sabers are sheathed and returned to the "carry" position. If the arch will be formed outside as well, the bride and groom wait in the vestibule until the ushers are in place at the chapel or on the steps of the church.

At the reception following a military wedding, you might feature regimental decorations and music, including miniature flags and the theme song of the groom's branch of the service. At a seated reception, military guests are shown to their places in order of rank. The highlight of the reception comes when the bride and groom cut the cake using the groom's saber or sword.

Should the bride and her attendants be officers in the military, they usually choose to wear traditional dress as for any formal wedding ceremony. However, if the bride wishes, she and her bridesmaids may appear in uniform. (The bride generally prefers not to show her title on wedding invitations, although she may; again, see Chapter 5.) If both bride and groom are military officers, all members of the wedding party may wear full dress uniform, with the bride either in a formal wedding dress or her own dress uniform. All other procedures are the same as for any military wedding, including the display of the standards of the bride's military unit.

THE DOUBLE WEDDING

Any two sisters, close relatives, or good friends may wish to express their mutual fondness by sharing their wedding day; it is a savings, both emotional and financial, for their parents. What's more, double weddings can be quite splendid with their multiplicity of attendants and, usually, large number of guests.

A double wedding is most often formal, with each couple having their own set of attendants. (The brides may serve as each other's honor attendants, but this is optional.) Both groups of attendants dress with the same degree of formality, in the same or harmonizing colors. The ushers, for example, might all wear the traditional black-and-white formal suits, while one set of bridesmaids wears pale lavender, the other deep plum. Or, for a summer ceremony, one couple might dress their ushers in pale gray, their bridesmaids in deep apricot, while the other chooses a rich beige for the men, peach for the women. The brides wear differently styled dresses with trains and veils of about the same length.

Invitations are usually issued jointly (see Chapter 5), but if the brides are not sisters, separate invitations may be sent.

If the two brides are sisters, the older one usually takes precedence in the procession and recession. Otherwise, the order of the ceremony and the seating arrangements must be worked out carefully in advance. If a church has two aisles, the processions and recessions may take place simultaneously, one on each side, with each set of parents in the first pew on either side of their couple's aisle. When there is only one aisle, one set of parents may sit in the second pew or both sets may share the first pew. One couple might lead the procession, the other the recession.

With a single aisle, the two grooms walk in together behind the clergymember and take their places side by side, each with his own best man behind him, the future husband of the first bride standing nearer the aisle. Both sets of ushers, paired by height, lead the procession. The bridesmaids, honor attendant, and flower girl of the first bride come next, followed by the bride on her father's arm. The second set of attendants and the second bride follow in similar fashion. At a double wedding of sisters, a brother or other male relative may escort the second bride to the altar, or the father may escort his elder daughter down the aisle and to her groom, then return to fetch his younger daughter. In either case, the father can give both daughters away. Other possibilities: the mother escorts the second daughter; or, the father walks down the aisle with one bride on each arm. The problem with the latter suggestion is one of space, since two bridal gowns are difficult to fit side by side in the average church aisle. But at an outdoor wedding, or in a hotel banquet hall, where the width of the aisle can be adjusted, this would be possible. The attendants might walk, two by two, one sister's maid of honor paired with the other's honor attendant, and so forth.

On reaching the head of the aisle, the attendants usually separate so that those of the first bride are on the left, those of the second bride on the right. The two couples stand side by side in front of the wedding official, the first bride on the left. In a wedding of sisters, the father stands behind the older bride until he gives her away, then moves over to give his younger daughter away before he takes his seat. The ceremony may be divided into sections, with each couple completing each section in turn: first one couple speaks their vows, then the other. However, the final blessing may be given to both at the same time. Then each couple may kiss and turn to face their guests.

The recession is led by the two couples, one preceding the other, followed by the two sets of honor attendants, then the bridesmaids and ushers in pairs. When the brides have served as each other's honor attendants, the best men escort the bridesmaids up the aisle, the extra ushers bringing up the rear.

A joint reception, which may be especially large and lavish, always follows a double wedding. Sisters receive in the same line, with the older bride and her husband preceding the younger. The honor attendants may participate, but bridesmaids may be excused in order to keep the line to a manageable length. Fathers seldom participate, choosing instead to mingle with and greet their guests. When the brides are not sisters, each family may form a separate receiving line, including the bridesmaids if they wish.

The size of the wedding party and the available space determine whether it's better to have a joint table or separate ones. Each bride may wish to have her own cake, to be cut at the same time. Any imprinted favors or napkins may include the names of both couples and the date, or they may be ordered separately for each couple.

CANDLELIGHT CEREMONIES

When the wedding will take place in the late afternoon or evening, and the church is a relatively dark one, a candlelight ceremony can be beautiful. Meeting the proper church authorities very early in the planning stage, however, is most important. Local fire regulations may dictate the number and placement of the candles, and the secretary (sexton or verger) should be able to inform you of your limitations as well as the possibilities. Dimming the electric lighting, for example, may enhance the mood of the setting, but in such a case special spotlighting at the altar may be required for the clergy to see.

Placement of candles to shine throughout the church should be carefully considered—you'll want to keep them out of drafts caused by both air conditioning and natural breezes. Large candles on stands, perhaps decorated by the florist according to a seasonal theme (green boughs and red ribbon at Christmastime) or with the classic white flowers and satin bows, may be placed at the end of the pew. Another group of candles can define the area where you and your groom will exchange vows.

Acolytes, a pair of responsible boys or girls who are either special friends or regular assistants at the church, might proceed slowly up the aisle, lighting these candles well before the procession is to begin. They often wear the white vestments-over-skirts of the church, and should take their instructions from the officiating clergymember or his or her designate. It is less ceremonial but perhaps more practical for the ushers to make certain the candles are already glowing as guests arrive.

Added drama will come as your attendants make their way down the aisle, to a very slow wedding march. They will bear lighted candles, perhaps with sprigs of flowers at the base. The florist can provide holders that are easy to grip. Or, for a charming touch—not to mention safety's sake—the bridesmaids may carry hurricane lamps or old-fashioned lanterns that radiate a soft aura.

Candles may also take on symbolic meaning at the ceremony. Two candles might flicker during the service—one on the bride's side of the church, the other on the groom's. A taller candle can stand unlit in the center until the clergy pronounces the couple husband and wife. Then the bride and groom may carry their respective candles to kindle the one in the center, indicating the joining of their families. The lighting of the Unity Candle can have touching symbolism in an interfaith wedding, or in the creation of a new blended family of two previously married parents. In a reaffirmation service, candles can signify the flame of love kept alive through the couple's married years.

Once the recessional has occurred and before the ushers direct the guests to depart, the acolytes might slowly make their way back toward the altar, snuffing the candles row by row. This creates a more meditative close to the ceremony than is customary, and guests may reflect as appropriate music is softly played. The church lights may be raised gently before the guests file out. Or the guests may walk out quietly under the candle glow.

Any acolytes, of course, should be thanked with a tip, or gift, if more appropriate (a family member, for instance). When a niece or nephew serves as acolyte, a gift (perhaps a beautifully illustrated book or gift certificate for cassette tapes) would be fitting. If the acolyte is a teenager from the parish, ask the church secretary for gift suggestions.

THE WEDDING AT HOME

Your own home, or that of a close relative or friend, provides an especially warm setting for your wedding. It may offer just the right mood for the working couple who've decided to sponsor their own wedding. An attractive fireplace or a large floral screen will provide an appropriate background for a religious ceremony, with an altar table and kneeling bench brought in if necessary. Formal seating is not required, but you may wish to provide chairs for guests. Chairs are usually arranged on either side of an "aisle" formed by looped ribbons or ropes of flowers and greens.

Be forewarned, however, that to have a large wedding in your home is entertaining on a grand scale, and that may mean more preparation than you are able to tackle yourself. Organization and delegation of responsibilities are essential. Do consider hiring a wedding consultant to handle arrangements for flowers, bartenders, caterer. And, just about anything you need—china, potted plants, furniture, sound equipment—is available through rental agencies. There are extra things to think about, but if you stick to a methodical timetable, you'll have a wedding party that has easy elegance without adding to your pre-wedding stress. Everything will be in place, your wedding party and family dressed and calm well before the first guest arrives.

Your mother or a close friend usually greets guests at the door and directs them to the wedding area: "So glad to see you, Mrs. Kampenga! It looks as though you were able to follow Audrey's directions out here—now for more directions. Just through that hall and to your right. We'll all be gathering in the living room. And if you'd like to freshen up, the bathroom is straight upstairs." Your honor attendant (who is responsible for greeting the wedding official and showing him or her where to change) may assist. The groom's parents may mingle with the guests before the ceremony, or wait with their son and the best man until they take their places. Ushers are not customary, but a few male relatives or close friends of the groom should be designated to alert guests when the ceremony is about to begin and to escort the groom's parents and your mother to their places at the ceremony site.

The procession is a modified form of the traditional one, with the bridesmaids, honor attendant, and the bride and her father making their entrance from an adjoining room or down a staircase. Or you may enter alone, with your father meeting you at the foot of the stairs or at the entrance to the wedding room, and escorting you to your groom's side.

At the end of the ceremony, your groom will kiss you right away. The two of you will then turn to receive the hugs and good wishes of your guests. A recessional is not necessary, nor is a receiving line for fewer than ten guests. Otherwise, unless you have a great many guests, an informal receiving line is best, where the wedding party stands together for a few minutes to give everyone an opportunity to express their feelings. Then you and your groom lead the way to the reception area.

THE OUTDOOR WEDDING

A large and blooming garden at home is a favorite site for outdoor weddings, from very formal to informal. If your thought is to make it "an easy backyard wedding," take a good look to see if planting, pruning, or major landscaping would be required. It may be a simple idea, but not necessarily easy to achieve. If you do decide to go ahead with such a plan, it's an extra bonus that shrubs, a rock garden, or roses put in to spruce things up become living reminders of the splendor of your wedding day.

Procedures are similar to those for any other wedding at home. Pick the prettiest garden spot for the ceremony—before a trellis of fragrant roses, in a latticed summerhouse at the end of a pebbled garden path, beside a sparkling pool. Consult your florist for more ideas. Create an aisle with flowered standards or garlands of greens and, if your dress has a train, spread out a canvas to protect it. The procession is the customary one, omitting ushers unless you've also set up chairs for the seating of guests. And you may do without the recession entirely. Instead, you and your groom turn to greet your guests immediately after the kiss. You and your parents may form a receiving line, talking to each guest individually. Then you retire to the shade of a nearby tent or grove of trees for refreshments.

There are many other popular outdoor sites, including parks and meadows, beaches, and public forests. Each city chamber of commerce will have ideas for beautiful wedding sites. View any site with an eye to entertaining there. Does a meadow need to be cut back or sprayed for insects? Will the beach front need to be cleaned of debris on the wedding morning?

Clubs, historic sites, even private estates are sometimes willing to rent wedding reception space. Consult museums, historical associations, and travel guides to find locations in your area. Be sure to sign a contract that specifies what time your caterer and florist can arrive to begin setting up; the length of time your party can go on; that you are allowed to serve food and beverages; who sets up, who cleans up; precise fees.

Check to see if a permit is required for your chosen site and make sure guests know how to get there (send a map with the invitations if you think it's necessary). You may be required to leave a deposit to guarantee cleanup. If parking is limited, arrange for transportation by bus or "shuttle cars" from the nearest large parking area. If you are not near a house but you expect the celebration to go on for more than an hour—as most do—you will have to arrange access to rest rooms for your guests.

For any outdoor reception, place food in a shaded area that allows an easy flow of traffic. Waiters might circulate with trays of hors d'oeuvres. And, speaking of food, finger foods work best if guests are standing. Plates, forks, and glasses are hard to handle all at once.

When planning any outdoor wedding or reception, you'll be wise to prepare alternative possibilities (moving the wedding inside or renting a large tent for shelter) in case of bad weather on the wedding day. You might even enclose a small card with the invitation, giving this kind of information: "In the event of rain, the wedding will be held at Woodington Town Hall."

If you think you might use a tent, start making arrangements early. Tents are very popular, for they create a celebratory mood all their own. Scorching sun can create as many problems as rain, so many outdoor weddings include a tent, rain or shine. Even if you don't use a tent, you might erect a canopy or awning over the serving tables. A representative of the rental agency should visit your site to discuss your needs and tell you what's possible.

THE OLDER BRIDE

If you're an older bride for whom it's a first wedding, choose whatever traditions or fashions feel comfortable. If you're an older second-time bride, you might choose to omit the train and veil from your wedding attire, but all else is fine. You and your groom may issue the invitations and announcements yourselves or ask a sponsor to do so (see Chapter 5). You'll delight in wearing a long dress in a lovely shade of white or ivory, marrying in church with attendants at your side, and being escorted down the aisle by your father, brother, or other man of your choice. Like most women of any age these days, you may prefer wording such as

"Who witnessing these vows will support this couple in their marriage?" rather than the suggestion that you can be "given away." Your best look will be the style you've established for yourself—perhaps elegant simplicity: a classic silk shirtwaist in softest ecru with a delicately veiled hat. Bridal designers create for a wide span of ages and life-styles these days, and you are sure to find something that's even better than what you've always dreamed of.

Any custom, any tradition is suitable and permissible for brides of any age. It's really up to you. You can have a large and festive reception, complete with dancing, toasts, and wedding cake. After having lived on their own, many couples, of course, may pay for the party themselves. Although the mature couple may feel self-conscious about throwing the bouquet or garter, it's something guests look forward to; so go ahead and do it—gracefully, and in the spirit of fun.

A senior citizen wedding is a truly joyous occasion. It may be a second wedding for both the bride and groom and an infusion of *joie de vivre* for both as well. The celebration can be a gathering of children, grandchildren, and old friends. The groom might splurge on a new suit; his bride, on a silk dress; and each of them on some updated travel clothes to take with them as they set off on one of the most memorable trips of their lifetimes.

THE WEDDING OF A CLERGYMEMBER

When the groom is a member of the clergy, the ceremony usually takes place in the bride's church or synagogue with her minister or rabbi officiating. If the bride is a parishioner of the groom's, his superior or another member of the clergy of equal rank might perform the ceremony, frequently with the entire congregation invited. The bride wears a dress suitable to the formality of the wedding, while the groom may be married in his clerical clothes, in formal attire with a clerical collar, or in regular formal dress. The customs of his denomination and the formality of the wedding determine these details.

When the bride is the minister or rabbi, the ceremony is held at her place of worship, with the official of her choice performing the ceremony. She may wear either her clerical garb or a traditional wedding dress appropriate to the style of the wedding.

If one of your parents is a member of the clergy, he or she may officiate at your ceremony. If it's your father, another male relative may escort you down the aisle, and your mother may step forward to give you away.

THE CIVIL CEREMONY

Most civil ceremonies are quiet and intimate, performed in a courthouse, a judge's chambers, or the home of a justice of the peace. The usual guidelines for an informal wedding apply, with the bride and groom dressing in their best street attire and having only one attendant each. A small reception at the ceremony site, at home, or in a restaurant may follow—and because the very closest family and friends are on hand, it will be an especially warm occasion.

One popular version is for a couple to marry at a civil ceremony during the day—even exchanging vows they have written themselves—then invite a crowd to a gala reception at night. In this case, the couple would need two outfits—the bride, for example, wearing a suit during the day and changing to a sophisticated cocktail-length (just below the knee) or dance-length (mid-calf) dress for evening. The groom might wear a suit or sport coat to the ceremony, then change to tuxedo or dress suit later.

If it is a large civil ceremony performed at home or in a club or ballroom, procedures are the same as for a religious ceremony of like formality. Aisles may be formed between rows of chairs for guests, and the wedding party may enter in the standard procession. The reception usually begins immediately after the ceremony, at the same location.

Many officials can perform civil marriage ceremonies—from your town's mayor, justice of the peace, township committee chair, or governor, to a clerk of Superior Court or even a county clerk. But these laws determining who can marry you vary from county to county—so call your local marriage license bureau to find out what your own state statute specifies.

You can ask a friend of the family who is a judge or magistrate to officiate, or just have your ceremony performed by a judge at the county clerk's office during regular business hours.

FAR-AWAY WEDDINGS

Today a couple may meet in Washington, DC, have parents in Hawaii and Canada, and plan to relocate in Louisiana after the wedding. It may happen that one set of parents or some very dear friends cannot make the long trip to be present at your wedding. What to do? Plan a small wedding in your present town, then visit each hometown for a local reception. Take lots of pictures and blow up the best ones so the folks back home can have a feeling of being there. Or, ask the telephone company to rig up a conference telephone system that would broadcast the wedding ceremony to your parents in Hawaii and his folks in Canada. This service is surprisingly reasonable, probably far less costly than plane tickets.

If you will be traveling to a far-away wedding site, your planning will be more challenging. It's essential to try to delegate as much as possible to those on the scene, especially one person who can be your main liaison. You'll need to arrive a few days ahead to get your marriage license, and you'd be wise to plan extra days to handle all those last-minute details. Very likely, friends and family will be waiting to entertain you with a shower or bridesmaids' luncheon. Your fiancé should come along if he can. That way, the two of you can take time to relax with family and friends ahead of the wedding.

THE WEEKEND WEDDING

If you're a couple who value the people in your lives, but have been too busy for lengthy visits, a marathon wedding weekend may be for you. This allows you to really spend time with distant friends and relations, having fun together, while getting caught up on each other's lives. Your rehearsal might take place earlier in the week, leaving Friday evening clear for a buffet supper to greet everyone. Your ceremony may take place any time during the weekend, but for this kind of wedding, it's not customary to leave right after the ceremony. Enjoy the weekend, then go away on your honeymoon (this is popular with live-in couples).

Where to hold it? Take over a country inn, rent a church or grange hall, have everyone meet at a vacation resort. Arrangements for accommodations are up to you, but usually guests pay their own way.

A typical weekend schedule includes a Friday night get-together; small-group breakfasts and activities Saturday morning; the wedding Saturday afternoon (or Saturday evening after sundown for Jewish ceremonies); and a Sunday good-bye brunch. You can plan a variety of activities—slides or movies, sight-seeing, a pool party, softball game (bride's team against the groom's), or picnic.

If your group has a mutual interest, everyone can help prepare for, then participate in, your wedding. The members of your gourmet club can all help cook an exotic wedding feast; your antique car club pals can polish and decorate vintage cars for a post-wedding parade.

A WEDDING TRIP

When work pressures make it impossible for you and your fiancé to organize a wedding, party, and trip: simply go away and while you're gone, get married. Sounds like eloping? Yes, except in this case, family, friends, and children from a former marriage are invited too! Surely some will be able to join you at a common ground, such as the summer resort area where you and your fiancé met.

Getting married in a foreign country sounds romantic, but be very careful to find out about the legalities. In some countries, a long period of residency is required before a license to marry can be obtained. Tourist boards or foreign consulates would be able to help you find this out.

What about being married by the ship's captain while on a cruise? Not possible, unless he happens also to be a minister or a judge. It is fine, however, to be married by a clergymember while on board ship, so check with the cruise line. One might be coming aboard.

If it turns out that very few people can join you for this special occasion, just remember that any kind of private wedding—foreign, civil, or one held in the clergymember's study—can be followed later by an observance with family and friends.

THE RUSH WEDDING

Like many couples today, you may be scheduled to move across country to a new job, or to start graduate school—away from family and friends. Instead of leaving your hometown and then returning for a wedding, you can complete plans quickly, marry now and leave together. There are other reasons a wedding might happen quickly—tax advantages, a health problem in the family (an impending operation), pregnancy. These situations do not have to curtail the lovely wedding you'd planned, but you probably would be wise to choose less elaborate options given the time frame.

If you've less than six weeks' time, set priorities, make some compromises, delegate jobs, and you'll be amazed at how fast your wedding and reception plans will come together. A civil ceremony can be arranged in most states in a matter of days. If elopement is your choice, you can still make it festive. Wear a new dress and have flowers. Toast each other now, and again at a reception when you return home. The pictures you take now and on your honeymoon trip will also delight friends and family later.

11
Remarriage

The real purpose of etiquette has always been—and will always be—to help people feel comfortable and good about themselves. The "rules" and guidelines change as people change. With each passing year, remarriages make up a higher percentage of marriage statistics. No longer an unusual happening, a second marriage is viewed by the couple and families involved as a happy new beginning. Therefore, many of the traditions that are part of a bride's first marriage can be celebrated again. More important than agonizing over whether or not you can wear white (you can!) is bringing feelings of pleasure and happiness to all the members of your wedding community—you, your groom, your families, and your friends. This chapter is designed to help you and your fiancé consider your options and choose just the right ceremony and reception for everyone involved.

ANNOUNCING YOUR ENGAGEMENT

If you have children from a previous marriage, you'll probably want to tell them first. How you do so depends largely on their ages and on their relationship with your husband-to-be. If they know him well and are used to seeing the two of you together, the news probably will not come as a surprise. Once you've told them privately, you may want to plan some "new family" time together when you can all discuss your future. Every child will have legitimate questions and concerns about this proposed change in his or her life—"What will I call him (her)?" "Do I have to be nice to his (her) kids?" "Do you love him more than me?" Positive, straightforward talking about the issues these questions represent will make the adjustment period easier for all. (Reread Chapter 1 for more suggestions about discussing remarriage with your children and families.)

Let your parents in on the good news next. And, if you do have children, your former spouse and his parents should also be notified. Then spread the word among your friends and family. Women who have been widowed or divorced may enjoy having a new engagement ring to show everyone—and in deference to their new commitment, it should be the only ring they wear on the left hand until the wedding day.

Most second-time brides would like to see their engagement announced in the newspaper, and today there is no stigma attached to it. It's traditional, however, that those who are recently widowed or divorced wait and announce only their weddings. Check with the society editor about format and deadlines for both engagement and wedding news. Though your parents may make the announcement (see Chapter 1), if you've been on your own for a while, you may prefer: "Ann Jones and Mark Wilson announce their engagement. . . ."

Should this be your first marriage, but your groom's second, your parents may still announce the engagement in the customary way.

PRE-WEDDING PARTIES

A second-time bride usually doesn't receive quite as lavish a round of parties as she did for her first marriage. Your parents or other close relatives may hold a dinner in your honor, and you may even wish to give a cocktail party or brunch in your own home. Certainly, where there are children involved (yours or his or both), you'll want to plan a number of special get-togethers where you can all get better acquainted. Some of these might well include friends of you both, so the children can see how the two of you function as a couple as well as parents.

Because friends and family wish you as much happiness the second time as the first, showers and the giving of simple gifts have also become very much a part of the second-wedding celebration. You've probably made many life changes since your first wedding—job, community, friends, to name a few. Those planning your shower may not have known you when you first married. So, let yourself relish the excitement and good wishes your friends lavish on you.

In thinking up a party theme, the hostess might want to consider the style of your wedding (you and your fiancé should clue her in). If you're planning a small, informal ceremony/reception, you may prefer that a shower be a "That's Entertainment!" party, for example, with just a few couples on hand, and inexpensive games, books, records or tapes, and stereo/video accessories as the presents. Tell your hostess you would find a large traditional shower (for women only) overwhelming—that's why you decided on a small wedding in the first place. And besides, all these guests cannot be invited to a small wedding.

However your friends choose to salute your wedding, your response is always equally warm—delighted verbal thanks followed up with a written note and perhaps a small gift of flowers for the hostess.

PLANNING YOUR CEREMONY

A remarriage ceremony should be beautiful and sentimental, and reflect the dignity of your courage to make a fresh start and a new commitment.

If a remarriage ceremony is simple these days, it's not because etiquette experts decreed it must be so. Today's couples make decisions about their wedding based on common sense and their own personal style. Anything is possible. Each partner may bring a more realistic understanding of commitment to the marriage. They want their ceremony to be a reflection of their unique relationship.

You may want to do everything in a new way. You eloped the first time? Have the church wedding you missed, complete with attendants and floor-length white dress. You may have a few conservative relatives who feel this isn't proper. Ask your mother or a sister to let them in on the plans ahead of time, along with current thinking on remarriage etiquette. Surely they'll want to celebrate, too. You felt your opinions didn't count as your last wedding was planned? Talk through each aspect with your fiancé—scripture, music, vows, menus, gifts— and decide what you want. You felt overwhelmed by the size of your first wedding? This time, have an intimate ceremony—just family and a few close friends. Afterward, jam your reception site with all who wish you well.

Many second-time brides find the most appealing plan involves a small, intimate ceremony followed by a large, fun-filled reception complete with champagne, dancing, and wedding cake. This way you can include everyone you love in your wedding celebration, without risk of offending parents or relatives who may find a large ceremony inappropriate.

If you feel your first wedding was just perfect, then why not repeat it? It doesn't bother some families to sit in the same sanctuary, before the same clergymember, and watch the bride walk down the aisle again. But it makes some people sad, or at least pensive. And since this is a time for rejoicing in new beginnings, discuss this beforehand too. If everyone's comfortable (including you and your fiancé), go right ahead.

Conventional wisdom says that the groom's first wedding ceremony does not affect his remarriage plans, but he and his family have feelings too. Though you've dreamed of hearing your friend sing "Ave Maria," the solo sung at his first wedding, wouldn't it be more thoughtful to select "O Perfect Love" instead?

You and your groom should certainly have honor attendants and, if you invite more than fifty guests, ushers as well. If either of you have children, you may ask them to participate. It's an especially thoughtful way of including them in the wedding. A teenage daughter might serve as your attendant, teenage boys might usher, younger children may be flower girls, ring bearers, or pages. If you plan a very small ceremony, you may simply ask your children to stand with you at the altar to share more fully in the wedding ceremony; they might read a special poem or prayer, even escort you down the aisle together. But when children express a preference not to participate, it's best not to insist. And always check

143

with your ex-spouse before proceeding with plans that involve children by a previous marriage.

The smallest wedding you can plan is the civil ceremony—with just the two of you and your attendants. It might take place at city hall, in a judge's chambers, or at your or your parents' home. You might plan a small religious ceremony at a chapel, church rectory, or friend's home. Still another option is to include everyone you want and marry on a grander scale at a large hall, club, or church.

If you have remained close to your former in-laws, you may wish to invite them as well. But you are not obligated to do so, nor are they expected to attend. An ex-spouse is rarely invited to the wedding, but if yours is one of those unusual friendships, and you'd like to, do consider the feelings of others first—relatives who have not seen or spoken to him since the divorce, your children, your fiancé. Generally, it would be wiser to invite your ex-husband to dinner after you have your wedding pictures or videotape, sharing it with him in that way.

VISITING YOUR CLERGY OR JUDGE

As soon as you've decided on the size and type of ceremony you'd like, make an appointment for you and your fiancé to visit your minister, rabbi, priest, or other ceremony official. If you belong to a faith with its own divorce laws (Jewish or Roman Catholic, for example), you may have problems even though you have obtained a legal civil divorce. Expect the clergymember to bring up your first marriage during your conference. While many restrictions on the remarriage of divorced persons have been eased in recent years, you may still need not only your own clergy's permission but, in some cases, permission from higher church authorities as well.

In addition to setting the date and time, discuss all other plans for the ceremony: music, flowers, attendants, and the like. Your ceremony official may have his or her own suggestions—the use of the chapel rather than the main church, religious rather than secular music, special roles for your children. If for any reason the clergymembers of your own congregation are reluctant to perform the ceremony of your choice, it's best to find this out early while you still have time to seek another ceremony official. You may choose to look for another church or even marry outside the faith. That would be disappointing, though, if you had decided on a religious ceremony. So don't be discouraged. Ask other remarried friends for suggestions, call local churches and college chaplains, talk to the church headquarters in your state—you'll most likely find a clergymember who will marry you.

INVITATIONS AND ANNOUNCEMENTS

The bride and groom may issue their own invitations for a small informal ceremony. Send brief notes or telephone your closest friends and relatives. When more than fifty guests are invited, you may choose to mail printed invitations, using this wording:

> *The honour of your presence*
> *is requested at the marriage of*
> *Marcia Maureen Craig*
> *to*
> *Mr. Nathan Randolph Carter*
> *Saturday, the fourth of May*
> *at four o'clock*
> *Hotel Mark Hopkins*
> *San Francisco*

R.S.V.P.
1053 Shady Lane
Oakland, California 12345

The bride's name may be written in the more traditional fashion, "Mrs. Marcia Maureen Craig," or, for a widow, "Mrs. Albert Brendon Craig." (If the bride's parents issue the invitations, they use the appropriate wording described in Chapter 5.)

No matter how small the ceremony, the reception following may be as large as desired, with printed invitations issued by the bride and groom or by their parents. When a large reception follows a small ceremony, you might send formal reception invitations to all your guests with handwritten ceremony cards inserted for those who are invited to both.

Formal announcements sent after the ceremony frequently prove an excellent way to notify friends of your marriage. Your parents may "have the honour of announcing" your marriage, or you and your groom may send your own announcements reading:

> *Marcia Maureen Craig*
> *and*
> *Nathan Randolph Carter*
> *announce their marriage*
> *Saturday, the fourth of May*
> *One thousand nine hundred and eighty-five*
> *San Francisco*

"Mrs.," "Ms.," or "Mr." may be added to the names in the announcement.

All printed invitations and announcements may, of course, have a traditional look or a personalized design. Some brides with children issue their invitations in their children's names or announce the formation of a "new family," perhaps including a photograph of the bride and groom with all their offspring.

If you wish, you may also send an announcement to your local newspaper, including all the details of the marriage but omitting descriptions of the ceremony, your address, and the like. Such an announcement might read:

Marcia Maureen Craig and Nathan Randolph Carter, both of Oakland, were married Saturday, May fourth, at the Hotel Mark Hopkins in San Francisco by Justice James Howard of the California State Supreme Court. The bride is the daughter of Mr. and Mrs. Daniel Ackerman of Los Angeles. She is employed by the University of California. Mr. Carter is the son of Mrs. Leon Ball Carter and the late Mr. Carter of San Francisco. He is an accountant with the firm of Richardson and Level. Mrs. Craig's previous marriage ended in divorce. The couple will reside in Berkeley.

If you wish to include details of your ceremony or reception, check with the society editor regarding the requirements.

THE QUESTION OF NAMES

In the past, a woman who had been divorced used a combination of her maiden and married surnames (Mrs. White Smith) in any formal context. Today, it is common for her to use her given names and married surname (Barbara Lynn Smith) or her first name, maiden name, and married name (Barbara White Smith). Widows can, of course, go by their husband's first and last names (Mrs. Robert Herman), but may also prefer their given first name and married last name. When you remarry, you'll have the option of dropping your former married surname in favor of your new husband's name, creating a combination of the two, or keeping the name you are known by now.

If you have already established a professional reputation under your maiden name or your first married name, you may wish to keep that name for all business purposes, taking your new husband's name for social use only. Or, as is happening more often these days, you may wish simply to keep your name as it is now (especially if you and your children share a common last name). Another alternative is to drop your maiden name and retain your first married name to help in identification. Thus, if you have been known as Barbara Lynn Smith, you may now wish to go by Barbara Smith Jones.

To let your friends and colleagues know your preference, enclose a name card with your announcement, or add a line to your newspaper write-up: "The bride will retain the name Marcia Maureen Craig after her marriage."

WEDDING DRESS

Romantically lacy, long and white, or traditionally elegant street-length ecru or pastel—the second-time bride has more choice in wedding dress today than ever before.

On her wedding day, every bride must feel absolutely beautiful. Wearing a dress you love is a large part of feeling fabulous. Even if your ideas of style conflict with your groom's or family's, with common sense and sensitivity to everyone's feelings, you'll arrive at a second-wedding fashion style that suits you perfectly, and enthralls everyone else. Keep in mind that bridal white is now recognized as the color of joy and celebration, not only virginity, and all who know you will share these happy feelings with you.

When you are shopping, don't be afraid to visit the bridal shop—they do have wedding dresses that will seem just right for second weddings. You might see a tea-length, body-skimming, chemise-shaped dress edged in lace. Worn in white (or your favorite color) with coordinated patterned stockings and lace shoes, the look will encompass yesterday and tomorrow. Depending on the formality of the ceremony and the time of day, you may find a second-time bridal look that's anything from a white cashmere suit with a white mink cloche to a ruffly floor-length dress without a train (again, in white or your favorite color). You may wear flowers or carry a bouquet or flower-trimmed prayer book. Or, complete your wedding look with a dramatic picture hat, a wreath of fresh or silk flowers. The only other thing you might do without is the veil—long a symbol of virginity—unless it's an Orthodox Jewish ceremony, in which case a short face veil is required.

Aside from the type of ceremony you plan, other factors you may want to consider include your age (if dressing "age-appropriate" is important to you), your first marriage (whether you want a look that's similar or totally unlike that of your first wedding), your groom's wishes, and the feelings of your family or clergy.

You want to look as beautiful as you can because it's your special moment, a tribute to your groom, and a gift to all who come to share your joy. In the weeks preceding wedding day, visit a professional hairstylist for healthy hair care and perhaps a new flattering style. Spend a day at a beauty salon, having a facial, manicure, pedicure, and massage. This, combined with regular exercise and plenty of sleep, will make you a radiant bride.

Once you've decided on your wedding style, the rest of the wedding party follows suit. Your honor attendant, any bridesmaids, and the mothers choose dresses of the same length and of a style similar to your own. The men may wear traditional formal clothes if you choose a long wedding dress. For a semiformal or informal wedding, they wear dark suits, white shirts, and dark four-in-hand ties; children wear party dresses or suits as for any formal wedding.

THE CEREMONY

A large formal ceremony for a second-time bride today might include a small procession with the bride escorted by any person she loves. You may have your father do the honors again, or choose your son or daughter, or even your groom—just walk in together. A woman who has been divorced is rarely given away a second time, but then, few women today are "given away" the first time! A widow may choose to ask a brother, son, or her father to escort her down the aisle and give her away, but probably she, like other remarrying women, will prefer that parents pledge to "support," "bless," or "uphold" the couple in their marriage, if possible.

Even though they are frequently omitted, if a second-time bride wishes to include bridesmaids and ushers in her wedding party, she may certainly plan a regular procession and recessional. Just be sure to discuss plans with the ceremony officiant in advance.

At a small wedding, your trip to the altar can be made without much ceremony through a side or vestry door. You'll meet the groom and his best man, already waiting at the altar. After the ceremony, the couple turn to greet their guests. At a civil ceremony—in a judge's chambers, perhaps—decorations and music are usually omitted, but otherwise the procedure is similar, with the bride and her attendant entering the room to find the groom and his best man waiting.

Once you and your fiancé talk about what your wedding means to you both, you'll see ways to express your ideas through your ceremony. For instance, if getting married is a religious commitment, choose a church setting. If your marriage will be based on equality, exchange rings. When children are part of your life together, include them in your wedding. They can be your attendants or altar boys (see Chapter 6). Your vows to each other might be followed by a family vow or a prayer of family unity with each member adding a phrase. Light a Unity Candle, a touching symbolic ritual for families (see Chapter 10).

You'll want this wedding to be appropriate, yet be an expression of you and your groom. You might prefer an alternate scripture reading, prayer, or response; your clergymember can explain the options. Feel free to express a style that's you—with flowers, decorations, music—as long as you stay within acceptable bounds for the ceremony site. A Victorian mansion may restrict candles as a fire hazard, for instance. If you feel "too young" with a wedding nosegay, choose a more dramatic way to carry flowers, such as a lovely array of spring flowers resting against your arm (an "arm bouquet"). Design wedding music that's unusual yet dignified. A medley of love songs, played on a harp, would be a surprising—and moving—prelude. Any idea for personalizing your ceremony (see Chapter 9 for suggestions) with your own vows, choice of readings, may be included in second weddings as well. Just check with your clergymember.

CHILDREN

Even if your child seems to have adjusted to the idea of your remarriage, wedding day may surprise all of you by making him or her feel insecure. A parent should take time for extra emotional support in the days preceding the ceremony, then plan to have a grandmother or aunt nearby for hugs and reassurance during the festivities. Young children also need physical supervision, so you are not distracted by the need to discipline them (out of concern for their safety) during your ceremony and reception.

If your children are too young or choose not to participate in the ceremony, include them in other ways. Assign them seats of honor to which they'll be escorted (wearing corsage or boutonniere) just before the seating of the bride's mother. Mention their names in a special prayer. Before the ceremony, they could pass out hymnals, programs; at the reception, put them in charge of the punch, hors d'oeuvres, balloons. Ask your teenager for a list of current songs the band might play. The important thing is that children feel loved and very much a part of this happy occasion.

Give each child a gift to commemorate the day. Any child would love the promise of a future date with the two of you (tickets to the circus, a hockey game); or, something fun to use immediately—a camera, an engraved locket, a tape recorder.

THE RECEPTION

Make it as extravagant a party as you wish, complete with all the wedding traditions—receiving line, dancing, wedding cake, and champagne. You might omit such first-wedding customs as tossing the bride's bouquet and garter, the white cake decorated with tiny bride and groom, and the exit through a shower of rice. Instead, consider icing or trimming your cake in a pretty pastel and garnishing it with fresh flowers; have guests line up to wave and call good wishes as you leave for your honeymoon.

You and your groom may head up the receiving line yourselves while your parents circulate among the guests. And, even if some guests bring you gifts, it's always best (and safest) to avoid any package-opening ceremony. Your reception may follow all the procedures for a first wedding, including the "first dance," the ceremonial cutting of the cake, and rounds of toasts from your parents, honor attendants, children, and friends.

If you or your groom have children, you may want to make a special effort to include them in the reception fun—perhaps planning your ceremony for afternoon instead of evening so they'll be wide awake, offering them special seats of honor at the bride's table, even (for a very small wedding party) letting them be the ones to choose a favorite restaurant as the reception site.

Ask your photographer to capture the many moods of this day by catching the reactions of the children: your daughter's face when her new stepfather asks her to dance; his son concentrating on balancing the ring pillow; the two of them clinking their glasses together in a vigorous toast. Include "family" poses—your groom with his children; you with your own children; and the whole new family together.

WEDDING GIFTS

Every wedding—first or second—marks a new beginning for the couple involved. Although gifts should not be expected at a second wedding—especially from those who attended your first wedding—friends often want to send something to express their good wishes for your future.

Once you've decided to marry, register your gift preferences at local stores. At first you'll think you don't need anything. How quickly you'll have a wish list! Now's the time to add special serving pieces to your good flatware pattern, or cater to your new hobby—French country cuisine—with an assortment of casserole dishes in wicker carriers. If you'd planned to make do with the china from his first marriage, you may find the past associations too strong. Put it away for his daughter when she marries (this can be a sentimental gesture she will appreciate) and start out fresh with a pattern that reflects the way you and your new husband entertain. Try to list items in all price ranges—including small kitchen gadgets—so that someone who spent quite a bit on a gift the first time has as many choices as your new acquaintances do. Do tell your attendants and family members where you're registered, so they can spread the word.

If it's the groom's second marriage, his friends are not expected to send gifts, but they frequently do. A first-time bride, even though her groom has been married before, will receive gifts from most of her guests and may display them (see Chapter 17).

Written thank-you notes must be sent to everyone who offers a gift, just as for a first wedding. Your child, parents, dearest friend, may be touched to receive two thank-you notes: one from you expressing your ongoing love and appreciation for their participation; the other from your groom sharing his feelings too.

WHO PAYS FOR WHAT

If it is a second marriage for both you and your groom, you'll probably split the wedding expenses yourselves. There are many ways to divide the costs, depending on the financial status of each partner. Some popular methods are to assign expenses in advance (you pay for your dress, the flowers, the cake; he pays for the church, the reception site, the champagne); to have one person pay for the ceremony expenses, the other for the reception; or simply pay bills as they come up, then total receipts after the wedding and reimburse the person who paid more.

If it is the bride's first marriage, or if she is a very young widow or divorcée, her parents may offer to pay for the wedding. Or, if the couple are not yet in a financial position to pay for the wedding, either set of parents may offer to assist them, and the couple may accept if they wish.

Sometimes couples with a limited budget find that they must choose between lavish flowers and a sit-down reception dinner. Only you and your fiancé can decide which is more important to you, and prioritize your spending accordingly.

THE HONEYMOON

One thing you should try not to skimp on is your honeymoon. Don't feel a honeymoon isn't necessary "this time around." Make sure you get away, even if it's just for a few days. You'll need some time for rest and relaxation after the exciting but nonetheless exhausting events surrounding your wedding. And surely some time spent together—just the two of you, away from family, friends, responsibilities—is a perfect way to begin a new marriage.

If you have children, plan a two-part honeymoon. Go over the itinerary of *your* trip with the kids, explaining where you'll go and who will take care of them while you are gone; but also tell them about the *family* trip you've scheduled two weeks later. With their sights set on "their" honeymoon, (white water rafting, visiting Washington, DC), the kids will likely be content to stay behind when you and your groom go off by yourselves. Bring back souvenirs, postcards, and lots of photographs to share with them. For your honeymoon destination, choose any place except where either of you went "the last time." As romantic as it was then, now it's tied to the past. With so many wonderful vacation places to choose from, you should have no trouble picking a lovely spot that's new to both of you.

12

Unexpected Situations

Etiquette offers guidelines for our social actions so that we can respond with assurance. But when the unpredictable happens, it can throw us into a tailspin. For at least six months prior to your wedding, you'll check and recheck every little detail of your arrangements. But little mishaps will still occur, despite your planning and rehearsing. Keep in mind, though, that while gaffes such as kissing the groom before the clergymember gives his blessing, or a mischievous ring bearer singing "Row, Row, Row Your Boat" during a prayer may make you want to die of embarrassment at the moment, you and your guests will have plenty of time to laugh over them in years to come. A sense of humor is basic to getting along in life—and a wedding is no exception.

When something goes wrong, try not to panic. Assess your options and choose an alternative plan quickly. Friends and guests can help. For instance, a cousin could go pick up an organist whose car broke down. If the photographer doesn't show up, everyone can help with candids. Forget your vows? Your clergymember will help you through. Despite these and other assorted wedding ceremony upsets, the end result is almost always accomplished: the two of you are finally married!

CEREMONY

What if someone gets sick? Should someone special, such as your grandmother or your roommate, get too sick to come to your wedding, it is a disappointment, but use a cassette tape recorder and candid photographs to capture your wedding highlights so you can share them together later. When an attendant gets sick, the "show must go on," so find a substitute or just continue without that person. When a parent is too ill to come, there are several options. If you have a few days' notice, there may be time to hook up a special telephone line to let your parent listen in from a hospital bed. Otherwise, you can ask another loving relative to stand in; and be sure you pay tribute to your absent parent during the service.

Rehearsals and plenty of rest tend to keep people calm, but during the ceremony, the sight of all those guests and the beauty and solemnity of the occasion may undo even the most reliable of bridesmaids. If tears, a bad case of "nerves," or a fainting spell threaten to upset an attendant, be on hand with a sympathetic smile or humorous word. One bridesmaid (hopefully, the most reliable of all) should carry an emergency kit of smelling salts, facial tissues, and safety pins for crises (or, tuck it under the front pew ahead of time). If members of the wedding party feel faint, they should sit down immediately and put their head between their knees until the light-headed feeling passes.

It's rare, but if a heart attack or real health emergency occurs, the ceremony should be interrupted until medical assistance arrives. If either of your honor attendants is unable to go on, the wedding must stop until a replacement (who signs the marriage certificate) is designated. Remember, once you've spoken your vows, even if the ceremony is cut short—you're already married!

What if there's a blizzard? Unpredictable weather throws a snag into many a wedding. If a storm threatens, make arrangements with a snowplow operator to clear out the church parking lot or your own driveway. You might rent several four-wheel drive vehicles for reliable wedding transportation or airport pickups.

Even though you've planned your reception in a museum garden, or a horse-and-carriage getaway, no one can guarantee you cloudless blue skies. That's why it is so important to have a backup location for anything planned outdoors. Torrential rain? Hire some teenagers to escort guests from cars to church with big beach umbrellas. If your problem is a heat wave, you will need to provide extra water for flowers. If the electricity can handle the extra strain, borrow small air conditioners or electric fans. Otherwise, buy inexpensive hand-held fans of paper or bamboo (have someone decorate them if there's time) and put them in the pews.

What if the organ breaks down? While organ tones are majestic, other instruments (trumpet, flute, strings) can also provide lovely wedding music. Locate an instrumentalist through city orchestras, the local musicians' union, or a college music department. A piano or portable organ can easily be rented or even moved from your home. Without an organist at the last minute? See if someone from another church can be hired to play for your ceremony. Or check with the church to see if a relative or friend would be allowed to play the church's organ. The best solution may be recorded music. Records or tapes of wedding music should be available in most music stores. Ask someone to serve as operator to control the sound and length of play.

What if I spill something on my wedding gown? Everything imaginable can go wrong with clothes—zippers stick, trains get stepped on, hats blow away, dresses get spotted and seem to shrink mysteriously. When you purchase your gown, ask what emergency cleaning tips are recommended for your fabric. Have safety pins and a needle and thread on hand for emergency repairs. Or, if it looks good, move your flowers to hide the spot or tear. Do try on your wedding clothes one week before the wedding, both standing and sitting, to be sure that all those wonderful pre-wedding parties haven't added some unwelcome pounds. It's a busy time, but keeping up a steady exercise regimen will help you look and feel better.

Since you probably aren't used to walking in a long dress, and certainly not one with a train, it's a good idea to hold a practice session at home with your maid or matron of honor. She needs to know how to arrange your train so you (or your father or groom) won't trip over it. With a little practice, you should be able to coordinate your turn with a graceful swirl.

What if something happens to the ring? Rings can cause many worries. They can fall off the ring bearer's cushion; the best man can drop one and it can roll under the pews. Generally, the best man should keep the ring in his pocket (not on his finger, where it can get stuck). Secure the ring on a ring bearer's pillow with ribbon (or use a fake ring on the pillow and keep the real thing safely in the best man's pocket). Warm weather and tension can make your hands swell, so you may want to rub your ring finger with baby powder or a tiny bit of petroleum jelly before walking down the aisle. If the ring is really lost, or forgotten at home, borrow a substitute from an attendant, or use your engagement ring upside down for now. Later, ask your clergymember to bless the real one.

What if an "unwelcome guest" turns up? Most adults know that an invitation is a prerequisite to attending a wedding. If your ex-mother-in-law or your ex-spouse were to sit unobtrusively in the back of the church, their motivation might simply be to share your happiness. Your response would be to greet them warmly at the close of the ceremony. If, however, it appears that your ex-spouse is ready to cause trouble, the ushers should be prepared to show him to the door rather than let him disturb your ceremony. If a cat or dog wanders in during the service, an usher or family member should attempt discreetly to lead it out of the building. If it's harmless and quiet, just let it sit and watch.

RECEPTION

What if the band that shows up isn't the one I hired? When you went to preview Dan Singleton's Combo, they sounded great, but you've never seen this group before? Popular bandleaders may have several groups operating under their name. Be sure to get a contract in writing specifying exactly which musicians will appear.

Contracts are essential to every aspect of reception planning. They should state the date and time of service delivery, specifics such as what flavor icing, how many waitresses, what color flowers, how many bottles of champagne, how long the breaks between musical sets.

If your reception is in an out-of-the-way place, give everyone a map with phone numbers for home and reception site attached so there can be no "we just couldn't find it" excuses. To avoid mix-ups, confirm all your plans by telephone a week ahead *and* the day before the wedding. A good friend or honor attendant can undertake this chore, then be on hand to check delivery arrivals.

If the liquor or food has gone astray, or the wrong order appears (a graduation cake; sandwiches for twenty-five instead of a buffet for one hundred guests), don't wait too long to seek substitutes. Check with the store or your caterer, but if the problem cannot be rectified quickly, send ushers or the bride's brothers scurrying to delicatessens, bakeries, liquor stores. Once you've made other purchases, do not accept a late delivery.

HONEYMOON

What if we miss our plane (boat, train)? Of course, you'll try your utmost not to start off your honeymoon trip with the added stress of being late for your transportation. But if something unforeseen happens, phone ahead to release plane or train space or warn the cruise line if you possibly can. An airline will rebook you on the next available flight (even another line's). Amtrak will put you on the next train, but charges a penalty (now 5 percent or a minimum $5 per ticket) if you haven't canceled. The agent of the cruise line or the local port authority will advise you about chartering a launch (if the ship's in sight) or flying to meet it.

What if our luggage disappears? Occasionally it happens, so be sure to hold onto your claim checks and notify an airline agent immediately. Do not leave the airport without filing a loss report (or your claim may not be honored later). If you're left luggage-less in a strange town, the airline will give you up to $25 each to buy necessities and will reimburse you 50 percent after 18 to 24 hours for reasonable clothes purchases (appropriate for the local weather). After about forty days, they'll settle claims up to $500, allowing for depreciation.

What if there's a foul-up in our accommodations? If your double bed turns out to be twin beds, or the special room you requested isn't prepared for your arrival, stay calm and ask to speak to the senior hotel staff person on duty. Present your reservations confirmation slip and ask that things be straightened out as quickly as possible; usually that's just what will happen. But if your reservations cannot be honored, the hotel should first try to upgrade you to a higher priced room at no extra cost to you; or, find accommodations for you at another hotel. It is annoying when plans are upset, but some good can come of it. To make up for your inconvenience, there may turn out to be complimentary drinks, food, or activities. Remain gracious when dealing with the hotel personnel (and each other). Do mention that you are a honeymoon couple, and they will try to find a way to make things right for you.

13
Your Reception

A buffet that seems to never end, the band with the best beat in town, a night full of hugs and kisses, and maybe even a few happy tears. Is that the wedding reception you have in mind? Or do you look forward to something more casual, more intimate—just you two, your parents, and a few close friends around a big table at your favorite inn, enjoying the specialty of the house? As long as it affords your friends and family an opportunity to greet you and wish you well, your wedding reception may be either of the above—or anything in between. Champagne, punch, or another beverage suitable for toasting the future, along with some kind of wedding cake, are the only things you really need.

You may hold your reception at home (indoors or in the garden), at a private club, church hall, large ballroom, or restaurant. Serve punch and cake, cocktails and hors d'oeuvres, or imported champagne and a five-course meal. Make it a breakfast, a luncheon, or an afternoon tea. Even when your budget is limited, a simple reception for all your guests may add more to your wedding pleasure than the most elaborate feast for only a few.

RECEPTION TIMETABLE

Here's a schedule for the most common kind of wedding reception, a light buffet for two hundred, lasting about three hours. If you are having a more lavish menu or inviting guests who love to party, then you must, of course, allow more time. Do adjust this timetable to your plans.

The reception is about to begin: Cars arrive at the reception site with bride, groom, and all the members of the wedding party.

The first half-hour: The bridal party forms the receiving line and guests begin to pass by. Drinks are poured as guests mingle. If there are table-seating cards, guests may pick them up now.

After one hour: The buffet is announced, and the members of the wedding party are seated at the bride's table. The guests line up for the buffet, while the members of the wedding party are served at their own table. At this point, the best man will rise to propose the first toast to the bride and groom. The groom may return the best man's toast, then toast the bride, his new in-laws, then his parents. The bride, too, may follow suit with her own thoughts and expressions of gratitude. After all the toasting is finished, the musicians resume playing.

After one and one-half hours: The first course is cleared from the head table. The musicians strike up the dance music, and the "first dance" begins. The other traditional dances follow, then the rest of the guests may join in the dancing.

After two hours: The tables are cleared of food, and the musicians signal it is time for the cake-cutting ceremony. Bridesmaids and ushers line up on either side of the table while the rest of the guests gather round to watch. The bride and groom cut and share the first slice, then give each other's parents their pieces. The cake is served to the guests.

The last half-hour: The single women all cluster in a convenient spot, and the bride throws her bouquet. The bride's garter may then be tossed by the groom to a group of assembled bachelors, although this is optional. Then the bride and groom slip away to change into their going-away clothes and return to say good-bye to their parents. They run out to their car in a shower of rice—and they're off on a long-awaited honeymoon. When the parents are ready to leave, they signal the musicians to stop playing and for the bar to close. They then bid farewell to all their guests.

Incidentally, it may be wise to appoint a very close friend or couple to handle the schedule, should any snag have to be discussed with the caterer, banquet manager, baker, or florist. This permits the father of the bride to attend to the wedding guests. These special helpers should be pointed out to the caterer and identified with corsages or boutonnieres, and thanked after the wedding with a personal note from the bride's parents.

THE RECEIVING LINE

Traditionally, your mother, as hostess, is the first to greet guests, followed in order by your groom's mother, you, your groom, your maid or matron of honor, finally your bridesmaids. If the fathers wish to join the line, each stands to the left of his wife. At a small wedding, you may wish to simplify things by including just the parents, wedding couple, and honor attendant. Usually, the best man, the ushers, and child attendants do not participate in the line, nor do the fathers, who prefer to circulate among the guests, making sure that the party gets off to a good start. In the interests of keeping the receiving line short at a very large reception, bridesmaids, too, may mix with the guests instead of standing in the line.

If your parents are divorced, your mother usually stands in the receiving line

THE RECEIVING LINE: 1. Mother of the bride 2. Mother of the groom 3. Father of the groom (optional) 4. Bride 5. Groom 6. Bride's honor attendant 7. Bridesmaids (optional).

alone or with your stepfather, while your father circulates among the guests. But, many problems can be avoided by having no fathers stand in the receiving line. If your father is co-hosting the party, however, or if many of his friends and family attend, ask him to join the line—but not stand next to your mother, as this might be uncomfortable for them both. (It also confuses guests who might not otherwise realize your parents are divorced.) Since each family situation is different, you will have to judge how many people to have in the receiving line and how to arrange them. You may be very close to your stepmother and want her included as well as your mother. She and your father might stand to the left of the groom.

If you have no mother or stepmother to receive your guests, your father may stand at the head of the line with your grandmother, a sister, or an aunt. When the reception is hosted by persons other than the bride's parents, they are the first in line to meet the guests. If you are hosting your own reception, of course, you and your groom stand at the head of the line.

If your wedding is not being held in your hometown, or, if English is not your mother's native tongue, you might consider having an announcer. The role of the announcer is to stand at the head of the line, ask the name of each guest, and then present the guest to the bride's mother. The announcer may be someone who is very familiar with the couple's friends.

The purpose of the receiving line is for the parents and principals to greet the guests and receive their good wishes. It is acceptable for the parents and the wedding couple to circulate through the reception hall for the same purpose. But the receiving line can be more efficient, and that way you're sure to speak to each and every guest. How to make sure this does not become a lengthy ordeal for everyone? Set up the line in a convenient spot near the entrance where guests can move down it easily, directly into the refreshment area. (Traditionally held at the reception, the line can also be at the ceremony site so it doesn't hold up the party.) Many a receiving line has not assembled for the arrival of the guests because the wedding party was off in another room having pictures taken. Being absent will get your party off to a disappointing start. Schedule the pictures with family before the ceremony and be prepared to take group poses very quickly after the service, or at some point later in the reception. Keep the line as short as possible; save conversations for later when you visit each table; ask waiters to pass refreshments to those in line and to place a few chairs nearby for those who become fatigued.

All the women in the line may wear their hats and gloves, but men should remove theirs. You might hold your bouquet in your left hand, or set it aside to show your new gleaming wedding band. The bridesmaids, if they participate, always keep their flowers in their left hands.

Guests going along the line are introduced to each person in turn, and move quickly on to allow room for those behind them. Your mother, for example, might start with, "Celia, I'd love you to meet Gene's mother, Rosemary Hart." As your mother shakes hands with the next guest, your groom's mother says a brief word. Then you might announce, "Aunt Celia, here's Gene. Gene, her family, the Rangers, are the ones who sent those terrific balloon wine glasses." Now, your groom: "Your glasses are *my* size—thank you! Celia Ranger, have you met Jill's maid of honor and college roommate, Andrea Shields?"

The idea is to keep conversation short, but still give some small fact that will help people remember one another. Although you precede your groom in line, he may reach out to introduce you to his own relatives and friends. After the last guest has been welcomed, you two may move to take your seats at the head table, start the dancing, or cut the cake (at the cocktail reception).

THE GUEST BOOK

A guest book (sometimes called the Bride's Book) is a lovely keepsake. And it's a unique way of preserving the names of those friends and relatives for whom your wedding day is special too! At the reception, you'll want to set your book in a prominent place, such as on a pretty table near the entrance to the reception hall or at the end of the receiving line. You would ask the last attendant in line to point guests in the direction of the book. Later in the reception, ask a teenager or one of the ushers to circulate the book to be sure everyone's had a chance to sign.

SEATING ARRANGEMENTS

The focus of the reception room is, of course, the bride's table, where all the members of the wedding party are seated. The table, which may be of any shape, is sometimes elevated on a dais. It's usually covered with a long cloth of white lace, damask, or linen fabric. Make certain the decorations are low—bouquets and candles or garlands of flowers, greens, and ribbons—so that the guests' view of you and the bridal party is not obstructed. Unless the table is round, seating is usually on one side only, with you and your groom in the center, bridesmaids and ushers in alternating seats on either side (see sketch). Attendants who are married to each other, however, need not sit together.

THE BRIDE'S TABLE: 1. Bride 2. Groom 3. Bride's honor attendant 4. Best man 5. Bridesmaids 6. Ushers.

When the wedding party is a small one, the husbands and wives of married attendants, your parents, and the officiating authority (and spouse or assistant, if any) may join the bride's table. Otherwise, there is a separate parents' table with your mother and father in the places for hosts at opposite ends. The groom's father sits at your mother's right, the wedding officiant at her left, the groom's mother at your father's right, the wedding officiant's spouse or assistant at his left. These are the places of honor. You may also arrange two parents' tables, one for your parents, one for your groom's, so that more relatives and friends may be among those given a seat at the parents' tables.

Even if divorced parents have gotten along famously so far, it's best to seat them at separate tables for the reception. Each is seated with his or her own family and friends. Seat your groom's parents at the table of the parent who raised you. You will both want to spend time with each group.

At the reception following a Jewish wedding, the parents and grandparents of the bride and groom, the rabbi and cantor and their spouses may be seated at the bridal table, and the bridesmaids and ushers seated among the other guests.

Place cards mark each place at the bride's and parents' tables, but are optional elsewhere. Guests may be left free to find their own places with special friends, or you may do a complete seating plan and designate each place, putting people

SEATING AT THE RECEPTION

The host and hostess sit at a table with the groom's parents, clergymember, etc. The other parent and stepparent sit with friends and relatives.
1. Bride's mother 2. Bride's stepfather 3. Clergymember, spouse 4. Bride's grandparents 5. Groom's mother, father 6. Groom's grandparents 7. Bride's father 8. Bride's stepmother.

together who haven't met yet but might enjoy doing so. In this case, you may want to have table numbers on cards placed near the entrance to tell each guest where to look for his seat ("Mr. and Mrs. A. Cohen, Table 9"). Each table is then clearly numbered. The place cards may be plain white or have a small design, such as a religious wedding symbol or a sprig of dried flowers (acacia for "friendship"). The guest's name is written in the most simplified form: "Mary Smith" or "Mrs. Smith" rather than "Mrs. John S. Smith"; "Mayor Burke" instead of "The Honorable Joseph P. Burke." If two couples have the same surname, first names or initials must be used: "Mrs. Robert Smith" or "Mrs. Joseph Smith"; "Mary Smith" or "Margaret Smith." The place card is usually placed on the folded napkin, which rests on the service plate. Otherwise, place name cards above the dinner plate. It's also a nice surprise for guests to find a pretty favor—such as lace-wrapped almonds, or candles tagged with your names and wedding date—at their places. A special table for children, with games and books available after the meal and a pair of teenagers to supervise, may be appreciated by parents who wish to enjoy your reception without having to worry about what their youngsters are up to.

BLESSINGS

When all the guests are seated for the reception meal, your clergymember or a family representative may give the blessing. Not everyone is comfortable doing this, so be sure to arrange this ahead. The Jewish blessing, *Hamatzi,* is spoken over a large braided challah on the bridal table, often by the rabbi or the two fathers. Pieces of the challah are then passed to the guests. The *Sheva Berakhot* (wedding grace after meals) may be recited after the cutting of the cake, by the rabbi, cantor, one or several members of the wedding party or family, who are permitted to say this traditional Hebrew prayer. In the Orthodox Jewish tradition, it would be spoken by a man rather than a woman. Guests should not leave until this ritual ends the meal.

THE HEAD TABLE

At the head table, you and your wedding party will be facing the guests and in full view. Help keep the table pretty by placing bouquets attractively, leaving it free of clutter. Because the head table remains the focus of attention, it looks best if everyone follows these rules for best behavior.

Voices: Besides keeping the volume of conversation to a moderate level, those at the head table should lead the way in keeping quiet during the "little" ceremonies—when the clergymember is reciting a prayer or the best man is reading aloud a congratulatory telegram.

Makeup and attire: Men keep jackets on; ladies, shoes, for the duration of the party. Do not freshen up your makeup or comb your hair at the table.

Smoking: It looks out of place in your wedding finery. Particular times to refrain from smoking are when seated at the head table, posing for pictures, or standing in the receiving line. Anyone who wants to smoke should slip away briefly.

Equilibrium: Even though you're excited, try to eat something to curb the effects of all those champagne toasts. If any member of the wedding party gets a little too inebriated, it's best to escort him or her outdoors for a time.

REFRESHMENTS

A wedding reception should always include a wedding cake and a beverage suitable for toasting your happiness. Champagne is traditional, contributing to the overall "special occasion" feeling. It is appropriate at any hour, and you may serve it during the entire reception or only for toasts. Ginger ale, white grape juice, or any punch may be substituted for champagne, but coffee, tea, and water are not generally used for toasts. Therefore, tea receptions usually offer a choice of alcoholic or nonalcoholic punch. Champagne punch and mixed drinks are popular in many areas as well.

All daytime wedding receptions were once called "breakfasts," but the term is rarely used today. After a morning wedding, however, you might still serve a real breakfast: perhaps cooling fresh fruit, shirred eggs, hot sausages, and muffins. Luncheon fare (a light soup, chicken casserole, and broiled tomatoes) complements a high-noon wedding.

Ceremonies starting between one and four in the afternoon are typically followed by a tea or cocktail reception featuring light nibbles, such as open-face sandwiches, nuts and mints, or a buffet of hot and cold hors d'oeuvres. A hot buffet or a sit-down dinner of at least three courses is the most common follow-up to an evening wedding. Your caterer or banquet manager will help you plan the menu and advise you on the quantities needed. An at-home reception may be an opportunity to show off some of your family's favorite recipes (make these dishes ahead and freeze them), but unless you have hired someone to help, or your friends have volunteered to thaw, heat up, and serve these dishes, this is a very big undertaking for an already busy day. It is most courteous, of course, to serve guests the amount of food they would expect at the particular hour when the reception takes place, and sensible to time your wedding accordingly. If you are trying to cut reception costs and wish to offer only champagne and cake, for example, you might plan a wedding at two o'clock in the afternoon; after a church ceremony at noon or thereabouts, most guests would be hungry for lunch.

YOUR WEDDING CAKE

Even if your wedding is attended only by two witnesses and your parents, you'll probably want to celebrate with a cake—it's been an important part of weddings since Roman days. The familiar frothy white confection called bride's cake is usually several layers or tiers of light pound, sponge, or white cake, although any flavor (including chocolate or spice) may be chosen. Cakes today are sometimes artistically shaped as getaway cars, fantasy castles, or other whimsical shapes. Atop your cake there may be real flowers set in tiny glass vials, a tiny music box that plays the "Wedding March," the traditional sugar wedding bells, or the old standby: bride and groom figurines.

Because tradition has it that a piece of the bride's cake under a single woman's pillow will lead her to dream of her future husband, it's customary to cut the cake and serve it at the reception, with extra slices provided for guests to take home. Napkins or tiny boxes might be supplied to those who wish to take pieces of cake with them. If you won't be having a groom's cake, do freeze the top layer of the bride's cake to share on your first anniversary.

The less familiar groom's cake is traditionally a dark, rich fruitcake, frequently iced to match and used as the top layer of the bride's cake. Seal the groom's cake in a tin with brandy (as you would a holiday fruitcake) to eat on your anniversary. Or make this cake the one you'll pack in individual boxes to distribute to your guests as favors.

Spotlight your wedding cake (and keep it safe from accidental jostling) by setting it on a separate table; cover the table with a white cloth and trim the base of the cake platter with flowers, greens, or bridesmaids' bouquets.

You'll cut the wedding cake just before dessert at a luncheon or dinner reception, just after guests have been received at a tea or cocktail reception. Your groom places his right hand over yours and together you cut into the bottom layer with a ribbon-tied silver knife. The bride and groom traditionally share the first slice as a symbol of their willingness to share each other's household from then on. It is a loving gesture for the bride to give her new in-laws their pieces after that, then the groom to serve his in-laws. The rest of the cake is then cut (by a friend designated in advance or by a member of the caterer's staff) and served to the guests.

DANCING

Although dancing is not necessary, it does add a festive note to any wedding reception. An orchestra is the ultimate, but a string trio, piano, or even a stereo will do also (see Chapter 14). At a hotel or club reception, the area in front of the bride's table is usually cleared for the dancing. At home, you might set aside one whole room or have a temporary dance floor laid down at the end of a large living room. For a garden reception, guests may dance on the terrace or on a temporary floor set up by your caterer under a tent or over a pool.

You and your husband will want to lead off the dancing, circling the floor alone to your favorite tune. What usually happens next is that you are claimed by your father, while the groom dances with his mother-in-law. If your parents are divorced and this would be another difficult choice—to dance with your father, or with your stepfather who raised you—you may invite everyone to dance immediately following your first dance. Another solution: let one escort you into the wedding ceremony, the other have the first dance. The father of the groom and the best man dance with you after your father, while the groom dances with his own mother and your honor attendant. The order of these traditional dances is optional, but they are usually completed before the guests join in. (It's not necessary to dance through an entire song.)

At a very large reception, you may want guests to begin dancing as soon as they've been through the receiving line and the music begins. Your father might see to it that this happens. Then, after you've caught your breath from greeting guests, the musicians signal everyone to clear the floor with a pause in the music or an arresting fanfare and you and your groom begin the traditional first dance. You'll probably dance with each usher; your groom, with each bridesmaid, before the dancing ends. It is also customary for each man in the wedding party to dance with many of the women present (including the young girls, who would *love* to be asked) and to be sure to request a dance with each bridesmaid and both mothers.

TOASTS

Toasts to and from the happy couple add to the celebratory feeling of every wedding reception. They may begin any time after the receiving line has ended and everyone has been served a glass of champagne or other bubbly beverage. The best man always proposes the first toast, wording it any way he likes. And he may follow the two steps in proposing any toast: include a reference to your relationship to the person or persons being honored, and add a thought about their future good fortune. The best man might, therefore, say: "Here's to Sharon and Gary. I wanted to come to their wedding so much, I introduced them! May their lives be full of the kind of happiness we are enjoying here today." When the best man has completed his toast, everyone except you and your groom rises and drinks to it.

The groom usually responds with thanks to his best man and a toast or two of his own—to you, to his parents, or to his new in-laws. You might then rise to offer your own toast: "To my husband, the most wonderful man in the world. To my new family, with thanks for raising such a loving and supportive person. And to my parents, for all the love and strength they've given me. May we all have many, many more memorable days together." Other members of the wedding party may then propose additional toasts if they wish. All those present, except the person being toasted, should raise their glasses to each toast. At the end of the toasts, the best man may read aloud any congratulatory telegrams or letters sent by absent friends and relatives.

OTHER RECEPTION ACTIVITIES

Ethnic dances are popular at weddings because they involve everyone and provide a link to the past. In fact, weddings are one place young people learn these dances. If you have not been to many family weddings, or, if your groom's traditions are very different from your own, you may be surprised when relatives start up the dance. Ask your parents what to expect. Here are a few:

Die Mezinke Ausgegeben: When the last child in the family marries, Jewish mothers are honored by being seated in the center of a circle while guests dance around them. They may also be presented with flowers.

Dollar dance: This is derived from an old Polish custom in which the men who dance with the bride fill her pockets with money or pin bills to her dress. The money is given in place of a gift. Today a bride of Polish descent might carry a special purse to receive gifts of money.

Greek handkerchief dance: The leader (at a wedding, the groom) is linked to the next person (the bride) by the handkerchief. Others hold on hand-to-shoulder and the dancing weaves around the room.

Tarantella: This is a very lively Italian folk dance in $6/8$ time, danced by couples with quick hops and tapping foot movements.

A popular contemporary feature of wedding receptions is the Grand March, led by the bride and groom to music by the band. The couple link arms and lead the attendants and guests in a lively march around the room, and sometimes outside and around the building.

The wedding couple then form an arch with their arms. Two by two, the wedding guests pass under their arms, then form another arch to make the "bridge" longer. When all the guests have followed suit, the bridge disbands with the last two passing all the way back through to kiss the happy couple who started it all. All come back through until just the bride and groom are left. Following the Grand March, a second receiving line is formed beside a table filled with cake boxes, cigars, and perhaps shots of liquor for the guests. It's a chance to say good-bye to the couple who will have a last dance and depart.

Your reception might include entertainment. Some couples plan slide shows of their childhood and romance; friends might stage a scene from a play or read suitable poetry; your college glee club, do a rendition of "your song." A bride and groom with either talent or confidence might even perform themselves; or write their own commemorative wedding song, with humorous lyrics, and sing it to a familiar tune. You might hire a wedding entertainer, such as a comedian or mime. Your bandleader or master of ceremonies may improvise with announce-ments and occasional jokes. But if this is the type of entertainment you'd rather do without, make that clear ahead of time.

Traditions are always turning up at weddings. You may be given a spectacular toasting cup called a *coupe de mariage,* a two-handled silver goblet shaped like a bowl. A German version resembles a girl with a cup on her head. The cup is tipped toward the bride, then the groom, when they drink to a toast.

If you hear lots of glasses clinking, it means everyone wants to see you two kiss. It may seem silly, but just go along with the custom!

THROWING THE BOUQUET AND GARTER

Just before you leave to change into your going-away clothes, word is passed to the bridesmaids and other single women to gather at the bottom of a stairway, under a balcony, or at some other convenient spot. If your going-away flowers are part of your bridal bouquet, remove them first. If you've carried a prayer book instead of a bouquet, you may toss the floral decoration and ribbon streamers. If you've had a large cascade of long-stemmed flowers or wish to save your own bouquet, you may toss a token bouquet made up by your florist especially for this purpose.

Some brides turn and throw the bouquet over a shoulder, but if you'd like to aim at your sister or a dear friend, you may want to face the group as you throw. Tradition holds that the woman who catches the bouquet will be the next to marry.

There is another light-hearted tradition that may be observed, but only if the bride wishes. Her garter, most likely of blue satin, may be thrown to the single ushers and other bachelors. The groom removes it from her leg, then (according to local custom) either the bride or the groom may toss it over their shoulder. The man who captures it is destined to be the next to wed! Sometimes, with much fanfare and drum roll from the band, the man who catches the garter places it on the leg of the proud possessor of the bride's bouquet. If you include this tradition, be sure your photographer snaps a picture of the lively scene.

RECEPTION PRANKS

Part of the fun of weddings is the humor that goes into planning decorations for the couple's car, a "ribbing" sung to the tune of your college song, or a funny telegram sent to the honeymoon hotel. But sometimes, with the flush of celebration, good judgment goes out the window. It's not amusing to have your reservations changed from a double to single room, your plane tickets canceled, or your car's paint job ruined by whitewash lettering. And, no one likes an expensive, formal country club reception interrupted by a rowdy "let's throw the groom in the pool" scene. The bachelor party is the right time for these spirited pranks. A word to a wise usher by the best man will help keep the fun at an appropriate level.

PLANNING TWO RECEPTIONS

If you and your groom live in a city far away from your parents' homes, or if your groom's hometown is a long way from your own, you may wish to marry at one location, then hold a second reception later at the other for all the friends and family who did not travel to the wedding—including those of a divorced parent not with you that day. Such a reception may be similar to the first, with printed invitations issued by your or your groom's parents (see Chapter 5), a wedding cake and champagne or punch, flowers, dancing, and another round of toasts.

More commonly, a second reception is simply a large cocktail party or buffet, hosted by the two of you with friends and relatives just enjoying themselves and wishing you well. (Your first reception may have been dinner for the few friends who accompanied you to your city hall ceremony.) The receiving line, bouquet and garter toss, and shower of rice may then be omitted, and invitations are often informal notes or telephone calls. If you are planning this party from a long distance, do engage the help of friends or relatives who can help find a suitable location, hire a caterer, and generally organize the festivities. Thank them with a gift of flowers or a special memento similar to those you gave your wedding attendants.

Your groom's parents may also wish to host you at a reception for their hometown friends. They may issue printed invitations (again, see Chapter 5), and stand in a receiving line with the two of you to greet guests. A champagne toast from your father-in-law to you, and one from you or your groom to his parents would be appropriate. Otherwise, the reception may be the same as for any other party at the chosen time and season.

LEAVING THE RECEPTION

When the toasting's done, the cake's been cut, and the bouquet thrown, you and your groom will slip away to change, then depart in the traditional shower of rice. (Young children or friends may distribute pretty packets of rice or birdseed to guests.) Some couples, though, opt to stay until the very end, since it may be a long time before they see all these special friends again. In the confusion, don't forget to bid a special farewell to all of your parents. Their happy memories, and yours, will increase in value with every passing year.

14
Wedding Music and Readings

Choosing music you love is one of the most natural ways to add meaning to your wedding. Whether you're planning an elegant cathedral ceremony and a lavish reception or an intimate exchange of vows beside the mantelpiece at home, use music to create a mood of both solemnity and joy for your marriage ceremony and to lend a festive note to your reception. A favorite poem or Bible passage can also personalize your wedding—as much for your guests as for you and your groom.

MUSIC: WHAT AND WHEN

For the traditional ceremony at a church or chapel, the music might begin with a soft prelude lasting about half an hour while guests are seated. Just after your mother has been seated is the traditional time for a soloist or choir to sing, or a small ensemble group to perform. You'll certainly want a majestic processional to herald you and your wedding party down the aisle; perhaps another solo after your vows; and, of course, a triumphant recessional. The organist might conclude with a lively postlude as guests file out.

You may choose to trust the church organist's selection of appropriate numbers for the prelude and postlude from the wealth of beautiful music available. Or ask to hear several different possibilities, then pick your favorites. There are so many lovely classical pieces appropriate to the occasion that you might even want to visit the listening room of your local library for several sessions before making your final decision.

The "Bridal Chorus" from *Lohengrin* ("Here Comes the Bride") and the "Wedding March" from Mendelssohn's *A Midsummer Night's Dream* are two very popular processional choices. But do consider something with more personal meaning—perhaps the regal "Rigaudon" by André Campra or the exuberant

"Bourée" from Handel's *Water Music*. For solos, "Oh, Promise Me" remains ever popular, but you might also choose from current love songs and movie themes, folk and country ballads, classical works, maybe even that "first song" you two ever danced to. Ask your organist, choir director, cantor, or a musically informed friend to suggest some possibilities. Check also with your clergymember—there may be a listing of appropriate music for weddings to which he or she can direct you. (The New York City Cantors' Assembly, which is Conservative, publishes such a list.)

Some suggestions you might consider:

- For the processional:
"Prince of Denmark's March"—Clarke
"Fanfare"—from *The Triumphant,* Couperin
"Sarabande"—*Suite No. 11,* Handel
"Trumpet Tune"—Purcell
Theme from *Love Story*—Sigman, Lai
"Lover"—Rodgers and Hart
- During the ceremony:
"First Organ Sonata"—Mendelssohn
"Jesu, Joy of Man's Desiring"—Bach
"Deck Thyself, My Soul, with Gladness"—Bach
"Sheep May Safely Graze"—Bach
"Canon in D Minor"—Pachebel
"A Wedding Prayer"—Williams
"Wedding Song" ("There Is Love")—Stookey
"One Hand, One Heart"—from *West Side Story,* Bernstein, Sondheim
"Somewhere"—from *West Side Story,* Bernstein, Sondheim
Theme from *Romeo and Juliet*—Roto, Kusik
"Hallelujah Chorus"—from the *Messiah,* Handel
"Sunrise, Sunset"—from *Fiddler on the Roof,* Harnick, Bock
- For the recessional:
"Fugue in C Minor"—Buxtehude
"Psalm 100"—Knecht
"Rondo"—*Masterpiece Theatre* theme, Mouret
"Let There Be Peace on Earth"—Miller, Jackson
"Benedictus"—Simon and Garfunkel
"Speak Softly Love"—theme from *The Godfather,* Roto, Kusik

Be sure to listen to every suggestion until you find just the pieces you want. The use of traditional or contemporary secular (nonreligious) music should, of course, be cleared with the clergy officiating at your service. You will probably find your own memory of the service enhanced by a processional that is more majestic than popular.

There are a number of ways to add your own personal touches via your choice of musicians as well. If you've a string or woodwind quartet, a group of madrigal singers, or a trumpeter in mind to enhance the processional and recessional, ask the church or chapel organist to suggest some names. (But remember, in many areas, you'll have to pay the church organist whether you actually employ him or not.) You might also call local high schools and colleges for the names of string quartets and soloists.

Do you want to include the people you love in your wedding plans? If they are professional musicians, or almost as good, let your Aunt Eleanor play the prelude on the piano and your music-major roommate offer a solo after the vows. Or, invite them to take the stage at the reception where the mood is lighter. Thinking of singing yourselves? Consider it carefully; even the most seasoned performer can get wedding-day nerves, and it may be most effective for you to simply say your vows with clarity and confidence.

Whoever the musicians, give them plenty of time to practice, make sure you include them in the wedding rehearsal, and pay them promptly—professionals, on the day of the wedding (frequently in cash); friends, with thoughtful gifts (see Chapter 17), perhaps distributed at the rehearsal dinner.

Singing a hymn together gets everyone participating. Your clergymember can lend you hymnals and offer suggestions. Do read through all verses and eliminate any inappropriate ones. Words can be printed separately or in a wedding program if hymnals are not available.

There are many lovely possibilities for hymn choices. Here are just a few:

"Praise to the Lord, the Almighty the King of Creation" (S. Gesanbuch), a strong hymn of praise to begin your service.

"Joyful, Joyful, We Adore Thee" (Henry Van Dyke), fitting words on a day when everybody's happy.

"Day by Day" (L. S. Berg), an old hymn popularized in the show *Godspell*, about the most important things in life.

"Morning Has Broken" (Eleanor Farjeon), a haunting Gaelic melody with a message of hope—every day is a new beginning.

"Blest Be the Tie That Binds" (Lowell Mason), lovely thoughts to share with friends and family gathered around.

"Lord Dismiss Us With Thy Blessing" (W. I. Viner), the first verse is especially nice for ending your service.

MUSIC FOR PROTESTANT WEDDINGS

Usually a Protestant ceremony means you can have both popular and religious music. It is likely to be performed by the church organist, soloist, or choir who will all be familiar with wedding procedures and can offer a wide variety of selections for you to choose from. If you request something out of the ordinary, be sure to allow the musicians plenty of time to learn and practice it.

MUSIC FOR CATHOLIC WEDDINGS

Some Catholic clergy may ask that you avoid popular music in favor of religious selections and the hymns sung at regular Masses. Ask about this beforehand. Sometimes a choir sings; more often, a soloist. "Ave Maria" is probably the favorite, but consider other possibilities such as César Franck's "Panis Angelicus" and the "Ave Verum" by Mozart.

MUSIC FOR JEWISH WEDDINGS

Secular music, including the usual wedding marches, is permitted at many Reform and Conservative weddings, but Orthodox rabbis may prefer you use only traditional Hebrew music. The cantor traditionally chants the Seven Blessings and may perform other solo pieces if requested. Ask the rabbi and the cantor for suggestions on both traditional Hebrew songs and contemporary Israeli music.

MUSIC FOR WEDDING RECEPTIONS

A string trio in the background, a pianist in the corner, a small orchestra on a raised platform, even a stereo or tapes—music brings a special note of festivity to every reception. If you're having a band or orchestra at your reception, ask friends, the local musicians' union, college music departments, or music schools for suggestions. Do hear them play ahead of time—either at an audition you arrange, or by visiting (briefly) another party at which they are performing. Pay particular attention to how they dress, the type of music they're playing, the length of time they actually play. Once you've selected your musicians, give them a list of your favorites, as well as those of your closest family and friends. A mix of current popular hits and old standards will give everyone from your grandmother to the best man something to hum to.

Here are some favorites for reception music: "We've Only Just Begun," popularized by the Carpenters; "I Love You Just the Way You Are," a Billy Joel classic; "Tales from the Vienna Woods," composed over one hundred years ago by Johann Strauss; "You Light Up My Life," once a favorite solo selection as well; "Somewhere," from *West Side Story*; "Just in Time," an upbeat tune from *Bells Are Ringing*; "People Will Say We're in Love," an old favorite from *Oklahoma*; "Younger than Springtime," very popular with older wedding couples.

Other songs turning up at wedding receptions today: "You Are the Sunshine of My Life," as sung by Stevie Wonder; "Your Song," "I Need You to Turn To," "Kiss the Bride," as sung by Elton John; "Endless Love," as sung by Lionel Richie; "Evergreen," as sung by Barbra Streisand; "And I Love You So," as sung by Don McLean; "Here, There, and Everywhere," "In My Life," as sung by the Beatles.

172

. . .

If there'll be dancing, be sure to let the band know how swinging you want the party to get—and which song you want for your "first dance." Provide the music to "your song" ahead of time. If you do not specify a tune for your first dance with your father (how about "The Time of Your Life," Paul Anka?), the band will likely strike up "Daddy's Little Girl," "Sunrise, Sunset," or "Yes Sir, That's My Baby," which are frequently used.

You may also ask the band leader to help coordinate the rhythm of the reception. He may be able to signal guests when you enter the room (probably with "Here Comes the Bride"), when you're ready to cut the cake, and when you're leaving. Do specify which songs you wish played at each point, especially if you're not fond of "The Bride Cuts the Cake" done to the tune of "The Farmer in the Dell."

If there is a song you would like played that is not generally known, an obliging group will gladly take the sheet music from you ahead of time so they can rehearse the tune and play it beautifully just for you.

Taped, pre-recorded music is a good alternative when live music is not available. There are cassettes of wedding music, dance tunes, hits from the twenties and fifties, or any other period you favor. You can rent wedding tapes from many music stores. Or, ask a music buff friend to pre-mix your selections on one long-playing tape. Of course, you'll need audio equipment—if you can't borrow, rentals are possible—and you must check your reception site for adequate electrical outlets.

READINGS FOR WEDDINGS

Whether you and your groom compose your own poem or prayer to accompany your vows, or choose a verse from another source, a brief reading can express special thoughts you wish to share with the guests at your ceremony.

The point in the service known as *The Word* is the time for readings, both sacred scripture (the holy writings of any faith) and secular scripture (any writings meaningful to you).

Sacred scripture: Before you choose your scripture selections, read many translations. Different wording may make one seem more meaningful—but remember, not all versions are acceptable in every church. See your clergymember for approval, or other suggestions.

On love: You will find biblical words on true love in I John 3:16; 4:7-19; John 15:9-17; I Corinthians 13; Song of Solomon 7:11-12; 8:6-7; Ephesians 5:1-2.

On husbands and wives: The Bible speaks about the roles of husband and wife, showing the need for mutual respect. Comments are found in Proverbs 17, 20, 25-29, 31:10-13; Hosea 2:21-22; Ephesians 5:28-33; Ruth 1:16.

On marriage: The married state is extolled in Hebrews 13:4; Ecclesiastes 4:9-12; Matthew 19:4-6; Mark 10:6-9.

On home and family: Verses that speak of the beginning of a new family relationship include Matthew 7:21, 24-27; Ephesians 3:14-19; Proverbs 24:3-6; Psalm 127:1-2, 128.

On praise and joy: It's such a happy day, with so much to be thankful for. Include words of praise such as Psalm 8, 118:24, 150; Isaiah 61:10-11; Jeremiah 33:10b-11; Ecclesiastes 9:7-9.

Secular readings: There are four kinds of readings, each with its own beautiful style. Inspirational prose—from texts in philosophy, psychology, or religion—can make a statement about your convictions. Authors such as Rollo May, R. D. Laing, Paul Tournier, Denis de Rougemont, and David Viscott are worth reading. Song lyrics, from show tunes or love songs, are a sentimental choice. Borrow an anthology from the library and start humming. Poetry expresses deepest feelings in symbolic language. Read from e.e. cummings, Robert Frost, Rainer Maria Rilke, Sarah Teasdale, Kahlil Gibran, Shakespeare, and others. Novels and plays can paint a vignette of love. You probably have favorites, but notice the work of John Updike, Thornton Wilder, Neil Simon, and Anne Morrow Lindbergh.

Do check your clergy or librarian for other ideas. You might include beloved friends or brothers and sisters by asking them to recite the reading for you. Natural points for the readings to be offered are before the vows and after the exchange of rings. To follow along, each guest might enjoy having his or her own copy of the reading, perhaps included in a wedding program distributed before the ceremony.

15
Your Wedding Flowers

Awedding just wouldn't be a wedding without flowers. They bring beauty, color, and a wealth of tradition to marriage ceremonies and receptions, from very formal to informal. Picture now the effect of lush greens at the aisles of a whitewashed chapel, pastel carnations against a dark-paneled altar. Or, rose-filled vases creating an aura of romance at home, floral garlands encircling the catering-hall bandstand.

Consult your florist in the early stages of planning. He or she can advise you on the most appropriate flowers for various uses (if they'll be dancing until the small hours, the mothers will want flowers that look fresh a long time), tell you which will be most readily available at the time of your wedding, and show you samples of the various types and shapes of bouquets as well as dozens of blossoms you've probably never seen or heard of before. The florist might also suggest some attractive arrangements and color schemes to go along with your own ideas. You can have any flowers you like, even out of season, thanks to hothouse growing and air shipping. But in-season flowers—chrysanthemums in the fall rather than tulips—may cost less and look more natural in your setting.

WEDDING BOUQUETS

The bride and her attendants traditionally carry a bouquet at all but the most informal weddings. It may be anything from an armload of flowers to a small nosegay, but it should be scaled to your height and complement your dress. A cascade of feathered chrysanthemums, for example, might overpower a petite bride in a street-length dress, but be stunning for a tall bride in a long, flowing gown.

The bride's bouquet, traditionally made up of all-white flowers, is usually mixed with ivy, the symbol of fidelity, and other greens. Some favorites: white roses, orchids, carnations, stephanotis, lilies of the valley, and gardenias. But many others are chosen in season: Easter lilies make lovely spring bouquets, summer arrangements frequently include baby's breath or Queen Anne's lace, and white poinsettias look most festive at Christmastime. Today, color blended with white or all-color bouquets are also popular alternatives for brides—they can range from two or three dramatic tiger lilies to a nosegay of bright-hued carnations or a woodsy bundle of yellow freesia.

Be sure to give your florist a complete description of your dress, including a sketch and fabric swatches, if possible, so he or she can recommend an appropriate style for your bouquet. If your waist and skirt are scattered with appliqués, for example, a crescent cascade might mask these pretty details, while a round colonial nosegay of flowers would not detract from them. Incidentally, although the groom customarily pays for the bride's flowers, if it is a formal wedding, the bride still chooses them. (She and her family may also pay for them if they wish.)

Afraid you won't want to part with your flowers when it comes time to toss the bouquet? Have a replica or smaller version of it made up especially for this purpose. Then you will have the pleasure of hearing someone close to you cry, "I've got it!"—and of keeping yours as a memento.

The bridesmaids and honor attendant usually carry similar arrangements of the same flowers, but the maid or matron of honor frequently carries a different shade or a contrasting color to set her apart. It is not necessary for your attendants' bouquets to be duplicates of your own, but they should be similar in design and mood. If you plan on daisies, for example, your bridesmaids might carry daffodils or cornflowers, but not formal orchids.

Various colors of roses and carnations are popular for bridesmaids' bouquets the year round, but some of the most attractive arrangements feature seasonal flowers. In spring, your bridesmaids might wear pink dresses and carry dogwood, lilacs, or anemones. Yellow daffodils and forsythia are also pretty. For bridesmaids in a summer wedding: red and white peonies, multicolored sweet peas, or pink and red larkspur. A fall wedding? Consider russet chrysanthemums mixed with autumn leaves or sheaves of wheat. If you'll be married in December, you might plan a red-and-white color scheme using poinsettias, roses, or holly. You may want to include each bridesmaid's favorite flower (or birth flower) in bouquets that match in every other way. Before ordering, ask if anyone has an allergy to a particular flower. A sneezing bridesmaid (or bride!) can create havoc, but with planning such a situation is easily avoidable. Whatever you choose, be sure to give your florist a complete description of your bridesmaids' dresses and a swatch of fabric to guide him or her in designing appropriate bouquets.

Flower girls traditionally tote baskets of loose petals to be strewn in the bride's path, but remember, petals can cause someone to slip. Instead, today's flower girl often carries a miniature bouquet of flowers arranged in a basket, attached to a muff, or fashioned into a nosegay. Rosebuds, violets, lilies of the valley, or other dainty blossoms look very sweet.

FLOWERS TO WEAR

The bride at an informal wedding usually chooses flowers for her dress or for her wrist instead of a bouquet. White orchids are popular with many brides, but you may wear any flowers that complement your outfit—even a muff woven of greens and daisies. For your informal wedding, where yours may be the only bouquet, leave the choice of flowers up to your groom. He may surprise you with something sentimental—peach roses just like the ones he sent you after your first date. If you have a formal wedding, the orchid or other flowers from the center of your bouquet can be removed to pin on your going-away outfit. Or you may have your florist make up a fresh arrangement to wear for traveling.

The mothers and grandmothers of the bride and groom are customarily presented with flowers to wear at the wedding. These may be made of any flowers that harmonize with their dresses, but personal preferences should be taken into consideration. Some women, for example, like nothing better than roses, but a mother with her own rose garden may well find a cluster of cymbidium orchids more unique for the occasion. Giving someone special—your grandmother, the young girl passing out programs at the church door, the friend who read the poem in your ceremony—a corsage or boutonniere is a thoughtful way to honor them, too.

PRAYER BOOK FLOWERS

In a formal or semiformal wedding, you may carry a flower-covered prayer book instead of a bouquet. This may be a new book purchased for the occasion or an old family Bible or missal. Whether new or old, the book may be covered in white silk or satin to complement your dress. Although you may choose any flowers you like, white orchids, with the addition of a cascade of smaller blossoms or ribbon streamers when the bride wears a long dress, are classic.

FLORAL HEADPIECES

Although silk flowers are much more common these days, headpieces made of real orange blossoms or other light flowers are still worn by some brides and bridesmaids. These are usually made in the shape of a crescent that fits across the top of the head or in a circle that sits on the crown. Such headpieces may be attached to a small comb or held in place with hairpins. Sometimes bridesmaids wear a single bloom (held by a comb) in the hair. A veil can be attached to the bride's headpiece but is not necessary for the bridesmaids. Another option is for the bride to wear her headpiece and veil for the ceremony, then change to a few pretty hair flowers for reception dancing.

BOUTONNIERES

The groom and every man in the wedding party—the best man, ushers, and fathers—traditionally wear a boutonniere on the left lapel. White carnations are the usual choice for everyone except the groom and his best man, who may wear a white rose, a sprig of stephanotis, or a stem of lily of the valley, an age-old symbol of love. You and your groom might follow this sentimental custom: Remove a flower from your own bouquet and pin it to his lapel. If you tell your florist your plan, he'll wire the flower for easy removal.

FLORAL DECORATIONS FOR CEREMONY AND RECEPTION

Ceremony flowers may vary considerably with the location, the size, and the style of the wedding. In general, elaborate floral decorations are reserved for very large, formal weddings. But a simple chapel sometimes needs more decoration than an ornate cathedral. Discuss what is permitted and what has been done in the past, first with the proper authorities of the church. Then ask your florist to visit your wedding site (if he hasn't already) to offer new ideas.

Regardless of the size and mood of your wedding, you'll want to have at least one vase of flowers on each side of the altar. You may also have a number of other arrangements. Imagine dramatic sprays of flowers attached to the aisle posts instead of just ribbon bows. These may be placed on every second or third pew, or only on those pews reserved for relatives and special guests. If you're being married in a church with plain windows, you might put an eye-catching arrangement of flowers in each windowsill. When guests are not expected to fill the church, it's nice to have a bank of ferns, palms—potted flowers to mark the section needed for the ceremony. Ropes of flowers interspersed with ivy or smilax may also be used to partition the church, or they may drape the altar rail.

You may choose any flowers you like, including favorite blossoms too fragile to be used on bouquets. Or have your altar arrangements made of the same flowers carried by the bridesmaids. Even the most attractive home or club needs greens and flowers to form a simple aisle and a decorative background for the ceremony.

Banks of ferns, baskets of cut flowers, or rows of potted plants may partition the room into the appropriate sections. You might place a screen of greens and flowers behind the altar or kneeling bench, or post a *huppah* woven of flowers and greens and add ropes of ribbon intertwined with tiny blossoms to indicate an aisle.

Reception flowers may also be as simple or as elaborate as you wish. Carry out your wedding color scheme by repeating the flowers in your bridesmaids' bouquets. Or select something different to harmonize with the surroundings. It's customary to have floral centerpieces on dinner and refreshment tables, and these may be anything from a few sprigs to a long garland of blossoms. You might even choose individual cuttings, small potted plants, or bud vases that guests can take home—for a long time to come they'll be saying, "Remember the wedding where . . ."

Be sure that all the arrangements on the bridal table are low enough to give an unobstructed view of the wedding party. You might place your bridal bouquet in the center of the table, with those of your attendants lined up on either side of it. The cake table is usually decorated with garlands or other small floral arrangements; the cake itself may be topped with flowers, a particularly elegant touch. You may also use floral screens and banks of ferns to form a background for the receiving line. It is a setting that will make guests feel truly welcome.

When you are selecting flowers, your florist can advise which ones are currently in season—that's when they are least expensive, most abundant. Some wedding favorites—gladiolus, baby's breath, roses, mums, statice, carnations, stephanotis, gardenias, cymbidium orchids—are available the year round. And, of course, any flower can be imported at extra cost, varying with distance, perishability, and availability.

Every flower expresses a sentiment. You might carry red and white roses (unity), your bridesmaids might hold double daisies (participation). Arrange yellow lilies (gaiety) into reception centerpieces, purple anemone buds (expectation) into a honeymoon corsage.

THE LANGUAGE OF FLOWERS

Bachelor's button	Hope
Bluebell	Constancy
Buttercup	Riches
Camellia	Perfect loveliness, gratitude
Carnation	Pure, deep love
Daisy	Share your feelings
Forget-me-not	Do not forget
Honeysuckle	Generous and devoted affection
Ivy	Fidelity
Jasmine	Grace, elegance
Jonquil	Affection returned
Lily	Purity
Lime	Conjugal bliss
Marigold	Sacred affection
Red rose	I love you
Sweet pea	Meeting
Violet	Faithfulness
Wood sorrel	Joy

In a way that everyone can appreciate, flowers symbolize the beauty of the wedding service and a marriage growing in love and devotion.

YOUR FLOWER GUIDE

Choosing flowers that will be in season will help keep you within budget. Here, a chart of regional availability.

FLOWERS	SOUTH				NORTH				MIDWEST				SOUTH-WEST				WEST		
	SPRING	SUMMER	FALL	WINTER	SPRING	SUMMER	FALL	WINTER	SPRING	SUMMER	FALL	WINTER	SPRING	SUMMER	FALL	WINTER	SUMMER	FALL	WINTER
ALSTROMERIA White, purples, yellows	•	•	•					•	•	•	•	•	•				•		
AGAPANTHUS White, purples, blues	•						•	•	•	•			•	•	•	•	•		
ANEMONE White, purples, reds	•							•	•	•			•					•	•
CALLA LILY White	*	*	*	*	*	*	*	*	*	*	*	*	*	*	*	*	*	*	*
CARNATION White, yellows, reds	•				•	•	•	•	•	•	•	•	•	•	•	•	•	•	•
CHRYSANTHEMUM Many shapes, all colors	•	•	•		*	*	*	*	•	•	•	•	•	•	•		•	•	•
MARGUERITE DAISY White, pinks	•	•	•		•	•	•		•	•	•		•	•	•	•	•		
FREESIA White, yellows, purples, reds	•	•	•	•	•	•	•	•	•	•	•		•		•	•	•		
GARDENIA White	•	•	•	•	•	•	•	•		•	•	•	•	•	•				
GLADIOLUS White, yellows, reds, purples	•	•	•	•	*	*	*	*	•	•	•	•	•	•	•	•	•	•	•
BABY'S BREATH White	•	•	•	•	•	•	•	*	•	•	•	•	•	•	•	•	•		
LILY OF THE VALLEY White, lilac-pinks	*	*	*	*	*	*	*	*	*	*	*	*	*	*	*	*	*	*	*
LILAC White, purples, reds	•	•	•	•	*	•	•	•	•	*	•	•	•				•	•	
RUBRUM LILY Pinkish-white with crimson spots	•	•	•	•	•	•			•	•	•	•	*	*	*	*	•	•	
NERINE LILY Pinks, reds	•	•	•	•	•	•			•	•	•	•	•						•
CATTLEYA LILY Purples	•	•	•	•	*	*	*	*	•	•	•	•	•	•	•			•	
CYMBIDIUM ORCHID All colors but blue		•	•		•	•	•	•	•	•	•	•	•				•	•	•
DENDROBIUM ORCHID All colors	•	•	•		•	•	•	•	•	•	•	•	•				•	•	•
MOTH ORCHID White, reds, purples					•	•	•	•	•	•	•	•	•				•	•	•
ROSES (STANDARD) All colors	•	•	•	•	•	•	•	•	•	•	•	•	•	•	•	•	•	•	•
ROSES (BABY BUDS) All colors	•	•	•	•	•	•	•		•	•	•	•	•	•	•	•	•	•	
STATICE White, pinks, purples	•	•	•	•	•	•	•		•	•	•	•	•	•	•	•	•	•	•
STEPHANOTIS White	•	•	•	•	•	•	•		•	•	•	•	•	•	•	•	•	•	
TULIPS All colors	•				•	•	•		•		•	•			•	•		•	

All information courtesy of Teleflora.   *These are available, but may be expensive.*

16
Your Photographs and Publicity

Your marriage ceremony will be over in a few minutes, your reception in a few hours. But your photographs, bridal portrait, wedding candids, videotape, and newspaper clippings are keepsakes you'll treasure for years to come. Through them, you and your groom will be able to relive some of your happiest moments and share those precious memories with your family and friends.

YOUR BRIDAL PORTRAIT

This is your most important wedding photograph, since it is the one that may be published in the newspaper and displayed in your new home and in those of your relatives. Keep both purposes in mind when you choose your hairstyle, makeup, and background so you'll be as proud of the way your portrait looks twenty years from now as you are when it first appears in print.

Most newspapers require that wedding photographs be submitted at least ten days before the scheduled publication date—so plan on having your portrait taken about a month before the wedding. If the proper facilities are available, you may arrange to have your portrait taken at your bridal salon during the final fitting of your dress. Otherwise, make certain you have your dress delivered in time to go to your photographer's studio. There you can be sure of having the lighting, background, air conditioning, and calm surroundings necessary for best results.

Your bridal portrait should look as if it were made on your wedding day, so be sure you carry along all the proper accessories—shoes, slip, gloves, jewelry, prayer book. If you wish your flowers to show, give the photographer a detailed description of your bouquet so he can provide an appropriate silk replica. Do take his advice on hair and makeup into consideration, but also strive for your own prettiest, most natural look.

Your photographer will take several different shots of you in different poses, then supply proofs of a good selection. You may want to choose one pose for publicity purposes, another for your finished portrait; let the photographer help you decide about which poses will look best in the newspapers (they will be special glossy black-and-white prints).

Some newspapers will now run portraits of the bride and groom together. If you choose this option, you'll have to make suitable arrangements with your photographer. Your fiancé, of course, should also plan to wear his full wedding outfit for the picture. Incidentally, since the groom-to-be nowadays may even go shopping with his fiancée for her dress, you may wish to disregard the old superstition of him not seeing you before the wedding.

YOUR WEDDING CANDIDS

The person who photographs your wedding ceremony and reception should be someone with the knowledge and experience to get the kind of pictures you'll display with pride. A talented friend or general photographer may be able to handle the job, but a photographer specializing in weddings is usually more reliable. This doesn't mean that your friends should be discouraged from bringing their cameras to the wedding. Let them shoot all the pictures they want. As long as they don't have the complete responsibility, it won't matter if they get caught up in the festivities and forget all about snapping your grandmother with your father, or about taking the classic receiving line photo.

It is nice to include posed photographs in your wedding album to make sure no important people are missed. But the pictures that may be the most talked about long after are those that catch spontaneous action (the flower girl waltzing with her brother, a happy bridesmaid kicking her shoe off) and unconscious facial expressions—true "candid" shots.

Whatever you do, don't make your guests wait around while you and other members of your wedding party pose for the camera. Plan in advance to have your posed shots taken as quickly and unobtrusively as possible. If you want to be photographed with your parents or your bridesmaids, for example, allow time for these pictures to be taken at home as soon as you finish dressing. Since the bridal party leaves the church before any of the guests, you should arrive at the reception in time to pose for several pictures before the first guests appear. A formal shot of you and your groom might also be taken at that time. The ushers and best man can be photographed after the receiving line forms.

Although a competent photographer doesn't need coaching to capture the highlights of a wedding, he does need to know your personal plans and wishes, and the names of any people you don't want him to leave out. It's helpful to make a list of "not to be missed" pictures, then introduce the photographer to one or two guests who will point out your cousin Bobby, your groom's boss, and others on your "must" list. You should make sure that he's familiar with any regulations or preferences of the clergy, too. Some churches, for example, do not allow flashbulbs or altar photographs during the ceremony. This may apply particularly if you're thinking of having movies or videotapes of your wedding made. Check with your minister, priest, or rabbi, then be certain the photographer knows how to preserve the solemnity and dignity of your wedding ceremony.

Your photographer, a professional, will work out a contract with you. Be sure it specifies the number of rolls of film to be shot, the number of locations, the date and time, and how many finished prints are included in the fee.

GIFTS OF PHOTOGRAPHS

Customarily, the bride's family covers the cost of the wedding album, and it remains with the couple. The couple should also have a picture of each other to put on a desk or dresser at home or at work. However, having prints made for both sets of parents is a thoughtful gesture. At the very least, the groom's parents should receive six pictures: possibly a small-size portrait of the bride, the couple, all the members of their immediate family together with the newlyweds, both sets of parents together, the receiving line, the parents' table. These prints may or may not be bound into a miniature album or encased in suitable frames. It is not necessary to show the groom's family proofs, but this does give them the opportunity to select favorites which they would like to order for themselves.

Each attendant would certainly appreciate a small print of the whole wedding party, with the bride and groom. And the guests? Having someone on hand at the reception with an instant camera and plenty of film is one way you can honor them with a memory of being there. Your wedding candids can be useful for Christmas cards or framed prints for friends.

PRE-WEDDING PUBLICITY

In large metropolitan areas, the only advance publicity a marriage receives is the engagement announcement (see Chapter 1 for suggested wording). In many smaller communities, however, the activities surrounding an upcoming wedding make society-page news for weeks before the ceremony. Some papers report the details of showers and other parties given in honor of the bride and groom; others publish the wedding plans a week or two in advance. Such an item might read:

> *Plans for the marriage of Miss Cynthia Joy Dumbrowski, daughter of Mr. and Mrs. Frederick Hugh Dumbrowski of Briarcliff Drive, and Mr. Ronald Lloyd Felker, Jr., son of Mrs. Ronald Lloyd Felker and the late Mr. Felker of Omaha, Nebraska, were announced today by the bride's parents. The ceremony will be performed at the First Presbyterian Church of*

Lockport, with the Reverend Roland Saunders officiating.

Miss Dumbrowski will be attended by her sister, Mrs. Kevin McGovern of Lexington, Kentucky, matron of honor. The bridesmaids will be Miss Jessica Kramer of Baton Rouge, Louisiana, Miss Donna Calabrese, Miss Andrea Gould, and Mrs. Kenneth Bronson of Lockport. Miss Leslie McGovern, the bride's niece, will be flower girl. Dennis O'Connor of Omaha will be Mr. Felker's best man. Kevin McGovern, William Harris, and Stanley Janski of Omaha and William Hertz of Lockport will serve as ushers.

The ceremony will be followed by a reception at the White Hills Lodge.

Before submitting an item of this type, study your newspaper carefully to make sure it considers such information newsworthy, then follow the form usually used for such stories as closely as possible.

YOUR WEDDING ANNOUNCEMENT

It's customary to publish the details of a formal wedding in the couple's hometown newspapers. A morning wedding is sometimes written up in an evening paper the same day, but most wedding stories are published the day after the ceremony. Check with your newspaper in advance to learn its exact requirements and deadlines. Some, for example, require the bride to fill out a standard form and submit it to the society editor ten or more days before the wedding. Others want telephoned confirmation that the wedding has actually taken place before they will go ahead and publish the story. Usually, they will ask you to pay a fee.

If your paper does not supply wedding announcement forms, type the information double-spaced on one side of plain white 8½ × 11-inch paper. Be sure to include your name, address, and telephone number(s) (or those of someone in your community who can be called for verification and additional details) in the upper right-hand corner, just as you did with your engagement announcement. The date you'd like the announcement published should appear as well.

If you send a photograph with your wedding story, it should be a 5 × 7-inch or 8 × 10-inch glossy black-and-white print of your bridal portrait. Tape a typed line of identification to the photo in case it gets separated from the story. Enclose the picture, announcement, and a piece of stiff cardboard in a manila envelope and address it to the society-page editor—mail it or drop it off. If you send photographs to more than one paper in the same city, you may want to submit different poses to each. Of course, if you will be using a picture of the two of you taken on wedding day, your announcement will be delayed. A "together" picture can be taken ahead, though.

A typical wedding announcement reads:

Miss Patricia Clark Butler, daughter of Mr. and Mrs. Clifford Marion Butler of South Orange, was married this afternoon to Mr. Lewis Herbert Sullivan, son of Mr. and Mrs. Howard Mitchell Sullivan of Short Hills. Msgr. Patrick Flynn of Englewood, uncle of the bride, performed the ceremony in Trinity Church in South Orange.

The bride, escorted by her father, wore an ivory dress of organza trimmed with Venise lace. Bands of matching lace edged her chapel train and veil. She carried a cascade of white roses and stephanotis.

Miss Carla Butler, sister of the bride, was maid of honor. Bridesmaids were Misses Gloria Geller and Linda Kerr of South Orange, Mrs. Gino DeGeorgio of Teaneck, and Mrs. Francis Demery of Buffalo, New York.

Arthur Clay of Newark served as best man. The ushers were Neil Butler, brother of the bride, Nathan Freeman of Short Hills, and Harvey Lyons and David Chan of New York.

Some newspapers also publish descriptions of the bridesmaids' and mothers' dresses and flowers, the location of the reception, details of the newlyweds' respective educational backgrounds, career accomplishments, professional affiliations, grandparents' names, honeymoon plans, and other information. (For example, if you will continue to use your maiden name after marriage, you could include a sentence mentioning this.) Use published stories in your newspaper as a guide to how much or how little to include. Send copies of the newspaper announcement to college alumni associations, professional societies, clubs.

Small weddings, second marriages, elopements, reaffirmations can all be announced with their stories following the same basic format shown above. A prior marriage is sometimes mentioned in a line saying, "The bride's (or couple's) previous marriage(s) ended in divorce."

If your parents are divorced, the announcement would read: ". . . the daughter of Mrs. Clark Butler of South Orange and Mr. Clifford Marion Butler of Newark." If one of your parents is widowed, the standard phrasing is: ". . . the daughter of Mrs. Clifford Marion Butler and the late Mr. Butler." If your mother has remarried and you have been adopted by your stepfather, that information appears later in the story, perhaps reporting that your stepfather gave you away. Is it your groom's parents who are divorced? The usual wording can easily be adapted.

However and wherever people hear of your wedding, it is the best of news.

17
Wedding Gifts

The gifts you receive as a couple not only provide many of the basic needs for your new home, they are wonderful tokens of friendship as well. Only those persons who accept invitations to your reception are obligated to send gifts, but you also may receive presents up to a year afterward from others who wanted very much to attend but couldn't. You'll receive packages from people you don't even know, since it is customary for all gifts given before the wedding—including those from relatives and friends of the future groom—to be sent to the bride-to-be. However, nowadays it is also common for checks and gifts to be addressed to the groom-to-be and sent to him by friends of his family. A note would mention his bride-to-be and upcoming wedding.

Your fiancé, your mother, your honor attendant, the ushers, and your bridesmaids may all join in the fun and help open your gifts. Just be careful not to lose any enclosure cards. And keep accurate records of who sent what, to avoid mixing up gifts or forgetting thank-you notes. You need a wedding planning notebook, if you don't already have one, with a section for gifts. Request or buy a gift-record book from your stationer, bridal salon, or Wedding Gift Registry consultant at your favorite store as soon as possible. There is nothing more rude than not thanking a well-meaning friend or relative for a wedding present.

As you open each package, list the gift immediately in your book, adding an identifying description of the item, the name and address of the donor, the store from which it came (in case you want to exchange it later), the date it arrived, and the date on which you mail your thank-you note. If you expect a lot of presents, number your list and stick a corresponding number to each item. Then you won't confuse the silver candy dish from your great-aunt with the one from your fiancé's boss. Some gifts and wedding books include self-adhesive numbers for this purpose. You may want to recruit your honor attendant's help with the gift record.

REGISTERING FOR GIFTS

Listing your preferences at your store's Wedding Gift Registry is becoming a bridal tradition, and it will be a real pleasure for you and your groom to make your choices together. Registering is also a courtesy to guests—you spare them the time and effort of hunting for the perfect idea for you, as well as the possible disappointment of buying you something you don't want or can't use.

Be careful to list items that suit the budgets of all your guests, as well as the many gift-giving occasions they will attend for you. The oven thermometer your little sister brings to a shower will mean as much as the silver coffee service from your grandparents.

How do you let people politely know where you're registered? A shower hostess can note the store name on invitations, but you would never print it on wedding invitations. Your mother, his mother, and your attendants might also spread the word. Whenever someone asks what you would like for your wedding, you yourself can answer, "John and I are registered at Addington's. You might find something you like as much as we do there." Many people, of course, genuinely enjoy choosing gifts themselves, perhaps wrapping them prettily, and this will always be their privilege as gift-givers.

When you are ready to register, really use your imagination. Couples can register in all sorts of stores—camping goods, bookstores, wine shops, art galleries and museums, hardware emporiums, gourmet supply houses—wherever their life-style or interests lead them. Getting a fabulous audio system may be more important to you than assembling a complete set of china. Your guests will appreciate knowing.

You can register in several different cities if your families and friends are spread out. Register for linens in Dallas, his hometown; for silver in Denver, where your folks live; and for china in Chicago, where you and your groom-to-be both work. Or, if the store has branches, there's no problem. Most stores now have computerized listings. Guests will be able to make purchases at a branch of a store in which you've registered, and the computer will keep track of all the purchases. Another possibility for a couple moving to a brand new town: register at a store in that town. Some friends may be considerate enough to order gifts from that store to be delivered after you arrive.

If you both have an upcoming long-distance move, plan to buy a new home, or are entering a second marriage with too many possessions already, you may prefer gifts of money like many others today. Money is a most popular wedding gift, closely followed by silver, crystal, toaster ovens, and furniture. Your mother, sister, and close friends can discreetly spread the word that you prefer gift checks if anyone asks what you want. A monetary gift may take the form of a check, cash, gift certificate to a favorite store, U.S. Government Bond, or stock certificates. You may carry a pretty white purse to collect envelopes containing money and checks, if this is the custom among your family and friends. But even if you do, envelopes should then be given to a friend or close family member whose trustworthiness is beyond question. (When you change to your honeymoon travel clothes, you both can endorse them—now that you're officially a couple, most will be made out to you both—adding the phrase, "For Deposit Only.") This person can deposit the cash and checks in a bank or security account while you are away.

FAMILY PRESENTS

In some families, parents give the bride and groom something traditional in addition to a lovely wedding present. This gift might be symbolic, as it is in Lithuania, where parents give wine for joy, salt for tears, and bread for fruitfulness. Others are sentimental, giving a "piece of the home," such as an antique clock or favorite rocking chair. Your family might give an heirloom—grandmother's locket or a bottle of cognac purchased the day you were born. Some make the gift religious, a family Bible to record births, marriages, and deaths. In the Jewish faith, the bride's mother might give the groom a fine *tallit* (prayer shawl) of silk. The groom's mother could give the bride Sabbath candlesticks or a tablecloth. A Quaker couple might be given a "love quilt." These family gifts will be treasured always as a reminder of the special caring exchanged in families.

YOUR THANK-YOU NOTES

You or your groom must send a personal, handwritten letter of appreciation for each gift you receive, even one from a close friend you've thanked in person and see every day at work. The only exceptions to this thanks-in-writing rule are gifts from your husband and from your parents, although they, too, might treasure a special letter from you. (Imagine your parents reading again and again together your words of appreciation for the gift of money toward that down payment on a house. Your husband, too, will treasure this very special "love letter.")

Although the responsibility for acknowledging all gifts—received before, at, or after the wedding—has traditionally belonged to the bride, your groom can write thank-you notes as well, particularly for gifts given at parties he has attended, or for those that have come with his name on them as well as yours, especially if they are from people he knows best. After all, you will be enjoying your gifts together.

Start writing your thank-you notes as soon as you receive your first wedding gifts, or you may never catch up. Also, you'll find it easier to make your words of thanks for each thoughtful gift sound sincere and spontaneous if you tackle just a few notes at a time. When trying to write several dozen at once, you will find it difficult to make them all as enthusiastic as you—and the gift-givers—would like.

Thank-you notes need not be long, but they should be prompt. In general, you should try to acknowledge gifts that arrive before your wedding within two weeks of their arrival. Those coming later should be acknowledged within a month after your honeymoon. If you expect to receive more gifts than you could possibly acknowledge within this time, you may send printed cards to let your friends know their gifts arrived safely. These cards, which must be followed by personal notes as soon as possible, read:

Miss Ann Marie Brown
acknowledges with thanks
the receipt of your wedding gift
and will take pleasure in writing a personal note
at an early date

The classic thank-you note is written in blue or black ink on a good grade of folded notepaper in ivory or white. Your name or monogram may be printed or embossed on the notes if you wish, but you won't use your married name or initial until after the wedding. Colored, decorated notes also may be chosen. Remember that the most important thing is to make certain a thank-you is sent quickly.

A thank-you note to a married couple is traditionally addressed to the wife, with her husband referred to in the body of the note. Nowadays, you may address both if you prefer. Do mention your own fiancé or husband whenever possible. For example, "Dear Mrs. Clark, John and I are delighted with the beautiful vase we received today from you and Mr. Clark. . . ." Your groom should do the same when he is the note writer.

Each letter should be as warm and personal as possible. Everyone loves exuberant praise for something chosen with care and affection. Describe the gift itself and how you plan to use it. If it's one of those inevitable "mystery gifts" with an obscure purpose, refer to it by color or material. It's much better to say thanks for a specific "blue glass piece" or "silver container" than for a vague "lovely gift." Try to put at least one thought besides "thank you" into each note. You might include an invitation to visit, a comment about the wedding, or a word or two about your new apartment—some personal touch.

You may sign notes to relatives and close friends with your first name only, but use your full name to people you don't know as well. After the wedding, you may include your maiden name whenever necessary for identification. For example, you may sign yourself "Ann Smith" or "Ann Brown Smith," but never "Mrs. John Smith." If you plan to continue using your maiden name, you might take this chance to notify your friends by signing your notes "Ann Brown" after the wedding. Always put your full name on the envelope to avoid confusion.

Many couples find gifts of money difficult to acknowledge, but it can be easy if you just mention how you plan to use the money. The following would be an appropriate acknowledgment for a gift check:

Dear Uncle Ed,

Thank you so much for the generous wedding check. It was a wonderful surprise. John and I have added it to savings earmarked for a car—and thanks to you, we're almost there. We'll be driving around to see you soon!

Love,
Ann

A situation, again, that often perplexes the bride is when she unwraps a gift she can't identify—and months after the wedding at that. The idea is not to worry about your confusion but take advantage of it:

Dear Miss Martin,

Thank you for the beautifully engraved silver piece—it was such a nice surprise to find it waiting when John and I came home from work. There is a reason I've remembered you as someone who could always brighten a routine day. It felt like Christmas all over. Thank you again.

Sincerely,
Ann Brown Smith

If you haven't met the gift-givers yet—they are friends of your fiancé's family, perhaps—suggest a time when you might:

Dear Mrs. Robbins:

Thank you very much for the blender you and Mr. Robbins sent. Both John and his brother Larry tell me you serve some of the thickest milk shakes in town. Now we can too! I can't wait to meet you at the wedding. Again, many thanks.

Sincerely yours,
Ann Brown

When you receive a single gift from several relatives, bridesmaids, or friends, you should write each one a separate note. However, if the gift came from a large group (ten or more)—your co-workers, for example—one thank-you note addressed to the group is sufficient (but be sure to thank everyone in person as well):

Dear Friends,

Thank you, thank you for the place setting of china. Now John and I have service for twelve—just the right number to host the annual partners' dinner. How did you ever guess? Seriously, we do appreciate it—and I can't wait to get back with our honeymoon snapshots for you to see.

With much affection,
Ann Smith

What do you do when you really don't care for a gift and can't return it? Find something nice to say about it anyway or about the persons who sent it, for their feelings are undoubtedly very important to you. You can always bring the gift out when they come to visit, then put it away.

> *Dear Bob and Jan,*
>
> *Thanks so much for the gum-machine lamp! Ann and I haven't stopped talking about it—and it's sure to be a conversation piece whenever we have people over. You two are always so clever and so much fun, we intend you to be among our first guests. Thanks again!*
>
> *Best,*
> *John*

DISPLAYING YOUR GIFTS

Nearly everyone likes to admire wedding presents, especially when the gift he or she has given holds a place of honor. Some guests even wait until they've had a chance to look at the gift display before selecting their own wedding present.

See that your display is set up in a room that is not in constant use, arranging your gifts on rows of card tables covered with white tablecloths or sheets. You may start your display as soon as you have six or eight gifts, adding more as they arrive. One way is to group gifts into categories, with silver on one table, glassware on another, electrical appliances on a third, and so on. Another would be to borrow some store display tricks to create attractive groupings that mix colors and textures in an interesting way. Display only token place settings of dinnerware, flatware, and glassware. Scatter similar gifts so that it's not obvious to viewers that you've received twelve sets of salt and pepper shakers (a problem that can be avoided by registering). If you file your gift enclosure cards elsewhere, you can display just one set of exact duplicates, and each donor will think you've received only this. Do not put out gifts of money, or place modest gifts immediately next to very generous ones. Garlands of greens, small bowls of flowers, or clusters of ribbon from the packages make your array more festive.

Besides *not* printing your address or the date of the wedding in your newspaper engagement announcement, there are other ways to protect your valuable gifts. It's wise to take out a temporary floater policy insuring your presents while they are on display. Check with your insurance company, or your parent's homeowner carrier, to determine whose policy should include the floater.

The best kind of policy protects your gifts no matter where they are—car, reception, parents' home. Many people today hire a security guard, or ask a neighbor or the local police to keep an eye on the house during the ceremony—or at other times when the house will be empty.

Incidentally, gifts sent before the wedding are likely to arrive at the R.S.V.P. address indicated on the wedding invitation. This means the bride who will travel to her parents' hometown for the wedding may be counting on her mother to collect and display gifts. If so, you will certainly need to make special arrangements to transport the gifts to wherever you and your groom will be living. Perhaps a friend from your town who drove to the wedding would take some back in the car. If you would prefer they come directly to your residence, make a note of that when you register your gift choices and pass the word on through family and friends.

If your reception is held at home, guests will see the gift display then. But you may also ask friends to come by and see the gifts or give a special luncheon, tea, or bridesmaids' party to show off your presents. You might leave your gift display up for a week after the ceremony so friends and relatives can drop by to see it. With the predictable letdown that comes after any major event in life, and with you off on your honeymoon, your parents might welcome the company.

Expecting gifts at the reception? Try to discourage it. But if you know there will be packages, place a guard at a particularly busy public hall or in a restaurant. In either case, it is safest not to open and display these gifts at the reception—you don't want anyone's carefully chosen present to you to get lost! Do designate a place to store gifts, and someone to transport them home.

DAMAGED GIFTS

When you receive a damaged gift from a local store, return it for replacement. If it came from an out-of-town shop, write a letter of explanation and wait for instructions. Be sure to ask them not to tell the purchaser of the damage. More than one bride has neglected to make such a request, only to learn that the store did call the person—long after she'd sent a thank-you note making no mention of the problem.

If a broken gift was mailed by the purchaser, check the wrappings for an insurance stamp. Is it there? Then return the package with a note of explanation so that the gift-giver can collect the insurance and make a replacement. If the gift was not insured, however, don't mention the damage as it may make the person feel obligated to send another gift. Damaged gifts are not displayed unless they can be arranged so that the crack, dent, etc., doesn't show.

EXCHANGING GIFTS

No matter how careful you and your fiancé are about registering your gift preferences, you're bound to receive a few gifts you can't use. Some duplicates, especially of breakable items and of things you can always use more of (towels, blankets) are nice to have, but it is practical to exchange gifts you really don't need—as long as it can be done without the giver knowing. Never ask the giver where a gift was purchased so that you can exchange it, and don't mention duplication or exchange in your thank-you note.

RETURNING GIFTS

When a wedding is merely postponed, send an announcement to all the guests, keeping the presents you've already received (see Chapter 5). When a wedding is canceled, however, every gift—even those that have been monogrammed— must go back to the person who sent it. A note expressing gratitude and explaining that the wedding will not take place accompanies each present, but you need give no reason for the cancellation.

MONOGRAMMING

There was a time when almost every wedding gift—from silver to linens—bore a monogram when it arrived. Monograms are very popular today, but most brides who want something monogrammed have it done after the wedding. You might even ask the consultant at the Wedding Gift Registry to indicate your wishes on your preference list. That way you can avoid the "no exchange" rule that usually applies to monogrammed items and make sure your monograms will read exactly as you want them to (for example, if you are keeping your maiden name after marriage or designing a contemporary monogram that includes both your husband's and your first initials).

A monogram is a personal trademark that should be chosen with care. The most common style for silver flatware is a single initial engraved on the handles. Triple-initial monograms, in a variety of styles, are also popular. The bride's first, maiden, and married initials are the traditional choice, but you may also use your first initial, your husband's, and your married surname in the center. If your initials spell a word like BAD or JAR, think about a monogram in which the last initial is in the center and larger than the other two: bDa or jRa. Ask your wedding consultant at the gift registry about new trends in monogramming, such as a style for the bride who is keeping her own last name.

GIFTS FOR ATTENDANTS

It is customary to give each of your attendants a small gift as a token of appreciation and as a memento of your wedding. These need not be expensive, but should be relatively permanent items of a personal nature. Traditionally, each bridesmaid gets an identical gift, but honor attendants usually receive something a little more special. Or you may break with tradition and give each attendant a gift chosen especially for her or him—from a sewing basket or series of theater tickets to a special golf club.

The same is true for your groom's ushers and his best man. Gifts to your attendants are distributed before the wedding, often at the bridesmaids' luncheon and bachelor party or, if preferred, at the rehearsal dinner.

You may give your attendants almost anything you think they'd like, but the usual choice is something that can be worn for the wedding or that can be monogrammed and engraved with the wedding date. In the first category are gloves, pearls, necklaces, or earrings for the bridesmaids (or their dresses, if you wish to relieve them of that expense); studs, cuff links, tie bars, stickpins (or shirts and ties) for the ushers. Women's gifts that monogram nicely include bracelets, pins, pendants, pewter cups, business card or contact lens cases, and silver hair combs. Monogramming works well for men's money clips, belt buckles, key rings, or pewter mugs.

GIFTS TO EACH OTHER

There is no rule that says you and your groom must exchange gifts, but most couples do. They choose something they know will be treasured for years—for its usefulness as well as for its sentimental value. For example, you might give your groom a good watch, a pair of gold cuff links, a piece of luggage, or a handsome wallet. He might surprise you with a watch, too, or with fine jewelry, an attaché case, or a frame of sterling silver to hold his picture. Engraving or embossing the gift with initials, wedding date, and perhaps a few very personal words will remind you both of your special feelings for one another, and the deep commitment you have made to share the years ahead.

ANNIVERSARY GIFTS

Picturing the years ahead, you may find yourself thinking of anniversary gifts. Today, when couples work hard to make marriage last and regard each additional year together as the best reason to celebrate, gifts become a natural and lovely way to mark the happy occasion. From time to time, the festivities will resemble a "second" wedding reception, with vows renewed, family and friends on hand, champagne toasts. At the thirtieth or fiftieth, for instance, there could be a receiving line including adult children. Other years the couple might enjoy a romantic—and most private—candlelight dinner at a restaurant. In any event, a store's Wedding Gift Registry will often keep a list of gift preferences up to date to remind anniversary party guests (not to mention a forgetful husband or wife!) what the couple would still appreciate. The following is a list of anniversary gifts, both traditional and modern.

Traditional		Contemporary	
1st:	paper	1st:	clocks
2nd:	cotton	2nd:	china
3rd:	leather	3rd:	crystal, glass
4th:	linen	4th:	electrical appliances
5th:	wood	5th:	silverware
6th:	iron	6th:	wood
7th:	wool	7th:	desk sets
8th:	bronze	8th:	linens, lace
9th:	pottery	9th:	leather
10th:	tin, aluminum	10th:	diamond jewelry
11th:	steel	11th:	fashion jewelry, accessories
12th:	silk	12th:	pearls or colored gems
13th:	lace	13th:	textiles, furs
14th:	ivory	14th:	gold jewelry
15th:	crystal	15th:	watches
20th:	china	16th:	silver hollowware, sterling or plate
25th:	silver	17th:	furniture
30th:	pearls	18th:	porcelain
35th:	coral, jade	19th:	bronze
40th:	rubies	20th:	platinum
45th:	sapphires	25th:	sterling silver
50th:	gold	30th:	diamonds
55th:	emeralds	35th:	jade
60th:	diamonds	40th:	rubies
		45th:	sapphires
		50th:	gold
		55th:	emeralds
		60th:	diamonds

When giving anniversary presents, use your imagination. Paper on the first could mean anything from magazine subscriptions to stock certificates; silver on the twenty-fifth, a silver ice bucket or plane tickets west to the land of the silver screen. Feel free to interpret the traditional suggestions in a contemporary way as well. Luggage on the third anniversary could easily be vinyl; candlesticks on the fifteenth, glass that's crystal-clear. What if the husband wants a clock on the first anniversary to keep time through the coming years, and the wife a diamond to add to her ring? The most-wanted gift is always the best gift.

Whether for wedding or anniversary, gifts make memories. Through the years, you will look at them, touch them again and again. And each will remind you that there always have been people around you who want all that is good for you and for your marriage.

18
Wedding Guests

Wedding guests gather to witness the wedding ceremony and to wish the bride and groom well at the reception. Of course, nowadays, there are many styles of weddings. Depending on what the couple choose, a guest might receive an invitation to a very formal service and seated dinner at eight or a surfside ceremony at dawn. Each wedding style suggests an appropriate response, gift, and dress—a way, if you will, of letting the couple know you are prepared to share their happiness.

RECEIVING A WEDDING INVITATION

A formal, traditional invitation to a wedding ceremony and reception must always be acknowledged promptly. Answering in writing is most courteous, as this helps the wedding hosts keep track of replies.

A reply to a formal invitation is written on plain white or cream-colored notepaper in blue, blue-black, or black ink. A formal acceptance reads:

Mr. and Mrs. Joel Kageyama
accept with pleasure
the invitation of
Mr. and Mrs. Ernest Carr Burke
for Saturday, the fourth of April
at half after four o'clock.

It is not necessary to repeat the name of the bride and groom, but including the date and time indicates that these have been correctly understood. Including the location is optional. Wording and spacing should duplicate that of the invitation.

A formal regret is usually worded:

>Mr. Jean-Jacques DeLille
>*regrets that he is unable to accept*
>*the kind invitation of*
>Mr. and Mrs. Ernest Carr Burke
>*for Saturday, the fourth of April.*

A regret does not repeat the time or the place, merely the date. No reason need be given but you may, if you like, enclose a separate personal note to explain why you cannot attend and to wish the bride and groom a life full of happiness.

An informal note is nice for a handwritten invitation, or one that is of a contemporary, personalized design. You can use your favorite stationery. For example:

>*Dear Stephanie,*
>   *Rick and I are delighted to be included among the guests at Rochelle's wedding on the fifteenth of June at Central Methodist Church. We are looking forward to both the ceremony and the reception.*
>
>   *Affectionately,*
>   *Becky*

An informal note of regret might read:

>*Dear Stephanie,*
>   *Charlotte and I regret that we will be away on the fifteenth of June as my younger sister will be graduating that day. If we hadn't already made plans, you know nothing could keep us from Shelly's wedding.*
>   *Please give Shelly and Norman our best wishes for their future happiness.*
>
>   *Fondly,*
>   *Gary*

If a response card is included with the invitation, use that for your reply. You may slip it into a separate note should you wish to add a more personal message.

If you accept an invitation and then find an unexpected complication (an illness, or out-of-country business trip) will keep you from attending, you are obligated to write, telephone, or telegraph your regrets to the hostess with an explanation.

When considering an invitation, you can assume that children and others who may be living with you are invited only if their names appear on the inside envelope. If the hosts address the invitation "Miss Marx," then they expect her alone to attend the wedding—not other members of the household. If your children are invited, take them only if you'll be able to keep a close watch over them during the ceremony and reception. Otherwise, arrange to leave them home. Single guests should not bring a special man or woman friend along unless specifically asked—remember, a reception is a wonderful occasion to meet new people.

WEDDINGS OUT OF TOWN

Is the wedding out of town? At the time you accept the invitation, you may request a map or other written directions to the wedding site from the bride's or groom's family, if they are not already included—more and more they are. There will be nothing more disappointing to you and to them than your missing the ceremony because you were driving along every highway and byway in the area searching for the church. It won't hurt, either, to double-check the instructions you receive with the police in that city, or your own road map.

Wedding hosts have certain responsibilities to their guests—and guests have certain responsibilities in return. The bride's family must recommend places to stay, and should block out reservations at hotels and motels nearby. You yourself, however, should confirm your reservations and pay for your accommodations. Your host will probably have some sight-seeing suggestions so that you can go off and do some things on your own—the families will appreciate being left free to deal with last-minute details. The family, or friends of theirs, usually give some sort of welcoming dinner for out-of-town travelers; or they may have planned a breakfast the day of the wedding. At a weekend wedding, there will be many gatherings, meals hosted by friends of the bride. Do keep track of those who entertained you and send them thank-you notes (small gifts).

RECEIVING A WEDDING ANNOUNCEMENT

A wedding announcement does not obligate you in any way; neither a gift nor a personal acknowledgment is necessary. When dear friends are involved, however, it is a thoughtful gesture to send a personal note of good wishes to the couple, and perhaps to their parents as well. Feel like giving a gift? Go ahead! (You might want to find out what the couple needs by checking to see if they are registered.)

SENDING A WEDDING GIFT

Always plan on sending a gift when you accept a reception invitation. In the rare event you are invited to a wedding ceremony alone (if, for example, an illness in the couple's immediate families means a reception would be inappropriate, or if a group invitation has been extended to members of the church congregation), a gift is not required. Nor is it when a reception invitation has been declined. Attending the second wedding of the bride or the groom years after you went to the first? Traditionally no gift need be given, but a token of your happy feelings would certainly be appreciated. Of course, your gift choice this time will be somewhat different. Rather than flatware, give a serving piece, perhaps; or instead of a complete place setting of crystal, select two toasting glasses and a bottle of quality champagne. Knowing that they are combining homes, rather than creating one, think of items they would not buy themselves, or luxuries—outdoor patio furniture, a gift certificate to the video rental shop, a fabulous linen tablecloth to fit her dining table (and to match his china). If you cannot attend a reception but want to give a gift—feel free to do so.

A wedding gift should be sent to the bride at her home or at the R.S.V.P. address. If she's heading to another city for the wedding, find out when—so your gift can arrive before she leaves home. Have the gift mailed or sent directly from the store and enclose a gift card with a personal handwritten note. Gifts sent after the wedding are addressed to the bride and groom wherever they are living.

A wedding gift should be chosen with careful thought and an eye to practicality. Expense is not a criterion; a present selected with imagination and affection can please the couple most of all. If you are unfamiliar with their taste, it is best to play safe with a classic item that can be used in many ways—a Revere bowl, for example, can hold anything from mashed potatoes and mail to a bouquet of flowers. The easiest way to give the couple something they really need, of course, is to choose something from their list at the Wedding Gift Registry. Don't know the store? Telephone the bride's or groom's mother, maid or matron of honor, or the couple themselves. Though a gift may be sent up to a year after a wedding, most guests find it's best to shop near to the event, so as not to forget the occasion.

Money also makes a suitable, and always appreciated, wedding gift. Checks sent before the wedding are made out to the bride or the groom, and sent to that person's home; those given on wedding day or later, to the couple.

While packages are brought to the reception in many locales, seeing to it the gift gets to the appropriate home address beforehand is not only traditional but wise. That way, the couple can assure safe storage of the gift you've gone to the trouble and expense to provide, as well as make efficient arrangements to move it to where they'll be living.

After either sending your gift or delivering it in person, you can expect a thank-you note from the bride (or from the groom, nowadays). If, however, several months have passed since the wedding and there is still no acknowledgment, it is understandable that you would be concerned about the gift's safe arrival. You may phone to make certain the store from which you had the gift sent actually delivered it. Or have the post office trace your package—keep insurance receipts for items you mail. If the gift seems to have been lost or damaged, you may replace it, enclosing a note to the couple. But if all appears in order, it's up to you whether or not to ask them about the present. You may find it difficult to check without implying their manners are amiss. A casual remark made during conversation the next time you see them (or their parents, perhaps) is most likely to be received in the spirit it's given. "How's that warming tray working out?" may bring you exactly the reassurance you need—that the couple not only got it but already have used it at their first dinner party. Hopefully, this will be followed by an apology that they didn't get around to writing that thank-you note.

DRESSING FOR THE WEDDING

Wedding guests dress as they would for almost any other social event held at the same hour and season. Men usually wear suits; women, street-length outfits in any color except all-black or all-white (black is the custom for funerals, while white is the distinctive color of the bride on her wedding day). All this really means is that guests should not draw attention away from the bride and groom. A white linen suit, worn with a bronze-colored blouse, would be a striking, unbride-like ensemble for a female guest, as would a black dress with red stole or accessories.

Look at the invitation. It will not say "long dresses," but if the invitation is engraved, the wedding in the evening, and the reception a large one at a very sophisticated club, chances are formal attire would be appropriate. Traditionally, a bride who wanted her guests to appear in "black tie" had to let the word out to close friends and encourage them to spread it around, since this was not printed on invitations. Today, since parties are more informal, you may wish to print "black tie" on your invitation. An innovative wedding, perhaps one held in a meadow with a barbecue afterward, might specify "casual clothes," particularly if the reception will include an activity such as a baseball game or swimming. When in doubt, telephone the bride, her mother, the groom's mother, or anyone involved in the wedding preparations.

"Esther, what are you planning to wear to Wendy's wedding? I'm getting the whole family's outfits together, and we'll take our cues from you." Then help spread the word by telling any other guests what the family intends. The bride's mother may advise guests on whether pants outfits or bare-shoulder looks are appropriate for the church.

CHURCH WEDDING PROCEDURES

Guests without pew cards should arrive at the site of the ceremony thirty minutes before the appointed time, even earlier for a very large gathering, in order to have a choice of seats. People with reserved seats should arrive about twenty minutes before the ceremony begins. Guests arriving later than ten minutes before the ceremony should seat themselves quietly in the rear. If the ceremony is already under way, they should remain in the rear of the church until the wedding party reaches the altar, then seat themselves, unless an usher is stationed at the back to seat latecomers. One may not be "fashionably late" to a wedding. Travel arrangements should allow for inclement weather, traffic delays, finding an out-of-the-way church or synagogue. During the playing of the prelude guests have a chance to appreciate the beauty of the setting and reminisce about their soon-to-be-married friends.

When they arrive at the church, guests are met in the vestibule by an usher who generally asks whether they are friends of the bride or the groom. Seating on the right side of the altar is for the groom's relatives and friends, the left for the bride's, in Christian weddings. (The reverse is true for Jewish weddings.) A friend of both bride and groom says so and is seated in the best available spot. A woman guest takes the usher's right arm and is escorted down the aisle to her seat. Her male escort walks a few steps behind them. Sometimes the usher will simply lead the way, so a couple can walk together. He may let you know that both sides are sitting together—sit where he suggests. It is customary for guests and ushers to carry on polite conversation in low tones as they proceed down the aisle. Quiet talk with other guests is also permitted until the wedding procession begins.

It is not necessary for guests to carry out unfamiliar rituals, especially if their own faith would leave them uncomfortable doing so. However, it is polite to follow the lead of the families seated in the front pews. Generally guests of another faith are expected to stand when the families stand, but may remain seated rather than kneel. In Orthodox or Conservative Jewish congregations, all men and all married women cover their heads. It would be polite for a Christian man to accept the *yarmulke* (skullcap) distributed at the door for his use. Women should check with the bride's relatives to determine what's proper. The family will appreciate your concern about doing the right thing.

The bride and groom may request certain personalized rituals to be part of the ceremony—such as congregational hymn singing, exchanging hand clasps and a brief greeting with others seated nearby. Guests will want to participate and enter into the spirit of the occasion.

If you find such touches meaningful, by all means tell the couple and their parents later at the reception; otherwise, withhold comment at least until the wedding day is past.

After the recessional, guests remain in their seats until the ushers have escorted the families of the bride and groom, including the grandmothers and other close relatives, out of the church. Frequently the ushers will indicate the time to leave by returning to stand at the sides of the pews, signaling guests to file out row by row. Incidentally, should you need directions to the reception site, rest rooms, and so on, the ushers are the people to ask.

AT THE RECEPTION

All reception guests pass along the receiving line, greeting and shaking hands with everyone. A guest who doesn't know the bride's mother introduces herself so she can pass her name down the line: "Hello, Mrs. Atkins. I'm Indira Shakib, Glenda's old friend from music camp. I really did enjoy the violin solo." It's customary to make some remark about the wedding, the bride, or the newly married couple, depending on how well you know the persons involved. It was once traditional to congratulate the groom and to wish the bride happiness—since the groom "caught" the bride, but never the reverse. Today, however, equality is a watchword of most relationships, and both husband and wife will be happy to receive your congratulations.

Considerate guests move quickly down the line so that others are not kept waiting behind them. Women wearing gloves may keep them on in the receiving line.

Once past the line, guests sign the Bride's Book (guest book) and go directly to the area where refreshments are being served. (If the receiving line has been held in the church vestibule or on the church steps, this means the ushers will point the guests on to the reception site.) If the reception is to be a seated luncheon or dinner, guests should seek their reserved places, or choose a seat at one of the unreserved tables. At a tea or cocktail reception, guests may serve themselves and circulate, introducing themselves to one another whenever necessary. After the wedding party take their places at the bridal table, the traditional toasts are proposed. Every guest should drink every toast (but not necessarily finish the glass), whether his beverage preference is champagne, iced tea, or ginger ale. After the toasts, the meal is served or the bride and groom cut the cake. At a tea or cocktail reception, the festivities may begin long before the cake is cut. And at a very large reception, the father of the bride may see to it that dancing is well under way before the couple appear on the scene for their traditional dance with each other and with their parents.

Wedding receptions have no specified length, although three hours is average. Guests usually remain as long as the bride and groom remain. After they have made their going-away dash through a shower of rice or rose petals, guests find a member of the bride's immediate family, if possible, and say something like, "Thanks for a really enjoyable evening, Mrs. Atkins. It was a beautiful wedding; I'm sure you must be proud of Glenda." The host and hostess are inundated with farewells? Phone or write the next day: "I had a wonderful time!" Guests may linger until the bride's parents signal the end of the party by ending the music, closing the bar, or preparing to leave themselves.

19
Going Away

The reception should be great fun—and you and your groom can stay as long as you wish the party to go on. Being the guests of honor, you are traditionally the first to leave, and people may take their cues from you. If your reception time is fixed—you have the Royal Arms Blue Room for two hours— you will need to keep festivities on schedule. Your departure will be the signal that the party's over. There is no reason, of course, that your family and friends cannot continue to dance, dine, and drink if your parents (or other wedding hosts) are on hand and eager for them to do so. In this case, making your departure while the festivities are in full swing may give you that elated feeling that comes from knowing things are going even better than you hoped. Staying till the end? Make sure guests feel free to go. If you've planned to stay all along, place a program of events on each table. Or, announce (in the form of a thank- you toast) just before you cut the cake that you're having so much fun with all your terrific friends, you've decided to stay. Some guests will then feel free to leave after the cake-cutting ceremonies; others will stay as long as the partying goes on—and that can be until dawn if you choose.

SAYING GOOD-BYE

When you are ready to leave, simply pass the word on to your bridesmaids and other single friends to prepare to catch your bouquet; and, if you wish, alert single groomsmen and male guests that the garter will be tossed. Once the laughter and excitement have died down, you and your groom can slip away to change into your going-away clothes.

Your honor attendant goes with you to help, and the best man accompanies the groom. Both of you should make sure your going-away outfits are comfortable and suitable to your method of transportation. Will you be taking a cross-country trip in your car? Good-looking pants and tops for you both, with a sweater or jacket in case it gets cool, make sense. If you'll be off on a cruise, a sporty dress is appropriate; a blazer and trousers may be best for your groom. But, if your destination is a rugged mountain campsite, do not leave in your blue jeans and backpacks. Better to depart in stylish outfits (surely you'll use them when you return, perhaps for an evening or two at a fine restaurant) that keep the mood of your glamorous wedding. Also consider where you'll be staying that first night. You may want to arrive in a wrinkle-free suit and heels at a city hotel; at a small-town inn, in separates. The classic accessory for a woman on this special occasion is a flower corsage to complement her outfit. A casual look might call for flowers in the hair. Sometimes these flowers will be part of the bride's bouquet, and detached from it before it is tossed to the single women.

When you are both dressed, your honor attendant should notify your parents so they can come to say good-bye in private. This is apt to be a sensitive time for all of you. Let your parents know how much you appreciate everything they've done: "Mom, everyone was saying how good the food was; thanks for your help with the menu. Dad, I'm glad you thought to get insurance for all those presents; you've always looked out for me so well." When your groom has finished bidding his own parents good-bye, he will come for you and thank your parents. Your honor attendants, incidentally, can see to it that your wedding clothes are returned to wherever you wish after the reception's over.

You may be tempted to leave the reception quietly through the back door, but your guests will never forgive you if you try to sneak away. Supplies of rice, or birdseed, will be handed around to the guests while you are changing (these are preferable to paper confetti and flower petals, which are hard to clean up and easy to slip on). Young friends or brothers and sisters will love carrying out this assignment.

Most couples hold hands and run under that shower of good wishes from their friends as they dash to their getaway car. The best man will have taken care of putting the luggage in the car and keeping practical jokers away—it is his responsibility, too, to see that any decorations that might block the driver's vision or hamper hearing are removed. (Even so, it wouldn't hurt to give your own luggage a quick check before you leave town, just to be sure no prankster has emptied it.)

Newlyweds with a penchant for dramatic finales may choose a hot-air balloon, helicopter, horse and buggy, bicycle, motor launch, or even a saddled horse to leave the reception for that great adventure ahead—married life.

YOUR TRAVEL PLANS

It may seem ages ago that you poured over travel brochures. But, if you were thorough with your plans, your trip should be fun and worry-free. A travel agent will help you focus on small details and keep important things in perspective. Do be clear about your preferences, with each other and with the travel agent. What kinds of activities do you like? How much privacy do you want? How much do you want to spend? How much social life do you expect? Do you really want rest and relaxation? Your travel agent will be able to help with weather probabilities and tips on what to pack.

Some couples today favor active honeymoons—tennis, scuba diving, skiing, hiking, sailing. Others just want to be together, quietly getting to know one another. A wise pair does not attempt too much or take on a grueling schedule, for wedding festivities have a way of depleting your energy. A heavy sight-seeing tour might be more thrilling on your first anniversary; an island hideaway with private beach, just the ticket now. Do things, go places, that each of you enjoys.

As a precaution, have your travel agent reconfirm all reservations (travel, hotel, car rental), or do it yourself two weeks before the wedding, and be sure to mention any specifics: "Would you be sure to note that we want a double bed?"

TIPPING

Decisions about tipping can often be embarrassing and confusing. The following tipping guide is very general; factors such as quality of service and the economy of the country you visit should be considered.

HONEYMOON TIPPING

Whom to Tip	How Much to Tip	When to Tip
Airport—Porter	50¢ per bag	Delivery of luggage to check-in or curb
Ship—Cabin/Dining Room Stewards	$2.50–$3.00 per day per passenger (more for first-class passengers)	End of voyage
Bar & Lounge Stewards	15–20% of bill	With each bill
Porters	$5	When luggage is delivered
Train—Redcap	25¢ per bag for short distance	When service is performed
Sleeping Car Attendant	$1 per person per night	Each night
Dining Car Waiters	15–20% of bill	Each meal
Hotel—Bellboy	50¢ per bag, plus 50¢ for hospitable gestures—opening windows, turning on lights	When service is delivered
Chambermaid	25–50¢ for each service, minimum $2 per person per week	Each time service is delivered (a new maid may be assigned)
Doorman	50¢ per bag, 25¢ for hailing taxi	When service is delivered
Headwaiter	$5 per week for special service, $2–$3 for regular service	Upon first visit
Waiter	15–20% of bill when no service charge; 5% of bill with service fee	Each meal
Room Service Waiter	15–20% of bill in addition to room service charge	Each meal
Taxi Driver	15–20% for good service	Completion of ride
Instructors—Water Skiing, Horseback Riding, etc.	15–20% of bill (unless they own the business)	End of lesson
Golf Caddie	30% over the caddie fee with good service	End of 18th hole
Bus Tour Guide	75¢ per person per half day	End of ride

THE FIRST NIGHT

Chances are you won't be heading for your honeymoon spot until the day after your wedding. Where to spend the night should be a matter of convenience and comfort. A couple who've already set up housekeeping, hosted the reception in their own apartment, might simply say good-night to their guests and stay right where they are. Or you might choose a gracious hotel or cozy country inn. What to avoid: driving long distances when you're tired or feeling the effects of your celebration.

EN ROUTE

Many young marrieds are already seasoned travelers, but there can be surprises. When traveling by plane, allow plenty of time at the airport before your flight to check luggage, recheck seat assignments. When you make reservations, inquire about advance seat assignments (you'd hate to find yourselves sitting three rows apart), and now's the time too to ask for vegetarian, salt-free, or kosher meals. It may be possible to arrange for champagne on board—to get your honeymoon off to a sparkling start. Should your flight be delayed or canceled, resulting in problems with connections, or should your luggage go astray (pack all essentials such as passports, birth control pills, traveler's checks, prescriptions in a carry-on bag just in case), ask to see a special service representative and expect that they will rectify the situation by arranging lodging, a new flight, and money for replacement clothes. Tip skycaps for each bag they carry.

On overnight train trips, tip the porter every night for making up your berth and for giving you a wake-up call in the morning. There are also a few conventions to observe on board a commercial ship. Except for captains and doctors with professional titles, all personnel are addressed as "Mr." (or "Miss," "Mrs.," "Ms."). Finding out as soon as possible where you will be seated for dinner is customary as well. You may request table changes, but if you do, make it within two days after arrival and tip the steward for this service.

If you've traveled together before, you may already know each other's idiosyncrasies: you hate to shop for souvenirs; he thinks you bring too much luggage; he always cuts it too close to departure time; you panic if you're not half an hour early. Do make some compromises ahead of time, so this can be an enjoyable, loving time.

AT YOUR DESTINATION

At your hotel, your groom may sign the register for you both, although many hotels nowadays ask for the first names of the husband and the wife ("Mrs. Shirley Moore and Mr. Russell Moore"). Don't be afraid to say you're newlyweds!

You may be surprised with complimentary flowers, fruit, or champagne. The bellman should, of course, be tipped for carrying suitcases to your room. Any problems with the room should be directed to the assistant manager or manager at the desk. If you do not wish to be disturbed, it is essential that you hang the DO NOT DISTURB sign on the doorknob; otherwise, the staff may knock or even walk in earlier than you'd like. During your stay, leave a tip each day for the person who straightens up—perhaps on the pillow. Because staff assignments may rotate daily, waiting until the end of your visit to tip in a lump sum means the appropriate people may not be remembered (However, if service is included, extra tipping is not necessary until the end of your stay.) A call ahead to the desk will assure that your bill is ready when you check out.

In foreign countries, mastering the native words for "please" and "thank you" can help with service. Any tips you give should always be in the local currency; restaurants, of course, may include the gratuities in the bill. Be sure to ask. The passport you applied for before your wedding will have been issued in your maiden name. Taking a copy of your marriage certificate on your travels may, in this case, be wise. Mention this need to your clergymember in case you need to arrange to photocopy the original right after the ceremony. With evidence, you can visit the local American embassy and have your passport adjusted to indicate your new marital status, if necessary.

As soon as you reach your destination, it's nice to phone or telegram your groom's parents and your own to let them know you arrived safely and to thank them again for the wedding. Many couples also enjoy shopping for souvenirs to bring the people "back home." A special gift for those at work who lived through the trials and tribulations of planning—"I can't believe the caterer just called and said he couldn't get pink tablecloths!" "My maids still won't agree on a dress."—is sure to be appreciated.

Work out a budget for honeymoon spending, but remember to allow at least 10 percent for the unexpected—the dress that needs dry cleaning, the muffler repair, the trip to the doctor for an allergy shot. It's easy to get carried away with luxurious extras and souvenir spending, so make a list of intended purchases.

Now, and in the future, you won't always want to do the same things at the same time. There's nothing wrong with feeling that way on your honeymoon, and acting accordingly. Besides, his all-day diving trip, your tour of the ruins, will make fun dinner talk when you get together in the evening.

You may buy straw hats, jewelry, leather gloves, but your favorite memento will be the photographs you take on your trip. Remember to take turns behind the lens and occasionally ask someone to snap you both. Your pictures—eating that romantic breakfast on the patio, trying to close the bulging suitcase, climbing aboard the kite glider—will record this special first chapter of your married life. Take along lots of film.

YOUR HOME TOGETHER

When does the groom carry the bride over the threshold? After the honeymoon, at the apartment or house where they will make their home. This is one of the few very private traditions surrounding marriage, and a moment not to be missed.

Jewish parents, or close friends of the married couple, may observe the tradition of the "threshold gift." Candles, bread, and salt are brought to the new home to express the wish that there may always be light, joy, and plenty to eat in the home.

Let both sets of parents know that you're back, then plan an evening to have them over to hear more about your trip. Next, begin entertaining all the people whose help made your wedding so wonderful. Whether a large "at-home" reception, a wedding party reunion for bridesmaids and groomsmen, or a "screening" to show off your photos, snapshots, or videotapes—make this a genuine expression of your gratitude. Plan ahead to bring back some duty-free Caribbean rum— to recreate those luscious piña coladas—or incomparable French chocolates, to share a bit of your honeymoon magic.

When you begin summing up your memories, you'll both realize that your own wedding has a special beauty and meaning for you no other ceremony will ever match. Whether it's a simple family service or an elaborate celebration before hundreds, your wedding will always have a place in your heart. It is, after all, the beginning of your married life together.

20
Reaffirmation

Reaffirmation of wedding vows is a new tradition, which began among several religious groups over the last ten years. This popular ceremony gives every married couple, young and old, the chance to pledge their lasting commitment to each other all over again. The reaffirmation, while solemn, is not a legal act, so this time you won't need a license or certificate! At some point in your marriage, you may wish to demonstrate your lasting love in this way—on an anniversary, at the birth of a child, at a point when you can afford the "wedding of your dreams."

PLANNING A REAFFIRMATION

The many reasons couples decide to reaffirm their marriage vows will influence the style they choose for this service. Religious differences, pregnancy, a problem divorce from the past may steer one couple to a city hall ceremony or elopement. Now, days, months, or even years later, wanting the church's blessing on their earlier civil marriage, they find the church more accepting, even eager to create a private chapel service, or include their reaffirmation in a Sunday church or Friday evening synagogue service. Friends and family will attend this time.

To another couple, the reaffirmation ceremony is a way to mark a milestone in the relationship. On their fifteenth anniversary, they are overjoyed to announce that they still want to be married to the person their spouse has become. This couple might plan a trip to the ski lodge where they first met, taking along their children and any other families with whom they share happy times. In this setting, they'll repeat the vows that first united them.

A reaffirmation, or "Service of Blessing," as it is sometimes known, can take place any time after a civil wedding. Held very soon after, it would appear to be the wedding itself, except that the clergymember would omit "I now pronounce . . ." in favor of "I now announce that you are husband and wife."

Husbands and wives who have been married quite a while might choose to reaffirm their wedding vows on the occasion of a wedding anniversary. The couple can repeat the same vows they spoke so long ago, or write new ones that express the way their feelings for one another have grown. The service might resemble a wedding before a congregation in church, with the children included this time. Or, the clergy can visit the couple's home for a private ceremony. Afterward, a gala party is certainly in order.

For those who see renewal of their vows as a religious commitment, a clergymember is the right officiant. A judge appeals to those who want someone who represents the community to give sanction to their vows. But any authority figure may officiate at a reaffirmation, since unlike the actual wedding, this is not a legal function. At the family reunion, the patriarch of the clan might preside. A military commander would fill the role for a couple in the service; for a faculty pair, the college president.

The possibilities for reaffirmation vows are as endless as for the wedding itself. You'll want to make the celebration of your marriage special—ingenuity and a little more advance planning than usual will ensure that it's a smooth-running experience for all—especially for the two of you!

ANNOUNCEMENTS

Call the society editor of your newspaper to ask if your reaffirmation information should be submitted on their standard wedding announcement forms. They may ask you to write it up as a press release, telling why you decided to have a reaffirmation and how you planned it. If reaffirmations are uncommon in your area, the newspaper may just report yours as a feature story.

A reaffirmation announcement would include the same basic details as a wedding announcement (see Chapter 5). But, additional data should be included—number of years you've been married, names of your children, and that it is a reaffirmation of marriage vows. You might choose to include the text of your vows as well.

REAFFIRMATION SITE

If you had a church wedding the first time, you may want to go back and repeat the performance, complete with organist, attendants, clergymember; that is, if you can locate everyone. But a new site may be chosen. How about something practical (where you live now), scenic (a Spanish mission), sentimental (the chapel you visited on your honeymoon), or famous (a big city cathedral)?

Your own home can be the perfect setting. There, surrounded by happy memories and a sense of well being, you'll celebrate the achievement of being successful at marriage. And, if there's not enough room at your house, see if neighbors will pitch in by opening up their living room or yard to the overflow crowd.

Then there are romantic choices. You may want your reaffirmation in that art gallery where you first met. Or any place where you two enjoy a shared interest, such as the community theater. Picture a set from *Plaza Suite* to complement a dramatic reaffirmation. Later, friends might perform a memorable scene from the play. If your closest friends are at your vacation town, you may want to hold your ceremony there. A natural setting—the beach at sunset or a mountaintop campsite with friends gathered around—will renew your spirits and your vows.

PREPARATION FOR REAFFIRMATION

Most couples find reaffirmation a moving experience, one they want sanctified by a church or synagogue. Visit with your clergymember to discuss your feelings about the service, ideas for vows, music, readings. You'll learn about existing services and guidelines for writing your own. Reaffirmations are an annual event in some churches and synagogues, with couples coming together to rededicate themselves to their marriages. You might decide to participate in a group reaffirmation.

Worldwide Marriage Encounter, Inc. is a group dedicated to keeping married love alive. Whether you are just about to marry, or planning your reaffirmation, you may find that a marriage encounter helps strengthen and renew your relationship. Marriage Encounter holds weekend retreats away from home for married couples (there is also Engaged Encounter, Inc.). For two days, husbands and wives learn to share the intimate, nitty-gritty feelings they may find hard to talk about back home—everything from how much money to invest in savings to how often to make love. At the end of every weekend, all couples are invited to renew their marriage vows. For many, these weekends spark a desire for public reaffirmation. There are a number of groups with enrichment programs for couples, many of them with religious leadership. (See the Appendix for the names of a few.)

INVITATIONS

Your guest list will include some of your oldest friends and many new ones. To compile your list, read over the names in your wedding guest book. Remember, your friend Ellen was having a baby that day—maybe this time she'll make it! Check your Christmas card list and address book for other names. An invitation to a mutual friend could include a handwritten note: "I'd love to send an invitation to Gene and Judy Shaw—do you have their address?" If your children ask to invite a few of their friends to this family celebration, say yes—gladly. It shows they're proud too.

Use personal handwritten notes to invite guests if your reaffirmation is small;

cheery, colorful invitations if it's festive; printed or engraved cards if the mood is formal. Feel free to personalize your invitations with a wedding photo or your thoughts on renewing your vows.

The usual wording for reaffirmation invitations is as follows:

The honour of your presence
is requested at the reaffirmation
of the wedding vows of
Mr. and Mrs. John David Smith
Saturday, the eighth of March
at three o'clock
All Saints Church
New York, New York

A simplified reception card would read:

Reception
immediately following the ceremony
The Plaza Hotel
Fifth Avenue at 59th Street
Kindly respond
860 Park Avenue
New York, New York 10021

The wording for an invitation issued by children of the couple:

The family of
Daniel and Sarah Patterson
request the honour of your presence
at their reaffirmation ceremony
Saturday, the twentieth of June
nineteen hundred and eighty-five
at six o'clock in the evening
Bethany Memorial Church
201 Main Street
Bethany, West Virginia

R.S.V.P.
Ms. Jan Patterson
21 Highland Avenue
Wheeling, West Virginia 26003

REAFFIRMATION ATTIRE

If you are repeating the same vows, returning to your original wedding site, you may want to wear your wedding gown. Doesn't quite fit? This might be good motivation to diet, or have a dressmaker do some alterations. Then update it with well-chosen accessories. If you will be buying a new dress, you can choose a bridal gown, a stylish cocktail dress, or a formal evening dress. The woman who eloped may want a chance to wear a long white bridal gown; the one who had a church wedding may seek something practical, a sleek sheath or a shapely dress with tiered skirt of ruffles that she can wear again. Your reaffirmation dress may be floor-length, ballet-length, or skim the knee . . . and be white (but pale peach, ecru, or dusty rose are also very pretty).

The headpiece should be simple. Consider a charming beret, demure pillbox, or perhaps a floral wreath or combs with tiny blossoms. A wedding veil is not worn as it signifies virginity.

The rich colors and fragrance of flowers are a marvelous addition to your ceremony attire. For an island reaffirmation, wear colorful leis; for a garden ceremony, carry an armful of bright field flowers.

Complement your reaffirmation dress with the pearls he gave you on your wedding day; the diamond eternity ring he presented you on your anniversary; and, of course, your wedding ring, which will be blessed again if yours is a religious service.

Your husband would wear a tuxedo or a dark suit with a new tie. He, too, might wear the gifts of jewelry you've given him during your marriage. And, of course, he'll sport a boutonniere.

If those who stood with you for your wedding are able to reassemble, they should wear dress clothes of their own, the women in dresses of similar length and style. It's unlikely that they would still own their bridesmaid dresses, much less all fit into them. The men would follow your husband's lead.

Your own children will share the joy of this celebration with you. They may be your attendants this time, or play other roles in the service. Let them wear their best outfits, or buy each one something new. It is not necessary to have them wear matching clothes.

VOWS

Vows are the focal point of the recommitment you are making. One way to make sure your vows express exactly what you and your spouse feel is to write them yourselves. For example, you might make pledges relating to patience, a sense of humor, the ability to communicate: "I promise you, the man I have loved so long, to be more open about my feelings, to share equally with you the care for our children, Denise and Samuel, to respect your personal needs and beliefs, and understand that marriage for us means working toward an ever richer companionship."

Sitting down to write out vows makes you address long-buried issues between you, which can only make your relationship healthier. You might also want to thank family and friends for what they've contributed to your relationship, or make references to hardships you've come through.

If you want to, repeat the same traditional vows ("I, Mary, take you, John . . .") but have the clergymember insert "renewing their promise in the presence of God" into the service. Or look into the revised marriage services many faiths now offer. The Book of Common Prayer, for instance, asks guests to promise "to uphold these two persons in their marriage."

RINGS

During the ceremony, your clergymember will ask for your rings—your original wedding rings, or new ones that you will wear in the future. These will be blessed just as they were the first time. You will again present them to each other with a pledge of love.

For example: "We have lived and loved as we promised long ago in the presence of God, and our past and future are a circle unbroken . . . like the ring, with which I renew my pledge to you of never-ending devotion." Why not ask the clergymember to bless also the gifts you will be giving the children to remember this day—a gold charm, locket, birthstone ring.

RECEPTION

Your reaffirmation will really be something to celebrate—and what better way than with a reception. Your party can be anything you want, from a candlelit dinner for just family to a cocktail party for just about everyone you know. The party can be catered at your home, or held in a banquet hall, restaurant, hotel with a band to entertain. Don't overlook church or synagogue halls. A reaffirmation reception could feature finger foods and drinks, a hearty buffet, or a sit-down dinner. Do include some classic touches such as champagne and a festive cake. Still have your cake topper? Use it again!

This time, the two of you are the hosts and will be making the arrangements yourselves. Friends, relatives, children will all be willing to help. It may be a more carefree celebration, though, if you rely on wedding professionals such as a caterer, baker, or wedding consultant. As host and hostess, you'll spend time with each guest and oversee all the hospitality details. Socializing with good friends will be the most delightful part of the party. For a larger party, have a receiving line so you're sure to greet everyone.

Your reception can have some wedding reception traditions—cake cutting, first dance, toasts. Others—throwing the bouquet, for instance—do not seem as appropriate. Instead, choose another way to pass on your "good fortune" to your guests—give rooted sprigs of forget-me-nots (true love), ivy or veronica (fidelity) to each one to take home and plant.

Your party site can be decorated with floral arrangements, nostalgia items, blown-up pictures of your wedding. You'll want memories of this day also, so hire a professional photographer or videotape company to record all the happy moments. Everyone would have fun leafing through your original guest book; and, don't forget to provide another for guests to write new messages, good wishes, humorous recollections.

GIFTS

Gifts should not be expected for a reaffirmation, but some guests will want to bring them to mark the happy occasion. (You might list items with your department store's Wedding Gift Registry.) Or, to stress that this is a celebration of love, they could offer a gift of love: Suggest (by word of mouth, not in writing) that in place of gifts, friends make a donation to charity in your name.

Give your guests something by which to remember your reaffirmation, such as a picture of your family, a recording of "your song," a scroll with an inspirational passage that has shaped your marriage. If your ceremony was recorded, cassette copies can be made quickly and inexpensively. Your children and other family members will also appreciate having such a memento.

A SECOND HONEYMOON

By all means, take a trip, either now or in the near future. All of your preparations, and the excitement of the occasion itself, will rekindle romance. And romance is good for marriage! This may be when you take that trip you've dreamed of—back to visit the ancestral sod in Ireland; or, it may just be a chance to splurge for a weekend at an elegant resort. Give yourselves a little private time and space to reflect on all the joy you've rediscovered.

Appendix

1 Your Engagement

American Association for Marriage and Family Therapy
    924 West Ninth
    Upland, CA 91786
    (201) 429-1825
Diamond Information Center (information about carats, appraisals, choosing)
    1345 Sixth Avenue, 36th Floor
    New York, NY 10105
    (212) 708-5000
Engaged Encounter
    Dan and Lilly Gioia (national team)
    123 North Richmond Avenue
    North Massapequa, NY 11758
Interpersonal Communication Programs
    1925 Nicollet Avenue
    Suite 102
    Minneapolis, MN 55403
    (612) 871-7388

2 Wedding Customs

American Folklore Society
    c/o American Anthropological Association
    1703 New Hampshire Avenue N.W.
    Washington, D.C. 20009
    (202) 232-8800
The Bride—A Celebration, by Barbara Tober. New York: Harry N. Abrams, 1984. A look
    at the bride through history.

The Celebration Book of Great American Traditions, by Wicke Chambers and Spring Asher. New York: Harper & Row, 1983.

3   Pre-Wedding Parties

BRIDE'S Lifetime Guide to Good Food & Entertainment. New York: Congdon & Weed, 1984.

Entertaining, by Martha Stewart. New York: Clarkson N. Potter, 1982.

Wedding Shower Fun, by Sharon E. Dlugosch and Florence E. Nelson with SHOWER-WISE. Available in gift shops and from the publisher: Brighton Publications, P. O. Box 12706, New Brighton, MN 55112.

4   Planning Your Wedding

American Association of Professional Bridal Consultants
    29 Ferris Estates
    New Milford, CT 06776
    (203) 355-0464

"Booklet for Women Who Wish to Determine Their Own Names After Marriage." Published by the Center for a Woman's Own Name, 1983.

BRIDE'S Wedding Planner, by the Editors of BRIDE'S. New York: Fawcett Columbine, 1980.

EveryWoman's Legal Guide: Protecting Your Rights at Home, in the Workplace, in the Marketplace, by Barbara A. Burnett, Esq., consulting editor. Garden City: Doubleday & Co., 1983.

The Liturgical Press (catalogue of posters, banners, wedding bulletins)
    Saint John's Abbey
    Collegeville, MN 56321
    (612) 363-2213

March of Dimes (Birth Defects Foundation)
    Box 1275
    White Plains, NY 10605
    (914) 428-7100

The Marriage Contract: Spouses, Lovers & the Law, by Lenore J. Weitzman. New York: Free Press, 1981.

Planned Parenthood (Federation of America, Inc.)
    810 Seventh Avenue
    New York, NY 10019
    (212) 541-7800

SIECUS (Sex Information and Education Council of the United States)
    84 Fifth Avenue
    New York, NY 10011
    (212) 929-2300

5   Your Invitations and Announcements

C. R. Gibson Company (wedding invitations, thank-you notepaper, other stationery
   needs, gift items)
   32 Knight Street
   Norwalk, CT 06856
   (203) 847-4543
   (For a nominal fee, Gibson will send you "The Bride's Planner," a purse-sized
   organizer.)
Rexcraft (free color catalogue of invitations)
   Rexburg, ID 83441
   (800) 635-4653
Society of Scribes (Calligraphy Association)
   P. O. Box 933
   New York, NY 10150

7   Guide to Wedding Clothes

American Formalwear Association
   240 Madison Avenue
   New York, NY 10016
   (Send self-addressed, stamped envelope to receive their pamphlet, "Your Formalwear Guide.")
International Fabricare Institute
   12251 Tech Road
   Silver Spring, MD 20904
   (301) 622-1900
   Your member (IFI) dry cleaner can contact this organization for special wedding-
   gown care problems or for help with restoring an antique wedding gown.

8   Your Wedding Ceremony

The New Wedding: Creating Your Own Marriage Ceremony, by Khoran Arisian. New York:
   Vintage Books, 1973.
Two Shall Become One (Ceremony, Music, and Program Kit), available from:
   Today's Bride, Inc.
   1010 Nicollet Mall
   Minneapolis, MN 55403
Ways To Say "I Do," available from:
   Plumrose Publishing
   P. O. Box 30504
   Phoenix, AZ 85046

Words for Your Wedding, available from:
    Peggy Libby, Heron Books
    86 Winthrop Street
    Box 2439
    Augusta, ME 04330
Write Your Own Wedding, by Mordecai L. Brill, Marlene Halpin and William H. Genne.
    Chicago: Follett Publishing Co., revised edition 1979.

9 Religious Rituals

Cross-Currents: Children, Families & Religion, by Evelyn Kaye. New York: Clarkson N.
    Potter, 1980. Discusses the implications of an interfaith marriage.
Helen Latner's Book of Jewish Etiquette, by Helen Latner. New York: Schocken Books,
    1981.
*Jewish Wedding Book: A Practical Guide to the Traditions and Social Customs of the Jewish
    Wedding,* by Lilly S. Routtenberg and Ruth R. Seldin. New York: Schocken Books,
    1969.
*The Love Covenant: Preparation for Your Wedding Ceremony or Your Anniversary Celebra-
    tion,* by the Daughters of St. Paul. Boston, Mass: St. Paul Editions, 1983.
Mixing: Catholic-Protestant Marriages in the 1980's: A Guidebook for Couples and Families,
    by Barbara D. Schiappa. New York: Paulist Press, 1982.
Mixed Marriage Between Jew and Christian, by Rabbi Samuel M. Silver. New York: Arco
    Publishing Co., 1977.
Together For Life, by Joseph M. Champlin. Notre Dame, Indiana: Ave Maria Press, 1984.
    There is a regular edition for the wedding within the Roman Catholic Mass and a
    special edition for marriage outside Mass.

10 Special Weddings

Places: A Directory of Public Places for Private Events & Private Places for Public Functions,
    by Hannelore Hahn and Tatiana Stoumen.
Available from: Tenth House Enterprises, Inc.
    Box No. 810
    Gracie Station
    New York, NY 10028
    (212) 737-7536

11 Remarriage

Instant Parent: A Guide for Stepparents, Part-time Parents and Grandparents, by Suzy Kalter.
    New York: A & W Publishers, Inc., 1979.
Making It As a Stepparent: New Roles, New Rules, by Claire Berman. Garden City:
    Doubleday & Co., 1980.

Remarriage, G & R Publications, Inc.
   648 Beacon Street
   Boston, MA 02215
   (617) 267-1513
The Stepfamily: Living, Loving, & Learning, by Elizabeth Einstein. New York: Macmillan
   Publishing Co., 1982.
The Stepfamily Foundation
   333 West End Avenue
   New York, NY 10023
   (212) 877-3244

13   Your Reception

American Rental Association (publishes 16-page "Party Rental Guide")
   1900 19th Street
   Moline, IL 61265
   (309) 764-2475
Cake Decorating for Any Occasion, by Cile Bellefleur Burbidge. Radnor, PA: Chilton
   Book Co., 1978.
Home Weddings and Receptions, by Belle Barstow. Available from the author at 27 Ben-
   nett Lane, Stony Brook, NY 11790.
Wedding Cakes (pictures of cakes that can be duplicated by your own baker)
   Cal-Mex Supply Company
   279 Third Avenue
   Chula Vista, CA 92010
Wilton Book of Wedding Cakes, ed. by Eugene T. Sullivan and Marilynn C. Sullivan.
   Woodridge, Illinois: Wilton Enterprises, 1971.

14   Wedding Music and Readings

American Society of Composers, Artists and Publishers (for information about songs,
   reprinting)
   One Lincoln Plaza
   New York, NY 10023
   (212) 595-3050
The Golden Book of Wedding Songs (this and other anthologies of wedding music may be
   available at your local music store)
   P. O. Box 35
   Oradell, NJ 07649
Music departments of your city library may have classical, ethnic, popular, and historical
   wedding music. If yours cannot help, try:
   The Carnegie Library of Pittsburgh
   4400 Forbes Avenue
   Pittsburgh, PA 15213
   (412) 622-3105

Nancy Cook's Music Programs (a booklet and newsletter full of ideas and examples)
Box 620
1330 New Hampshire Avenue NW
Washington, DC 20036

The New Complete Book of Wedding Music. East End Music & Arts Library, Charles Hansen Music and Books, Inc.
1860 Broadway
New York, NY 10023

Union of American Hebrew Congregations (Reform) (have published specially commissioned music for weddings)
838 Fifth Avenue
New York, NY 10021
(212) 249-0100

15 Your Wedding Flowers

The Illuminated Language of Flowers, text by Jean Marsh, illustrations by Kate Greenaway. New York: Holt, Rinehart & Winston, 1978.

Simon and Schuster's Complete Guide to Plants and Flowers. New York: Simon and Schuster, 1974.

Teleflora (a pamphlet, "Your Teleflora Wedding Album," is available by mail; or stop in your local Teleflora florist and ask to see *Wedding Album*, a florist's guidebook available for ideas at most Teleflora shops)
12233 West Olympic Boulevard
Los Angeles, CA 90064
(213) 826-5253

16 Your Photographs and Publicity

Association of Independent Video Filmmakers
625 Broadway
New York, NY 10012
(212) 473-3400

Professional Photographers of America, Inc. (Wedding Photography Planning Kit available; includes a directory of member photographers)
1090 Executive Way
Des Plaines, IL 60018
(312) 299-8161

Videography. For information and national referrals contact:
Mr. Paul D. Kennamer, Sr.
P. O. Box 1933
Huntsville, AL 35807
(205) 882-9155

Wedding Photographers, International
    P. O. Box 2003
    Santa Monica, CA 90406
    (213) 451-0090

17 Wedding Gifts

The Complete Guide to Buying Gems: How to Buy Diamonds and Colored Gemstones with Confidence and Knowledge, by Antoinette L. Matlins and Antonio C. Bonanno. New York: Crown Publishers, 1983.

Consumer's Resource Handbook (for handling problems, inquiries regarding gifts or purchases; single copies free)
    United States Office of Consumer Affairs
    Consumer Information Center
    Pueblo, CO 81009

Gold Information Center (cleaning your gemstones, jewelry to buy for bridal gifts, appraisals, values of gold)
    900 Third Avenue, 26th Floor
    New York, NY 10022
    (212) 688-0474

The Greatest Gift Guide . . . Ever, by Judith King. White Hall, VA: Betterway Publications, Inc., 1982. Distributed by The Berkshire Traveller Press, Stockbridge, MA.

Insurance Information Institute (gift insurance)
    110 William Street
    New York, NY 10038
    (212) 233-7650

Jewelers of America
    Consumer Information
    Department B
    1271 Avenue of the Americas
    New York, NY 10020
    (212) 489-0023

Jewelry Industry Council
    608 Fifth Avenue, Room 902
    New York, NY 10020
    (212) 757-3075

National Housewares Manufacturers Association
    1130 Merchandise Mart
    Chicago, IL 60654
    (312) 644-3333

Say Thank You With Style. Available from Lark Publishing, Box 503, Capitola, CA 95010.

Sterling Silversmiths Guild of America (pamphlet on "The 20 Most Asked Questions About Sterling")
    1111 East Putnam Avenue
    Riverside, CT 06878

Write Thank You the Easy Way. Available from The Pen's Pal, Box 125, Hewlett, NY 11557.

18 Wedding Guests

Charlotte Ford's Book of Modern Manners, by Charlotte Ford. New York: Simon and Schuster, 1980.

Miss Manners' Guide to Excruciatingly Correct Behavior, by Judith Martin. New York: Atheneum, 1982.

The Amy Vanderbilt Complete Book of Etiquette, by Letitia Baldridge. New York: Doubleday, 1978.

19 Going Away

Adventure Travel, by Pat Dickerman (Adventure Guides, Inc., New York, NY). New York: T. Y. Crowell, 1978.

American Society of Travel Agents
71 Fifth Avenue
New York, NY 10022
(212) 308-7942

Amtrak (National Railroad Passenger Corporation)
400 N. Capitol Street, NW
Washington, DC 20001
(202) 484-7540

Away for the Weekend (series, i.e., "Great Getaways Less than 250 Miles from Los Angeles," by Michele and Tom Grimm). New York: Crown Publishers, 1984.

Caribbean Tourism Association
20 East 46 Street
New York, NY 10017
(212) 682-0435

The Compleat Traveler—Country Inns (by regions—5 U.S.) by Anthony Hitchcock and Jean Lindgren. New York: Burt Franklin & Co., updated for 1984–85.

Country Inns of America (series of Architectural Digest Books by Peter Andrews, George Allen, and Tracy Ecclesine). New York: Holt, Rinehart & Winston.

Cruise Lines International Association
("Answers to the Most Asked Questions About Cruising")
Suite 631
17 Battery Place
New York, NY 10004
(212) 425-7400

European Travel Commission
630 Fifth Avenue
New York, NY 10022
(212) 307-1200

The Great Weekend Escape Book, by Michael Spring. New York: E. P. Dutton, 1982.
Luggage and Leather Goods Manufacturers of America, Inc.
> (free pamphlet available by sending stamped, self-addressed business-size envelope:
> "Traveler's Guide to Luggage: How to Choose It and Use It")
> 220 Fifth Avenue
> New York, NY 10001

20 Reaffirmation

Association of Couples for Marriage Enrichment
> P.O. Box 10596
> Winston-Salem, NC 27108
> (919) 724-1526

Jewish Marriage Encounter
> Joe and Deanie Crane
> 199 Boston Avenue
> Massapequa, NY 11758

National Marriage Encounter
> 955 Lake Drive
> St. Paul, MN 55120

Reaffirmation: Renewing Your Marriage Vows and Values, by Susan Lane and Sandra Carter
> with Ann Scharffenberger. New York: Harmony Books, 1982.

Worldwide Marriage Encounter
> 1025 West Third Avenue
> Columbus, OH 43212
> (614) 294-3774

Index